FEAR & LOATHING IN PLYMOUTH 2003-2005

A TEENAGE DIARY

CLAIRE LE DAY

Published by Claire Le Day 2025
Copyright © Claire Le Day, 2025
Claire Le Day has asserted her right to be identified as the author of this work.

All rights reserved.
This book is sold or supplied subject to the condition that it shall not, by way of trade or otherwise:
a) be reproduced or copied in whole or in part and in any form or by any means without the publisher's consent; or
b) be lent, resold, hired out or otherwise circulated without the publisher's prior consent in any form of binding or cover other than that in which it is published and without a similar condition including this condition being imposed on the subsequent acquirer.
c) No AI training: Without in any way limiting the author's [and publisher's] exclusive rights under copyright, any use of this publication to "train" generative artificial intelligence (AI) technologies to generate text is expressly prohibited. The author reserves all rights to license uses of this work for generative AI training and development of machine learning language models.
The moral rights of the author have been asserted.

First published in the United Kingdom in 2025
ISBN: 979-8-2850659-1-3

Typeset by Ned Hoste

'He who makes a beast of himself gets rid of the pain of being a man.'
Samual Johnston (1809) quoted in Hunter Thomson's Fear and Loathing in Las Vegas *(1971).*

To James. Thank you for enduring yet another book of warm-up acts. x

PRELUDE

11TH JUNE 2023

LISTENING TO PITY PARTY BY IVORY LAYNE

This, in many ways, is a sequel, an older but certainly not wiser one. If 'The Diary of a Teenage Dirtbag' was a low-brow coming-of-age story, consider this its equally low-brow cousin. It's messy, it's embarrassing, and it's a rollercoaster of bad decisions.

By 2003, I'd shaken off the worst of my early teenage awkwardness, and with that, I unleashed a whole new level of chaos. I arrived at Plymouth University under the grand illusion that I'd matured. I would flick a switch and become the conscientious medical student I'd seen on TV. My 'diaries' would become 'journals', I thought, accurately documenting my arduous journey to doctor-dom. I was wrong. Sure, I studied (a bit), and I succeeded in the end goal of becoming a doc, but was my diary full of learning? Nope. Drunken misadventures and emotional meltdowns? Absolutely.

I found myself navigating a world not too far removed from Hunter S. Thompson's wild, drug-fuelled odyssey in Fear and Loathing in Las Vegas. Only my version involved a mind-altering obsession with boys that I cringe at even now. I spent more time chasing feelings than facts, more hours in sticky pubs than in sterile labs, and the only thing I ever dissected with any great detail was the meaning behind a text at 3 a.m.

I'm not proud of everything (anything?) you're about to read, but I think it's important to remember that we were all young, impulsive and selfish once. Maybe, as you read these pages, you'll remember your own reckless years. Maybe you'll laugh, maybe you'll squirm, or maybe you'll just feel relieved it wasn't you. Either way, here's the next instalment of teenage diaries; flawed, ridiculous, and wonderfully real. After all, I'd already conquered my teenage dirtbag phase. What was left but to up the ante?

MARCH 2022

Message from Artie: Good luck with your book (The Diary of a Teenage Dirtbag). I can't wait to buy a copy. Also if 'Claire Le Day' has a sequel of 'The Uni Days', I wouldn't mind. Plymouth was such a blur for me and it took me at least a decade to fully appreciate myself and those around me. I needed to grow and change (didn't we all?!), but I'm always happy to see you being happy.

Message to Artie: Thank you. I definitely don't think I've got it in me to do the uni days though! It may have been a blur but my memory was always of you being the perfect gentleman. It wasn't just you - I think we were all mega dicks at that point.

From Artie: Yeah, in hindsight my Plymouth memoir would give Fear and Loathing a run for its money. But our adventure was an important stone in my journey. Being mega dicks at points, aside, thank you for that.

To Artie: 'Fear and Loathing in Plymouth' - title of my next book… ha ha. I'm not going to lie, I'm a little more tempted now.

AUGUST 2022

To Artie: Ouft. Revisiting 2003 is rough.

From Artie: You're braver than me. Not exactly halcyon days!

To Artie: No. Right.

From Artie: Grey, rushing, grimy, overwhelming Plymvegas.

CONTENTS

1. Freshers Week
2. Artie
3. Bath
4. My 18th
5. Noel
6. Big Dick Dave
7. Lovely Northern Joe
8. Chloe
9. Easter 2004
10. Finn
11. Lily
12. The Sisterhood
13. Mumps
14. Joe in Edinburgh
15. Summer 04
16. Nico
17. Jersey Boyz
18. Marc
19. Shagopoly
20. Amity Place
21. Miles
22. Frank
23. Pete Bond
24. Christmas '04
25. Ed
26. Easter 2005

CONTENTS

27. Tom 'The Tipple' Morris
28. Edinburgh Fringe
29. Sexy Laurent
30. St Jacut
31. Ribs
32. Exeter

ONE
FRESHERS WEEK

**SUNDAY 21ST SEPTEMBER 2003 00.30AM
LISTENING TO WHERE IS THE LOVE BY BLACK EYED PEAS**

It was 2003. The year Apple launched iTunes, Beyoncé released "Crazy in Love", and low-rise jeans were somehow continuing to get even lower. It was also the year I arrived at Plymouth University, wide-eyed and under the illusion that I was about to embark on some grand intellectual adventure (and undoubtedly meet the love of my life).

~~~

I've arrived, baby. So long, Edinburgh, ya sucker. I can't believe it's actually happened… breathe… I am a university student! I've been here for a day and a half now, and IT'S AMAZING!

I. AM. BOSSING. IT.

I'm sharing a flat with two girls: Ellie and Lou (lovely), and three guys: Bruce, Mark and Sox. All very sweet and Bruce is HOT.

~~~

I am not in the least bit surprised to discover that I fancied the first man I laid eyes on.

I met Ellie when I was picking up my keys. She is ABSOLUTELY GORGEOUS… cheekbones up to her eyebrows and brilliant, green cat's eyes. I stared at her and had the rather sobering realisation that I would never feel attractive EVER again.

~~~

Ellie was breath-takingly beautiful, but her composed demeanour, which I now realise was likely shyness, initially made me think she was a little frosty. I was (of course) wrong. Ellie was both maternally warm and fiery as hell. By day, she walked with the grace of a ballet dancer, had a conscientious work ethic, hit the gym, ate her greens and fulfilled the role of 'mummy of the house'. When the sun went down, however, Ellie transformed. She dated jaw-dropping international DJs and dominated dance floors like she was possessed, teaching Lou and me to twerk fifteen years before we'd even heard of the term. Ellie was, by all accounts, very impressive.

~~~

We walked up to our flat and met the others. I was sooooo anxious but also: how EXCITING! I get to press reset on my adolescence - clean slate time. I feel like everything that has happened before today will disappear into someone else's memory. We're all 'passing go' at the same time… a true level playing field. This is my chance. Youth: Take Two.

Mark and Bruce couldn't take their eyes off Ellie from the second we both walked into the flat. This is going to be my invisible life now.

~~~

Mark was awkward, tall and hunched. The main descriptors for his hair and limbs being 'scraggly and white'. This culminated in an anaemic 'I've spent my teens avoiding sunlight and wanking in my bedroom' appearance. He was a sweet soul, though. Living with Mark for two years was a joy… kind, unassuming, funny Mark. Bruce was Mark's antithesis. His hair and upper body were rock-

hard and sun-kissed. He was an arrogant, surfing Jersey boy who, despite his exterior bravado, had just the right amount of insecurities and softness to balance 'it' all out.

Bruce moved back to Jersey and became a real-life Bergerac (police detective extraordinaire). He surfs by day and solves crimes by night.

~~~

Mum and Dad helped me unpack...

~~~

...the standard issue IKEA red checked bedding, an IKEA pink plastic desk lamp, a Fear & Loathing poster for above my bed, a brand new concrete slab of an HP laptop and an array of hipster troos, 'going out' tops, and chain belts.

~~~

... and we went out for dinner at the Barbican. I was eating quickly, desperate to get back to my new flatmates. Mum was lingering over her food and taking ages - so frustrating. We'd just spent ten hours stuck in a car together. Surely, we had nothing left to say to each other! There was, of course, a small part of me that felt ruffled about the prospect of saying goodbye. What I did not want was to prolong this agony and uncertainty, sitting, picking at a tagliatelle dish, unable to read my poker-faced parents.

They dropped me off at the pub before heading back up to Edinburgh. I was so excited, I leapt out of the car only to realise Mum was sobbing. I think I've only seen her cry a few times, and I didn't know what to say. Man, I'm a bitch. I can't believe I hadn't even stopped to think how my leaving would impact them. I was so worried about not settling in... I just didn't think.

~~~

This is the selfishness of immaturity. Is there a difference between narcissism and adolescence?

~~~

It broke my heart, and I could feel the tears forming, so I gave them both a quick hug and a kiss and walked straight into the pub.

I didn't look back.

What a night. I am so hyper!! Wow - this is great. I feel so happy. Bruce and I stayed up chatting most of the night after we got back. NOTHING HAPPENED… but it was quite nice just to share a bed with him… AS MATES! Everyone's been teasing us today, and apparently, Bruce "quite likes me", which, let's be honest, adds a little spice to life. Ahhh, I'm so excited… so many new people to meet, so much to do, and so much partaying! Right… I need some sleep. This is going to be FUN!

~~~

Ah yes, Partay as a verb. You monster.

~~~

MONDAY 22ND SEPTEMBER 2003 2AM
LISTENING TO CRY ME A RIVER BY JUSTIN TIMBERLAKE

If I didn't live with Bruce, I would definitely fancy him! Should I have given it a go when he was in my bed? I mean, maybe…

NO.

Right?

~~~

TUESDAY 23RD SEPTEMBER 2003 11PM
LISTENING TO RAPPER'S DELIGHT BY THE SUGARHILL GANG

Bruce and I had a weird 'we don't fancy each other, right?' conversation last night. No. Of course not. Flatmates. Friends. Nothing more. It's definitely for the best. Don't want to smoke my own stash… shit on my doorstep… is that the expression? Piss in my bed?

The flat and I danced all night in *Zanzibar*, and that's where I met Jean-Pierre, the ridiculously sexy South African. Seriously… drool. I swear, I turn to jelly the moment I hear that accent. He came back to ours, and we stayed up in the kitchen talking (such amazing chat!), then pulled the rest of the night in my room. I've been giddy all day; it actually felt like he liked me!

I saw him again tonight in *Roundabout* and he saw me, nodded, turned around and promptly disappeared. I don't get it. People are always so interested, and then it's like they get to know me and are like, 'Nope'. Why am I even surprised? I'm still me. Just me in Plymouth. Sheep's clothing and all that… Ahhh, I'm tired and in a bad mood.

I then pulled a guy called Robin Mills. He's the first fellow medic I've met, and we were both pissed. It lasted about two minutes; the first: alcohol-fuelled, the second: British politeness. We both withdrew after what felt like an appropriate amount of time and started laughing. We agreed that snogging each other felt freaky… like snogging your sibling. We won't be doing that again. I like him, though. Hopefully, we'll be friends.

~~~

Interestingly, Robin did snog my sibling about four years later. I'll always adore Robin, but could not yet recognise his awesomeness at this time. He arrived at university straight from the farm in rural Wales, and we were not on the same wavelength. I made fun of

Robin for things I am a little ashamed of, like his wide-eyed expression the first time he tasted curry, his skull and crossbones wallet, and his beautiful innocence. I was going to say he was naive, but actually, in retrospect, I was the naive and small-minded one. Robin has taught me so much over the years. Kissing technique not being one of them.

~~~

WEDNESDAY 24TH SEPTEMBER 2003 00.12AM
LISTENING TO INAUDIBLE MELODIES BY JACK JOHNSON

Bruce, Ellie and I spent the whole night drinking White Russians in Voodoo Lounge. What an absolute shit hole, but what. a. night. They're knocking it down and doing 241 cocktails until then. This meant we had to buy six at a time, but the round still managed to fluctuate mysteriously between £3 and £5. Man alive, am I full of milk.

It was around cocktail number four that I told Bruce and Ellie that I could murder a joint in order to fully embody The Dude. Ellie gave me the look that I'm getting used to, which means that we are NOT alike, and she soooo does not get me, but even Bruce looked baffled.

'What the fuck are you talking about?'

'You know! *The Dude*?! White Russians… *The Big Lebowski*?'

'Sorry, mate. No idea what that is. You Scottish people are weird...'

And in that moment, I felt oh so far away from home. NEITHER OF THEM HAD SEEN IT! Where even am I?

Jean Pierre is coming round in 15 minutes - YEAH!!!

~~~

THURSDAY 25TH SEPTEMBER 2003 3.45AM
LISTENING TO JUST LIKE A PILL BY P!NK

So last night with Jean Pierre, the South African, was a little disappointing. We stayed up for hours chatting, and we came to the conclusion that we'd be friends for the time being. It wasn't my conclusion at all. I don't want to be friends with sexy Jean Pierre, the South African. <u>AT ALL</u>. I could totally fall in love with him. I realise I may not be particularly discerning on that front but I could.

We'd just had THE BEST night; got pissed just the two of us, and he then came back to mine and chatted 'til 10 minutes ago. I'm totally falling for him. He's GORGEOUS, and everything he says makes me smile. Woof.

~~~

Woof?!? WOOF? Who am I? Lord Flashheart? I KNEW this book wasn't going to be any better than the last. It's arguably worse. How much longer do I keep ploughing through these diaries before I abandon them, realising it's just a list of boys I have no memory of with an 'I'm totally falling for them' annotation? One after another, inhabiting my thoughts for a few weeks before I realised they probably weren't the love of my life. How was I capable of falling so hard so quickly? I think part of me was just falling in love with the idea of being in love. Weren't we all? 'The Curse of The Millennial' (Not a Wallace and Gromit Movie).

~~~

SATURDAY 27TH SEPTEMBER 2003 4.40AM
LISTENING TO BEAUTIFUL BY SNOOP DOGG, PHARRELL WILLIAMS, UNCLE CHARLIE WILSON

God, I'm so gutted. I came so close to tears tonight. I've had an amazing day and night with Bruce, Mark, Lou and Ellie - man, they're great. How lucky am I to just be randomly placed with house mates that are brilliant? Very.

The boys upstairs came out with us, too. What a funny group of misfits. Rich is fast turning into one of my favs though.

~~~

Rich was different from the boys I had got used to befriending. Without wanting to use a derogatory term, Rich was a chav. He had a skinhead with a long fringe plastered down his forehead in approximately six down arrow spikes. He wore the shiniest of shell suits, drank lukewarm Carling and Rich's diamanté studs were bigger than mine. I loved him despite my snobbery. He giggled so freely, and his friendship felt honest and like one of life's simplest and purest pleasures. After only a few minutes of meeting Rich, I felt like fate would have guaranteed a friendship between us; anywhere, anytime.

It's a shame he turned out to be such a massive twat.

~~~

Jean Pierre, the sexy South African, came back to mine for about four hours, and we pulled a bit, and it got a bit feisty… friends-schmends.

It was awesome. He's so fucking HOT, then out of nowhere, he announced, 'No. Sorry, Claire', got up and just walked out. And that was that. OVER. ARSEHOLE. I'm so hurt. What was it? I really like him, and he just gave me a little taste of what I could have had. FUUCKKKK. THIS AGAIN. Is this life? Just a series of guys telling you they don't want you.

~~~

SATURDAY 27TH SEPTEMBER 2003 6.45PM
LISTENING TO WHEN I'M GONE BY 3 DOORS DOWN

This always happens when I like someone. There's obviously something inherently wrong with me. What do they discover? Is it my personality? Do they find a hairy bit that repulses them? What is it!?

~~~

SUNDAY 28TH SEPTEMBER 2003 4.20AM
LISTENING TO CRAZY IN LOVE BY BEYONCE (FT JAY-Z)

I am going to get no sleep tonight. Had about 10 million vodka red bulls cos they were two for £1. I can't stop thinking about JP - it's driving me mad. Fuck fuck fuck fuck shit balls fuck.

~~~

TUESDAY 30TH SEPTEMBER 2003 1.35AM
LISTENING TO DRIVE BY INCUBUS

I can hear Ellie having sex. I'm not trying to, but Jesus - she's a fucking animal. Go get 'em, tiger.

TWO
ARTIE

THURSDAY 9TH OCTOBER 2003 1AM
LISTENING TO CONCRETE SCHOOLYARD BY JURASSIC 5

I've got a boyfriend! Arthur Callaghan (Artie) and we've been together for a whole week. He's cute (although I reckon I'm a bit better looking), makes me laugh, and he's really affectionate. Bottom line… he's one of life's good guys, I think.

~~~

Artie was six feet tall with a mop of dark curls, cornflower-blue eyes, and a grin that was equal parts cheeky and geeky. He embodied skater chic, decked out in Volcom and sporting a beanie for every month of the year.

He had a long list of endearing qualities; he was funny, kind, loyal, reflective, sensitive, big-hearted, and endlessly supportive. But for all his strengths, Artie was trapped in an infuriating quest to find meaning in a bottomless pit of drugs.

Artie grew up in Bath with the support of a loving family and an enormous Georgian townhouse. Despite this, he cultivated an exterior better suited to his reprobate friendship group, which fostered in him a love of narcotics and board sports. He studied 'surf science', something I felt the need to repeatedly question.

'But what do you actually learn?! What IS it?'

I'm not sure Artie and I would have crossed paths before university, but there we were, both starting fresh and free of preconceptions or reputations. It was everything I had ever wanted. And in this world, where I could reinvent myself and be anything I wanted to be, seventeen-year-old me chose the most elusive of all identities; I decided to be cool.

After a miserable experience at school, I arrived in Plymouth determined to be untouchable. I'd watched plenty of would-be sociopaths win popularity simply by asserting it. So I went for it, tipped my chin up and faked it.

~~~

I met him last week in a very Romeo and Juliet-esque way. My bedroom window is right next to his flat's balcony. I'd spent ages trying to find a lighter before I gave up and stuck my head out the window to ask my (evidently stoned) neighbours (Artie and Mike). We ended up chatting and smoking for hours.

'You're going to have to stop smoking Marlboro Lights now you're a student, Claire.'

I looked down at my cigarette, failing to compute.

'It hadn't occurred to me… but yeah, I guess I will.'

'I'll teach you to roll. Come on.'

He grinned at me, and, at that moment, I'd have said yes to literally anything and marched with him into hell.

We met downstairs, walked to Plymouth Hoe and sat at the base of the lighthouse until sunset. This. Is. Fucking. Romance. It blew a gale all afternoon, but goddammit, he was going to teach me to roll.

~~~

ARTIE

I remember this as a Rocky-style movie montage for tobacco rolling. I no longer smoke (much) but still consider myself an expert roller. I am the (self-proclaimed) 'Finest Roller in the West' and able to create a beautiful (some might say perfect) rollie. Is this really something to be proud of? Absolutely, it is.

~~~

FRIDAY 10TH OCTOBER 2023 7.50PM
LISTENING TO GLYCERINE BY BUSH

I spent the day with Artie and his house mate, Kate. I think I'm a little bit in love with her…

~~~

Kate is now one of my oldest and best friends. She was the first to teach me that women were not to be feared, and that they were not all insecure, mean girls; she changed my life in that sense. Leaving Edinburgh and realising that the world was full of Kates filled me with relief and delight.

~~~

SATURDAY 11TH OCTOBER 2003 4AM
LISTENING TO SEVEN NATION ARMY BY THE WHITE STRIPES

I slept with Artie last night, and it was a bit weird. He lost his erection when he put the condom on and got really upset. I didn't mind - it's just one of these things. But he REALLY minded to the point that I thought, 'I hope this doesn't become a thing', but then we tried again a few hours later, and it was all good.

I'm a bit worried about not being that into him. We officially started going out today, but I think I still like JP. God, I'm a bitch.

~~~

SUNDAY 12TH OCTOBER 2003 11.45PM
LISTENING TO MUDFOOTBALL BY JACK JOHNSON

I'm so confused! I have so much work to do, and I've done nothing. I'm still with Artie Callaghan but I'm really not feeling it. His flat had a massive party last night, and I stayed over after getting stoned. I felt 'nothing'. I just don't have 'the feeling'. Ahhh, I don't know what to do. I still really fancy Sexy JP Le SA - he's so lovely, and we still end up being drawn to each other on nights out. He told me he really liked me and that I shouldn't be with Artie... even though I'm sure he doesn't want me. Is this a want what he can't get situation? I'll sleep on it. But JP's smile makes me SAAAAA... WWWWOOOOOOOON.

~~~

MONDAY 13TH OCTOBER 2003 00.25AM
LISTENING TO LAID BY JAMES

BIG NEWS IN CLAIRE WORLD. This is utterly amazing. I just managed to make myself orgasm. All by myself! Just a finger! Well-bloody-done me. I can die a happy lass now.

~~~

Every ounce of my being was screaming in pain as I was typing this. Just cut it, I thought. No one wants to hear about me wanking. URGH - STOP SAYING WANKING. But times have changed. THIS is feminism. Why do men get to own wanking? Generations of men and boys have dined out on masturbation stories. No one has forgotten The Pie in 'American Pie' or poor Mary's jizz-quiff in 'Something About Mary'. How would the 1998 audience have felt watching Cameron Diaz masturbate and then rub her... <genuinely don't know what word to use here without grossing everyone out>... in Ben Stiller's hair? Surely a scene with Alison Hannigan having sex with a baked good would have been deemed totally in-

appropriate and axed. But the other way round? A cultural milestone, no less. The subject has never been taboo for men… It's 'normal', it's 'funny', NOT doing it would be weird… 'unhealthy' even. But female masturbation makes a lot of people feel odd. I'm a little ashamed that my initial instinct was to delete the entry. Normalising female masturbation is such a powerful contributor to equality and the world I want for my daughters. 'Women wanking' should be talked about more openly without the previous need for humour, shock factor or, worst of all: FOR THE PLEASURE OF MEN!

Well, this has turned out to be a very cathartic love letter to all the women out there who feel embarrassment or even revulsion at the thought. To quote Noah Levenstein, 'It's perfectly natural'. So go for it. Have a wank, enjoy it, talk to your close friends and then publish it (sorry, Dad).

~~~

MONDAY 13TH OCTOBER 2003 9.15PM
LISTENING TO THROUGH THE WIRE BY KANYE WEST

Ah merde. I'm single, and I feel like the ultimate bitch whore fuck from hell. I broke up with Artie, and I feel horrible. He looked so upset and didn't know what hit him. AND THEN, to make everything a million times worse, he was really sweet and said he wanted to stay friends. Do I want to be friends with Artie? Do I ever! We have such a laugh together. I don't want to lose him.

~~~

TUESDAY 14TH OCTOBER 2003 9.15PM
LISTENING TO BOHEMIAN LIKE YOU BY DANDY WARHOLS

Right - I'm going to bed. I feel miserable and like there's a big cannonball sitting in my stomach. But I simultaneously feel empty.

The novelty of university has worn off, I have so much work to do, and I'm finding it really hard to pitch how much to do. It's the whole of medicine without so much as a starting point or framework. How is this possible? I have a horrible feeling I'm not going to make it. I'll drop out, drunk, single and fat with no prospects. I'll end up back in Edinburgh, and everyone will think, 'Well… no surprise there!'.

Damn - I can't let that happen. I'll end up flat-sharing with Gretchen, working a dead-end job, and probably falling pregnant after a one-night stand with a tramp.

NOPE. GET IT TOGETHER. DO NOT FUCK THIS UP.

Plus, I've clearly made a mistake dumping Artie. I've lost him. I feel so lonely, and it pains me to say it, but I miss home. I miss my parents and Chloe.

I'm so tired. Maybe that's it. A good night's sleep should sort me out. Enough bollocks chat. Bed.

~~~

MONDAY 20TH OCTOBER 2003 1.20AM
LISTENING TO IN DA CLUB BY 50 CENT

Things are A-OK.

Friday night - got really stoned with Artie and Mike (Artie and Kate's house mate). I stayed over and slept in Artie's bed with him. We chatted all night and I felt so close to him (and not just because I was physically so close to him!).

Saturday: I spent the day with Bruce, Mark, Lou, Ellie and the boys from the flat upstairs: Tommo, Rich, Trigger and the rest of the crew. We danced all night in *Zanzibar*, and I slept on Rich's floor after chatting with him until sunrise.

I went to JP's tonight, and we spent the whole night making a short porn spoof with two Henry Hoovers having a steamy affair with a Barry White soundtrack. 'Girl Henry' had a mop for hair, and some big red paper lips stuck on the front. It's hard to convey just how funny it was and hard not to fall in love with someone who makes you laugh that much. I just wish he felt the same. Ahhh… Sexy JP, the South African.

~~~

TUESDAY 21ST OCTOBER 2003 4.30AM
LISTENING TO SOMEDAY BY NICKELBACK

Woooo, JP and I pulled in *Zanzibar* tonight! I'm lying in bed thinking about how perfect he is. I am SO excited. I had some vouchers for free entry and nine drinks, and I finally had the courage to lean in and kiss him, and hallelujah - he kissed me back.

"Falling lasts forever if everything you know will catch you."
JP 12/10/03 2am

~~~

Geddadatown Bob Dylan. The fact that this didn't make me cringe my face off causes no end of agony to my adult brain.

~~~

WEDNESDAY 22ND OCTOBER 2003 2AM
LISTENING TO KINGSTON TOWN UB40

Oh goodness me, I'm completely stoned (which may explain the ridiculous girly, swirly, curly handwriting). At least it will make more sense than if I was drung… DRUNK! The past few days have been a bit weird. I was really worried JP had only pulled me cos he was drunk. Then last night, I went round to his and stayed the night, and tonight he came round and watched Hannibal with me, and we pulled again. He was so affectionate with me, constantly touching and kissing me. I refuse to believe he isn't falling for me too, but then… I'm just not sure. I reallllly like JP. I just have this horrible feeling it's all in my head. He's not over his ex. He loved her, and how am I supposed to compete with the perfect, rose-tinted memory of someone else? I'll never match up to this girl who is no doubt being remembered better than she actually was… I love his kiss… like Nutella. I could definitely eat some Nutella on toast right now. Pfff, I'm talking crap again. He left early this evening and I went and smoked with Artie, Mike and Kate next door. I think I'm going to knock the weed on the head. I can't carry on like this forever, plus it's really not very conducive to getting work done. It mustn't sneak out of 'summer life', into 'real life'. I don't want to be a stoner. It's October now, and it's on my doorstep whenever I want it.

~~~

FRIDAY 24TH OCTOBER 2003 5AM
LISTENING TO YOU CAN CALL ME AL BY PAUL SIMON

Last night was amazing. It was the first proper MedSoc night out - 'doctors and nurses themed' - not very original but understandable. I got ready with Kate and Connie next door, and Artie joined us for a few drinks. Life would be so much better if I liked him… more. I like him A LOT. I'm just not sure it's enough. I wore some surgeon's gown and they both went as nurses.

'Oh, come on, guys! We can't have all the girls dressed as sexy, slutty nurses and the boys as big men doctors! Surely that defeats… EVERYTHING! The guys won't be wearing nurse outfits.'

(Although, as it turned out, I was quite wrong on that front.)

~~~

I stand by this. When my youngest was three, she was shocked to hear that I was a doctor, 'like Daddy'.

'But you can't be a doctor! You're a Mummy.'

This must be my fault somehow. It's probably that doll I gave her when she was one... gender stereotyping and constant parental guilt; I'm such a clichéd millennial parent. 80s parents wouldn't have overanalysed this. Maybe there are instances where we could be more boomer.

~~~

We went to *Bar 38* and got ready for the three-legged pub crawl. I was strapped to Frank, this super cute first-year medic I hadn't met yet. Helloooooo handsome. We had such a laugh, went to *Cuba* for more drinks, went back to mine to pick up my NUS card and then to Artie's for another drink and onwards to *Voodoo Lounge*. I was texting JP the whole time and not getting much response. Had some more drinks and then (still tied together) got down to some seriously dirty dancing.

~~~

Oh, Frank, I'm sorry. I was OBSESSED with boys. Was there something wrong with me? I fancied EVERYONE.

~~~

We were all over each other, and I was completely fucked. Artie arrived and bought us both a drink, but then stormed off in a really bad mood.

~~~

Which bit of me thought I'd behave with a little more decorum at university?

~~~

Anyway, Frank and I walked home and finally cut ourselves loose at 3ish (self-proclaimed winners), and he went home.

Artie messaged after Frank had left, and we met out my window for a fag. He was stoned and drunk and emotional and told me he still liked me. I didn't really have much to say. I'm in bed now, just staring at my phone. Nothing from JP.

FUCK.

~~~

MONDAY 27TH OCTOBER 11PM
LISTENING TO FAMILY PORTRAIT BY P!NK

JP and I started officially seeing each other on Friday (via text) but I then didn't see him all weekend. I spent the weekend with Artie and Mike - I LOVE them. I could love Artie for sure… maybe in time. I like him more and more, the more time I spend with him.

I stayed at JP's last night, just pulling and messing about a bit - GREAT, but then I barely saw him today - I'm fairly sure he's not interested. The vibe is all wrong. He was supposed to come round tonight at 7pm and arrived at 8.30pm. He just stood in the doorway, looking at his feet.

'Sorry Claire, I can't stay - I'm going out. My house mates are waiting for me outside.'

Argh - why am I being such an idiot and liking him more as he pushes me away? I am so fucking grumpy.

I made my Dad's birthday card today. I miss home. I miss Maggie loads too - I'd love to live my Edinburgh life for just a few days. All the 'new' is draining. I spoke to her yesterday, and she said she'd been to St Andrews last week to visit Charlie - I had not realised this was still a thing! Argh - she still doesn't know about us hooking up behind her back just a few days after she'd left for uni. Amazingly, Charlie and I appear to have kept it a secret. He's such an arsehole, he doesn't deserve her. Anyway, she said he's really changed, living his fake new life (aren't we all?) with his new-found, poncy, snobby Ralph Lauren and Pashmina-clad friends. Ha - mine aren't. I'm yet to see Mark out of his Wolves shirt.

It's not fair. Everyone keeps nipping home for a weekend and I'm so cut off down here. I know that's what I wanted but I'm feeling so homesick. I'm so lonely despite having amazing friends around me like Artie and incredible house mates like Bruce, Mark, Ellie and Lou. They hardly know me, and they've been better friends than I ever had in Edinburgh. They're like France friends - real friends. But I feel really worn out and I need a rest and a proper meal. I need to smoke less, sleep more, drink less.

Pfff... I am, without doubt, going to die young.

Artie has invited Mike and I to go back to Bath with him at the weekend. It'll be great, and I'll get a chance to breathe a bit.

~~~

TUESDAY 28TH OCTOBER 2003 00.45AM
LISTENING TO LET'S PUSH THINGS FORWARD BY THE STREETS

The soundtrack for our (middle class) 'rebellion' of soft drugs and Avril Lavigne aesthetics was provided by The Streets. It allowed us to dabble in cannabis and lager tinnies whilst never really stepping too far from the safety of ska punk and Smirnoff Ices when no one was watching.

Ohh no. I wrote a poem again. A bit of me just died.

~~~

Angry Poem of Nonsense

>Fuck THIS SHIT
>I'm sick of it!
>No one understands,
>Life's not simple or bland.
>I'll just sit
>And think for a bit,
>Of what makes me sad,
>How I miss my Dad.
>I just want some care,
>My old friends, and a chair.

~~~

What rhymes with care?! Come on man! Care.. pear... hair... chair. Good one.

~~~

>I can't always keep going,
>Being happy and knowing,
>I'm treated like a fool,
>By people so cruel.
>For fucks sake I'm extreme,
>My mood swings - obscene.
>I love and smile
>and I hate with great style.
>This doesn't make sense.
>It's not my fault I'm dense.
>I'm just wasting time,
>'Till Artie comes in a while.

~~~

Oh my stars. Get the girl a Pulitzer.

ARTIE

WEDNESDAY 29TH OCTOBER 2003 7.16AM
LISTENING TO GRACELAND BY PAUL SIMON

Well, I'm about as confused as a confused person. Artie did eventually come round last night, cheered me up and stayed the night. What's wrong with me? I can tell him my deepest, darkest secrets. We spend so much time laughing together. He calls me 'greeb', which as far as I can tell, is an affectionate-emo-skater word. LOVE THAT. I could definitely fall for Artie.

~~~

Hmmm… dictionary.com has a somewhat different definition.
  Greebo
  An unkempt or dirty-looking young man.
  Oh.
  <Keeps googling>

  A greebo is a person who listens to rock/punk/metal music and doesn't follow fashion trends. They don't usually class themselves as being a greebo but are assigned that title by trendies/rudes. Some of them may look quite threatening but generally they are all-around nice people.
  Urban Dictionary

  In the 00s, the greebo was camouflaged by the broader nu-metal trend that saw every park-dwelling teenager dressed in the same three-quarter length shorts, ball chain necklace and a flannel shirt with a hoodie stitched into it.
  Vice.com

~~~

I love the smell of him. It makes me feel a little like William Macleod did. The smell is different though, like fresh tobacco, Jasmine, firewood and cocoa butter. I take a deep breath of him, and I do an involuntary little sigh. And his smile… I'm falling in love with his smile. It's so goofy, and his laugh comes straight from his chest… like his heart is singing… punk rock. Oh, I don't know. He doesn't seem to do any work and he is always at home getting stoned with Mike. What would my mum say…

JP came round last night. It's not going very well. He clearly has 10% of my up-for-it-ness. He came round early, and we kissed but nothing else. I started kissing his neck, but NOTHING. No reaction whatsoever. HE JUST LAY THERE like he was being kissed by a brick. His kiss is so delicate but there is zilch passion. He appears to have a rather heartbreaking but crystal-clear indifference to me. Claire - only marginally less boring than nothing… a filler… something to pass the time. I can see it now.

THREE

BATH

MONDAY 3RD NOVEMBER 2003 2AM
LISTENING TO FLUTTER BY BONOBO

I've just spent the best weekend in Bath with Artie and Mike.

Friday Night: We met up with some of Artie's friends at a party and got absolutely caned. Seeing him in Bath has changed the way I see him. In the opposite way that no one would like me in Edinburgh, Artie was in his element and waaaaay more fanciable on his own turf. He is AMAZING with his parents and brothers. His friends are so cool, it was hard not to feel intimidated. AND THE GIRLS! Good god, where do you even find such beautiful creatures?! (Bath obviously.) But they were the coolest things I'd ever seen. They all adored Artie, and I could tell they all craved his attention and, although friendly, were quite wary of me. Side eyes all round I guess. I hate that watching hot girls with him made me like him more. Am I always going to be this fickle?

Saturday: Artie was doing family stuff, so Mike and I went to meet Herbert McNash (who's doing his first year here now). I can't believe I used to fancy him! Sooo weird. It was comforting to see him though, even if it doesn't sound like he's having the best time in Bath. Poor Herbie, he is clearly unappreciated for who he is here, and it breaks my heart to see him depressed like this - he's not sleeping again. Bath's too edgy and underground for him*. He should have been in Cambridge, singing in niche medieval choirs and playing parlour games after dinner with other posh boys and their 170+ IQs. Instead, he's in a world where the druggie skater boys rule, and no one cares if you play five instruments unless one of them is a 2am guitar. Spending time with him made me remember Edinburgh properly, though, and I realised that Edinburgh life wasn't everything I'd built it up to be. I've done a classic rose-tinted specs/ absence that makes the heart grow fonder trick… but for a place.

~~~

*Ah yes. 'Edgy Bath'; Bristol's uncool big sister - home of Jane Austen, walking tours, The Roman Baths, The Royal Crescent and Bath Abbey. So 'underground'.

~~~

Artie came back to join us after lunch. I was so pleased to see him, I gave him a little hug, and he chuckled and messed up my hair before giving me a big kiss on the top of my head. It made my heart lurch.

We then spent the afternoon at *The Pig and Fiddle* with some of Artie's school friends. I reckon I would kill to be half as cool as them.

Artie's mum then made the most fantastic roast and spent all of dinner asking me questions and laughing - such a joy. We then skipped out again with our bellies full of a home-cooked meal and grown-up wine. I'd forgotten what it felt like to eat properly. No wonder I look like shit with my only sustenance being copious amounts of the cheapest drink in the supermarket/ bar/ pub, fags and a tuna and chip melt from Jake's when the munchies get the better of me. Ellie made me eat an orange last week, so I guess that's something. We ended up in this club called Babylon and I danced with Mike and Artie all night. It felt like it does when I'm with François and Marc. Proper friends and my hurts full to bursting. Finally.

When we got back, I wanted nothing more than to be wrapped up in Artie's arms. I knew I'd made a mistake ending it. This guy, man. SURELY, the love of my life is going to be this guy. How can it not?

Mike and I had a big mattress on the floor and Artie beside me but in his bed. We were both lying there listening to Mike snoring and staring at each other. I whispered, 'I think I want you back', and he mouthed, 'Yes, please', and pulled his duvet back.

~~~

There is so much that I have zero recollection of when reading these diaries. There are entire people (JP the SA for example) that have been wiped. I don't remember bars I supposedly spent countless nights in, and important conversations are like forgotten dreams, but this moment made it into my long-term memory. This has become THE memory for Artie, and with no hidden meaning attached, I can honestly say that I still love it.

~~~

I got in with him, and we pulled, and it felt completely perfect. This is right. Right? Mike told me earlier that a lot of people think 'I'm messing him about', which, to be fair, is accurate, BUT I'M NOT CONSCIOUSLY DOING IT!

It's moments like these that I can still hear Angus telling me, aged fifteen, that I'm a 'head fuck'.

~~~

WEDNESDAY 12TH NOVEMBER 2003 2.40AM
LISTENING TO ALL MY LIFE BY FOO FIGHTERS

I have had the most incredible week. Artie Artie Artie, you dazzling soul. We're back together and I cannot understand how I could ever have not wanted to be with him. It feels so right. He makes me laugh, he makes me shudder and he envelops me in love and kindness that I'm not sure I deserve. The weed is the only issue. I'm having to say no a lot, but I still feel like I'm smoking way too much.

Friday night: Artie and I went out, just the two of us and drank Terminators downstairs in the *Skiving Scholar*. Ouff. They're not called that for no reason...

~~~

We spent too many nights drinking Terminators. They were smoothie-thick, vulval-pink and of unknown aetiology. Sharing a Terminator before a night out was very much considered de rigueur in 2003/2004. If you google 'what's in a terminator at the Skiving Scholar?', *the top answer helpfully suggests 'Vomit, pus, coffee, soap and the juices of that bloke that hangs around Bretonside'. After much research, my sources suggest: beer, cider, 'a mix of 5 spirits' and Cheeky Vimto.*

~~~

On the way out, he had his skateboard, and he quite literally whisked me off my feet.

'C'mon on then, greebo, let's see if the skateboard can take us both.'

We got on at the top of the hill round the back of *Roundabout*. I wrapped my arm around him, buried my head into the back of his neck and skated off into the crisp moonlit night. We were quite quickly going too fast when we lost control and I was catapulted off. I'm worried I've broken my elbow. So funny though.

We just rolled around at the bottom of the hill in a messy, hysterical heap.

Saturday: I stayed in and I watched Jay, Silent Bob, Mike, and Artie get stoned.

Sunday: Watched *Top Gun* with the upstairs boys and laughed so hard with Rich - I love that big chavvy twat.

Monday night: We went to *Wonky Legs* for Mike's birthday. I ended up drinking too much. Drum and bass does that to me. I obviously don't like it that much if it's shit when I'm sober. I passed on the weed again before we went out and kinda wish I hadn't. I'd dance to anything to dance with Artie, though. So anyway, I overdid it on the booze, and Artie took me home. I slurred the whole way home about how much I like him - arghhh, I'm so embarrassed. I'm just hoping he was stoned and doesn't remember. Fuck's sake, Claire - I'm too old to be a massive drunken twat like this.

I think I'm anaemic too and I have this report due. Oh god. What am I doing?! I need to start doing some work. And should I buy some iron?

Artie and I finally slept together again tonight (since we got back together). He gets a bit stressy having lost his erection before, so I'm definitely adopting a 'no biggie' attitude. Haha… no biggie… ha. Life would certainly be better if we were all a little bit more liberal in our pun-usage. But also: I genuinely don't really care about it. I really like him and OF COURSE I like having sex with him, but it changes nothing if we don't. I'm fairly confident that everything'll be fine once it all works a few times. I slightly hinted that being off his face *may* not be helping, but he hated that, so I dropped it.

There is also a slight other problem… I assumed that JP had ended it through a total lack of contact… not a peep since I went to Bath but got a text tonight…

```
Text from JP: Hey babe. Can I see you
tonight?
```

Oops. Although it's clearly a drunk text.

```
Text to JP: Sorry JP. I thought you'd
disappeared.
```

```
From JP: Never from you babe…
```

Definitely drunk. I didn't reply. If he messages again sober, then I'll deal with it.

Now to dream about Artie Callaghan. The man of my dreams.

~~~

WEDNESDAY 11TH NOVEMBER 2003
LISTENING TO GONE BY JACK JOHNSON

I would like to write a wee note in respect for my cat, Figaro, who died last week. I loved that cat so much. We grew up together, shared a bed together and became adults together. Oh Figs. I'm sorry I wasn't there. He battled through so much shit in life and was always there for me. Poor Figsters - I hope you didn't suffer. Thanks for being an irreplaceable companion. My friend and brother - I'll always miss you.

~~~

THURSDAY 12TH NOVEMBER 2003
LISTENING TO PRETTY GREEN EYES BY ULTRABEAT

Sorry! Did I say I didn't care about sex with Artie?! <SCOFF> BOOOOOLLLLLLLOCCCCKS.

Artie and I had THE BEST SEX EVER tonight. I haven't had sex like that… it's been a while anyway.

~~~

SUNDAY 16TH NOVEMBER 2003
LISTENING TO LONELY AS YOU BY FOO FIGHTERS

Fucking hell. The strangest thing is happening. I'm falling in love. I'm actually falling for Artie Callaghan, the guy 'I wasn't that into'. I fall for him harder with every second I spend with him. I know from past experience that me loving someone is NOT GOOD, as I'll start to get paranoid. I'm a fake cool, perfect girlfriend until I actually like someone, and I turn into the world's worst clingy loser. It's something to do with knowing you've got something to lose. It's scary to think that Artie might go off me and with that thought goes my 'cool'. Poof.

~~~

MONDAY 17TH NOVEMBER 2003 2AM
LISTENING TO SMELLS LIKE TEEN SPIRIT BY NIRVANA

I went round to Artie's tonight, and he's pissed me off. He was hanging out with Mike and their 'new friend' Laura. Fucking Laura… she's absolutely stunning with her white elfin hair, flawless, makeupless face and her cool as hell greebo wardrobe.

She effortlessly takes all the drugs and laughs so freely with Artie. They look perfect together with their fucking matching beanies. They got royally fucked, but I didn't, as had so much work to do. I felt so self-conscious next to her. I was getting all sketchy thinking how much he fancies her. I think he's going off me. Is he bored of me? Are we in a rut already? For every inch I eek closer to him, he edges away. I'm like a Labrador chasing a ball out to sea.

~~~

TUESDAY 18TH NOVEMBER 2003 2.40AM
LISTENING TO HARD CANDY BY COUNTING CROWS

I've fallen in love with Artie. Artie Callaghan: the surf science, skating little greeb. It's almost like I made myself fall in love by simply thinking, 'I must not fall in love.' I know I *think* I've been in love a lot, but really, I think it's only been William and Gael. This reminds me so much of William. The jealousy I feel takes me right back. I'm turning into the attention-seeking, paranoid, jealous, love-sick psycho that treated William Macleod like shit. The last thing I want to do is hurt Artie like I did William.

I went next door tonight because I knew Laura was there, and I just couldn't leave them uninterrupted to fall in love. They were so baked. I asked if he would have a word with me in private.

'Looks like you guys are having a good night…'

I said it as coolly as possible, but the edge in my voice sliced its way through. I caught a flash of exasperation on his face, so I did the only thing I knew how, and I tried to kiss him. Pure desperation. But he wasn't even looking at me, and he kept looking back to Mike's bedroom, where we could hear Mike and Laura giggling away.

'Yeah, it's been great. Laura's awesome. You two would get on if you gave her a chance.'

'We do get on! I just don't want to get stoned all the time. I'd rather not fail my degree, thanks.'

'Greebs - you sound so stuck up saying shit like that.'

'I AM NOT STUCK UP! Anyway, do you want to come back to mine later?'

'Nah. I think I'll just hang here. Mike's just rolled a beaut.'

'Seriously?! Are you choosing drugs over me?'

As soon as the words came out my mouth, I wanted to stuff them back in. I've got such a stupid, MASSIVE gob. I was jealous of Laura, and I was jealous of drugs, and no one wears jealousy well.

'Look. We're cool, aren't we? I am not going to be given an ultimatum between drugs and my girlfriend. Although, if you keep acting like this, I'm not sure you want to know my choice. Goodnight Claire. We'll talk tomorrow.'

There was such control and finality to his voice. There was nothing left for me to say. Artie chose Laura and drugs over me. I got home, had a wee cry and finally got some work done. I've got community group in six hours now and Artie is slipping between my fingers. FUCK.

~~~

7.50AM
LISTENING TO ME AND JULIO DOWN BY THE SCHOOLYARD BY PAUL SIMON

I think I've blown it with Artie. I sent him this text in a moment of desperation and blind panic last night.

```
3.10am: You dont want 2b with me Art-
ie. Im such a horrible person. I hate
who I'm turning into. How can u b sure
u want 2b wid me?
```

Anyway, he called and was like, 'We'll talk tomorrow cos I'm stoned and that would be weird.' I wish I knew what he was thinking. Just a little reassurance would be amazing.

~~~

Oh, Claire. I was still just a child playing 'grownups'. You can smell the insecurity in this 3am scramble for attention. Of course, it makes me cringe, but that is (in part) the whole point of this story. This isn't me. Not really anyway. This is the unripened, self-centred version. This is the forgotten part. No one REALLY remembers what they were like as we conveniently erase texts like this from memory.

Teenage brains are still so raw, and they struggle to understand any perspective outside their own. The frontal cortex isn't fully developed until the age of 25 and this is the bit of our brain that manages emotions, impulse control and social interaction. There is a mental health epidemic in the under 25s, and I believe that it is largely because we are expecting unfinished brains to cope with the unrealistic burden of adulthood.

Am I insufferably patronising? Yes. Yes, I am.

~~~

6.30PM
LISTENING TO NERVOUS IN THE ALLEY BY LESS THAN JAKE

I feel like such a fool. If I could take that text back, I would. More than anything in the entire world. I just apologised, and he said we'd have 'a little chat', and he'd be round in fifteen mins. I've got a really BAD feeling about this. 'A feeling of impending doom' as they say in medicine. I'm worried. I don't want to lose him. I am terrified of how much I like him. Oh god, what's he going to say? Where the hell is he? I'm feeling a bit sick. I've been chain-smoking since I got home from University. AHH I'm so nervous.

~~~

WEDNESDAY 19TH NOVEMBER 2003 3.30AM
LISTENING TO COCOON BY JACK JOHNSON

Right. Quickly. I need some serious sleep but I need to vomit some words down. Artie came round, and I felt so ill, convinced he might break up with me.

'You were unreasonable last night, greeb. That's not like you. What's going on?'

'I know. I was. I'm sorry. I'm not sure what got into me.'

'We've been so intense recently, and we're spending a lot of time together. I don't want to say "it's too much", but you know what I mean right?'

'Totally.'

'Maybe we should slow things down a bit? Neither of us wants anything really serious, do we? I know it freaks us both out.'

<IT DOES NOT FREAK ME OUT AT ALL!>

'I agree. Let's see how things go.'

So I 'agreed' to this, and we were all cool, but I was secretly gutted because apart from the 'me being unreasonable' bit, I DID NOT AGREE WITH ANYTHING HE SAID! I love him, and I love spending all my time with him. I don't want to slow it down. I am all in, and surely the only thing I can take from this is that he's going off me, and he's not interested anymore. How has this happened? I love him, and I just have to pretend and hide it. It sucks.

FOUR
MY 18TH

MONDAY 24TH NOVEMBER 2003
LISTENING TO MR BRIGHTSIDE BY THE KILLERS

WHAT. A. WEEK.

It's been absolutely incredible.

This is my first-ever diary entry as a legal adult. Hellllooooo, eighteen-year-old Claire. Look out world, here I come.

Everything is fine with Artie. We're back to being great, and we've both kind of ignored the whole 'let's slow it down' thing. So. To summarise the coming of age…

Wednesday 19th November: I went out with Kate, drank a TONNE of wine and then went back to hers to turn eighteen with Artie and Mike. I love how freely she laughs. I'm not sure I laugh in such an unrepressed way… Anyway. We were all on their balcony at midnight, and I was shouting, 'I'm eighteen!' across the courtyard, with a bottle of rum in one hand and a spliff in the other.

~~~

I wouldn't have wanted it any other way.

~~~

Mike and Kate went to bed whilst Artie and I sat there for a few more hours. He had his arm around me, and we were listening to music as he stroked my leg. It felt like climbing into a warm marshmallow.

'Happy birthday, greeb… what's the plan now you're an adult?'

'Oh, you know… Go to the gym, go to some lectures, stop smoking…'

'Ha ha… very funny.'

'I'm glad we're ok now, Artie. I really don't want to lose you.'

'I feel the same.' He smiled and looked at me in a way that surely only exists in the world of love. SURELY?! 'Not being with you just wouldn't feel right now. I think we're pretty cool together. You're pretty cool…'

FUCK! I LOVE HIM SO MUCH! But the 'cool' was all a lie.

'I'm not cool, Artie.'

'Course you are, greeb!'

We then talked about our friends and charmed lives and he made a comment about me 'always being popular'. Pah! So I told him how very uncool and unpopular I was. I told him about how much I used to love Celine Dion and Shania Twain, all the horrific bullying, the spitting, the isolation, being called a fat, hairy pig at every opportunity. Psycho Jane turning against me. Fucking Gretchen trying to ruin my life for years. Tom Southall telling everyone I was a hairy man-beast. That fucking list I found by 'accident' of 'Reasons we hate Claire Le Day'. Mish having his 'affair' with me and discarding me like his used condoms. Ewen the Pervert trying his damndest to rape me last summer…

I didn't stop for breath as it all came tumbling out, and I had tears in my eyes as I kept remembering just how utterly pathetic I'd been. Artie grabbed both my hands, kissed me on the forehead and said, 'I wish they could see you now. I can't even picture you like that… You're so confident.'

I fucking will be, I thought.

THURSDAY 20TH NOVEMBER - MY 18TH.

It was such a cool day. I woke up having sex with Artie. Happy FUCKING birthday to me! It was so intense, and he whispered in my ear, 'I could lose my mind with you.'

~~~

I already have. I thought. My mind is well and truly lost.

~~~

Then he gave me my present - a three-pack of Volcom thongs… niche but brilliant. I wouldn't have said 'no' to a birthday 'I love you', but I'll settle for thongs.

I spent the day in *The Scholar*, and people came and went throughout the day. Herbie even came to visit for the day from Bath. I went back to the flat in the evening. Ellie, Lou, Bruce and Mark had balloons everywhere with champagne and cake and pressies all laid out for me. They'd made such an effort. It was so sweet. Ellie was making a huge fuss that I wasn't with my family for my 18th. They gave me a beautiful photo album that they'd got engraved and filled with pictures of us from the last few months and room for me to put 18th birthday pics in it.

'We can be your family while you're here, Claire' and Ellie gave me the biggest hug, followed by the others for a big group hug, and it made me cry. I felt so touched. I am so lucky.

We went back to *The Scholar* for Terminators and finished the night in *Destiny's*. Artie eventually took me home, and we had slow, drunken sex and talked until the sun came up. In the morning, he'd brought around a bag for breakfast, and he showed me how to cut up a mango. It felt like the sexiest thing I'd ever seen.

It is also the best and ONLY way to cut up a mango, a hack I love imparting on others - How do you eat yours? Peel, then chop? Loser.

MY 18TH

    Maggie Mcfarlane arrived at lunchtime on Friday - I've missed her so much! I couldn't wait for her to meet everyone. We had a chilled one in the *Union* on Friday night, and then, on Saturday night, we had my party in the flat. It was fancy dress, and it went impeccably. I had the best time and just kept thinking how much better it was than if I'd done it in Edinburgh. Kate made the most incredible cake, Maggie had made herself a Snow Queen costume which was insane! Trigger came as Homer Simpson, which was very impressive. Artie came as a geek, and I'm sorry, but YES! There was something so hot about his thick-framed glasses, freckles, bowtie and four-colour biro. YES YES YES, Artie. We all got fucked and went to *C103* and danced 'till closing. Had sex all night with Artie, and I think I love him more than William… more than Gael. It's hard to have perspective while I'm in the thick of it, I guess. Go telling me at fifteen I could love someone more… I DON'T THINK SO!

<div align="center">~~~</div>

TUESDAY 25TH NOVEMBER 2003 2AM
LISTENING TO BLACK OR WHITE MICHAEL JACKSON

Artie has been in Birmingham since Sunday, and he called tonight (admittedly quite drunk).

    'I miss you, Claire. It seems nuts, given that it's only been a few days, but there you have it.'

    What a breakthrough. Woohoo! I'm going to bed with the biggest smile on my face.

<div align="center">~~~</div>

THURSDAY 27TH NOVEMBER 2003 1.30AM
LISTENING TO HALO BY FOO FIGHTERS

Artie got back last night, and we had sweet, sweet, slow sex. Twice last night and twice this morning. I can't get enough of him. Everything is different when I'm with him; the world is varnished, my body feels springy, music hits me differently, jokes are funnier…

~~~

It's no surprise, really, that a disproportionately high number of people feel compelled to burn their teenage diaries when they're faced with nauseating content such as this.

~~~

I want the world to stop so I can retreat into a bed-sheeted world with him. I don't want anything to affect us. NO ONE MOVE. This level of intimacy has bubble fragility, and the 'pop' is inevitable. I feel like I'm just watching us, caught in a breeze, flying over a field of roses.

~~~

Watch out, William Blake - there's a new kid on the block.

~~~

SATURDAY 29TH NOVEMBER 2003 1.32AM
LISTENING TO BABY BOY BY BEYONCÉ (FEAT. SEAN PAUL)

I went out with the flat tonight, and I was trying to 'Wing-Wom' Bruce. We've been watching too much Top Gun, for sure. I reckon we watch it about twice a week. Anyway, wing-womming Bruce is not hard. I had a chat with him at the end of the night about all the weed (he hates it). So do I really. I don't want to be a stoner. I've decided I'm going to make a conscious decision to stop. I know I love my bubble, but as they say in *Jurassic Park*... life goes on. Haha! No, that's not right... 'Life finds a way' is the *Jurassic Park* quote. Still. I know what I mean... the world keeps turning and all that. I can't just shag and smoke weed all the way through University, then *Poof* I'm a doctor.

I went round to Artie's after we got home, and he was on his bed, high as a kite, with Mike and Laura. Man, I hate her. She looked insane. Mike offered me some spliff, but with my conversation with Bruce still ringing fresh, I didn't smoke. I felt tortured watching Laura and Artie in their own microclimate. Our relationship feels like a sand castle with a rising tide; I have no control, and the more I dig for it, the more it disintegrates. He likes Laura. I can tell, and there is nothing I can do to stop it. I had no choice but to leave, but he at least had the decency to see me out.

'I think I'm just going to leave you guys to it, Artie. I feel like we're on slightly different wavelengths tonight.'

'Don't make it a "drug-thing" again, Claire. You're just being sketchy.'

'I'm not... you're stoned, and I'm not, so I'm not feeling it. That's all. It makes me feel like I'm interrupting something...'

'You're making this weird, and I'm off my face and can't handle it. Goodnight, Claire.'

'Night.'

Shit.

~~~

SATURDAY 6TH DECEMBER 2003 4AM
LISTENING TO WHEN TOMORROW COMES BY THE EURYTHMICS

It was the medic Christmas ball tonight at The Imperial Hotel in Torquay. Artie and I were sat at a table with Frank, Robin Mills, Pete Bond, Kate, Connie etc - perfecto. Pete is fastly turning into one of my favourite people. Artie *almost* seemed jealous - I wish he had been.

~~~

Pete is fiercely loyal, brilliantly clever, and unapologetically silly. He grew up on the outskirts of Bristol, where legend has it that his mother once broke down in tears at a Catholic school, begging them to accept her tangerine-haired chess prodigy. 'They'll kill him at the local comp!'. Her success in getting him admitted sparked a lifelong soft spot in Pete for Catholic girls, a trait that followed him well into university. Still, Bristol's edge runs deep in him.

I knew Pete was special but initially mistook my feelings for love, swept up in a desire to keep him close forever. I was lucky enough that Pete being Pete, ensured I didn't totally blow it and let me keep him platonically. He was everything I ever wanted as a friend.

These days, Pete lives in Australia, where he's an Emergency Medicine consultant. He has two little sunset-haired Aussies of his own (though I'd bet they've still picked up a "cheers drive" for when they hop off the Melbourne buses). For all his competence, reliability and all-round sense, Pete is still very, very silly.

~~~

After dinner, Artie and I sat in the lounge, and he smoked a cigar and loosened his bow tie. I swear to god, it was the sexiest thing anyone has ever done. EVER.

'Shall we go for a walk around the grounds? Maybe share a little doobie-doo?'

It's fucking relentless with him.

'I'm good on the doobie front, but a walk sounds lovely. You, by all means, fill your boots.'

So we walked through the moonlit grounds, and he draped his jacket around me and held me tight around the waist.

'Well, I must say, tonight's been kinda fun. I thought I'd hate it with all your medic mates, but they're not anything like I thought they'd be.'

'I'm not sure what you were expecting, seeing as the only medics you know are Kate and I, but good. I've had an awesome night with you.'

And he stopped and kissed me and… I LOVE HIM! I would literally cut off a leg for him to tell me he loves me. It was the most romantic night of my life.

~~~

MONDAY 8TH DECEMBER 2003 2.45AM
LISTENING TO BLACK AND BLUE BY COUNTING CROWS

So, my period is now over a week late. SHHHIIIITTTTT. Lou went and got me a pregnancy test as I was in full denial mode, and she'd had enough of it. I told Artie, too, and he was VERY quiet. Anyway, it was negative. THANK GOD. I can't remember the last time I was so relieved, but it certainly brought a touch of reality to our sex-filled world. If I'm one of the 1% false negatives, I will cry a fucking ocean.

I went to the *Union* this afternoon with Rich, Tommo and Trigger from upstairs, played some pool and had a couple of snakey-bs. Artie came and met me after his lecture and we left to have food at his. On our way out, Artie lit a spliff, and we bumped into JP, the South African. He's hot, sure, but I felt nothing for him.

'Hey, babe,' he drawled. I felt Artie bristle next to me.

'Sorry bud, but who are you calling babe?'

I had never seen Artie get possessive or jealous. It was awesome! JP then genuinely looked surprised and said, 'that's my girlfriend'.

WHAT?!

'Err, JP, we haven't seen each other or texted in months. You can't possibly think that we're together?'

I looked over at Artie, but he genuinely didn't seem to give a toss anymore. He was staring off into the distance with a bit of a glassy stare. My Artie spotlight had gone out again. Was he stoned already? JP then burst out laughing.

'No, Claire! I was just yanking your chain. Anyway, nice to see you. See you around!'

Dick.

Artie and I went back to his and watched *Fear and Loathing in Las Vegas*, shared a bottle of red wine, and a spliff and then had some wonderful sex.

~~~

Wonderful sex? Weird adjective choice... title of my next Christmas film/stripper biopic...

~~~

Artie and Mike then had another spliff, and I sat and sketched them before Artie left me to go and play football.

~~~

What time was this!? I'd been to the Union, had a few pints, played pool, had dinner, a bottle of wine, two spliffs, a film and a double portrait... all before evening football practice? This doesn't make sense.

~~~

MY 18TH

WEDNESDAY 10TH DECEMBER 2003
LISTENING TO THIS IS A CALL BY FOO FIGHTERS

I feel sad. I haven't seen Artie all night. He's been on shrooms with 'Drug Twats', and it makes me feel like even more of an outsider to his 'group'. I fucking hate shrooms. WHY would anyone want to take a hallucinogenic? It sounds like the worst idea ever. I hate Artie doing them and I hate him being 'away with the pixies' without me.

I also hate how threatened I am by Laura. Why doesn't he love me? FUUUUCKKKKK.

~~~

Easy now, hormones...

~~~

SATURDAY 13TH DECEMBER 2003 3.20AM
LISTENING TO HEY YA! BY OUTKAST

I spent the morning in Tescos with Ellie, but I've hardly got any money left so I just bought some pitta breads, 4 x tins of tuna and a bag of apples. Hopefully, that can keep me going until the end of term. I really tried to budget but it's impossible! I spent the afternoon playing Monopoly with Bruce, Mark and Lou. And won - OBVIOUSLY.

```
Text to Artie: Hey Artie. How's your
night going? We're hanging in the flat
if you fancy joining? x

Text from Artie: Hey! Yeah good thanks.
I think i'll just stay here and hang
out with the boys tonight. Have a good
one. x
```

'Hang out with the boys' AND LAURA, no doubt.

Bruce and I then went out to the *Union* with Tommo, Rich and Trigger from upstairs, but I was in a foul mood. Artie said he 'wants to try E' despite his night on shrooms being a disaster (he called me crying and hysterical about the size of his hands.) THAT'S A FUCKING HULLUCINAGENIC FOR YOU! But now E? I know loads of people do it, but some guy died in Dance Academy during Freshers after doing E. He apparently drank so much water that he got cerebral oedema and coned. I get that it's relatively safe, but why would you forever want to live in a world that is less good than a drug-induced one? If you have an apple on E, every apple after that won't taste as good. If you have sex on ecstasy, you are forever doomed to a lifetime of 'ok… but it was better on E' sex. How shit is that?! I don't get it. AT ALL.

So I'm home now, and he said he'd come home in the next half an hour. He just picks me up when he wants, and I just take it. I've completely lost control of everything, and I feel so insecure about this relationship.

~~~

SUNDAY 14TH DECEMBER 2003 4.30AM
LISTENING TO TIRED OF YOU BY FOO FIGHTERS

I am so fucked off with Artie - he never came round last night. I just sat waiting for him like a big loser of a lemon. He didn't even bother to let me know. So I've been stewing about this all day, and I'm getting the impression that he doesn't give a shit anymore.

I went round to his tonight, and he proceeded to tell me how fucked he'd got last night, and they all went round to Laura's even though he told me he was 'all mine' after the *Union*… like I'm some possessive brat that won't share him. He just has all his fun with everyone else and then quiet nights with me. That's all we do! He gets REALLY stoned. I sometimes join in. We watch a film, have sex and repeat. Borrrrrrrring. But I'm completely in love with him, and he's fading away. Fuck him. I shouldn't let him be a shit with me just cos I love him. So I tried to tell him this tonight (not the love bit), but he got it all wrong, thinking I was saying we weren't spending enough time together, which wasn't what I was saying at all! And so he went on to tell me he needed his space once in a while and 'I didn't think you were the kind of girl that was overprotective like this' etc etc… ARSEHOLE! Who the fuck does he think he is making me out to be some crazy bitch? I'm SUPER easygoing. I give him shit loads of fucking space! Anyway, I left quickly after being made to feel like such a fool. I felt so emotional and worried that I'd say something I was going to regret.

I think unreciprocated love is a bit like a slow, painful death of the soul. You lose yourself trying to get what you can't. You become crazy, ugly and completely unlovable.

~~~

WEDNESDAY 17TH DECEMBER 2003 1.45AM
LISTENING TO TAYLOR BY JACK JOHNSON

Oh my god. I can't believe this is actually happening. Artie just dumped me. Oh my god. My blood is fizzing. Am I going to die?

His best friend from Bath, G-man, was visiting on Monday night. I had a big one with Artie, Mike, G-man and Laura. We went to *Wonky Legs* and I was having a good time but aware that I had basically not seen Artie all night. I came out of the toilets, and Mike told me that everyone else had left. At least Mike didn't abandon me too but I couldn't quite understand what was happening.

'I can't believe Artie just left without me. Did he say anything?'

'I think you just need to have a chat with Artie, Claire.'

'What? Why?'

I could feel the panic setting in, and I started to cry as my world cracked. Mike put his arm around me, and we started walking home.

'Don't cry, mate. You just need to have a chat.'

I already knew. We walked home in silence, and I tried not to think about anything. I knew that if I did, I would break. We got back, and Artie barely looked up from his joint.

'Mike said you wanted to have a chat. Is everything ok?'

'Not tonight, Claire. We're both fucked. We'll have a chat tomorrow. Goodnight.'

Once again. I was speechless. What could I say? Put the idea in his head, make myself sound crazy or vindicate my anxieties and trigger the inevitable. I went home and lay awake in bed, running through the endless possible conversations in my head.

I didn't see him all day, and I was just a nervous wreck.

```
2pm Text to Artie: Hey. Are you free
today to catch up? Xxx

Text from Artie: Maybe later but I've
got a tonne of work to do. I'll call
later.
```

Mike messaged later.

```
4pm This is ridiculous. Just come
over. I've put the keys through your
window. X
```

So I let myself in, and Artie, Laura and G-man were just sitting in front of the TV, stoned off their tits. Tonnes of work, huh? He was so cold with me and didn't even look up when I arrived. Laura was giggling uncontrollably. It probably had nothing to do with me and everything to do with her inane, drug-addled brain, but the paranoia had me in a chokehold. I was screaming and crying inside but tried to be the laid-back girlfriend Artie wanted me to be. I spent the whole day there pretending to be the 'cool girlfriend' but given how I was feeling, there was a 50/50 chance I was going to break. Before I knew it, Artie had just gone to bed. Tomorrow is our last day together before the holidays, and he clearly has no inclination to care. I asked Mike what Artie had said, and he told me I couldn't put him in this situation. So I woke Artie up.

Enough.

'What's going on? I don't care if you're fucked. You can't treat me like this. I can't wait for when you're not fucked for this conversation - that's just not going to happen!'

I could feel tears burning down my cheeks, and my heart was trying to explode out of my chest.

'I'm sorry Claire. I'm just not sure I'm feeling it. I'm not sure I know what I want. I like you, I really do, and you're incredible, but the "having a girlfriend thing" is sketching me out. Please don't make me have this conversation with you now. You deserve better. Tomorrow morning, I promise.'

So there you have it. It's over. I fell in love. Again. My heart is smooshed. Every time I breathe out, it feels like I might not be able to breathe in again. But I do, and the pain continues. This will take me a lifetime to recover from.

~~~

I recovered.

~~~

THURSDAY 18TH DECEMBER 2.30AM
LISTENING TO GOLDEN SLUMBERS BY THE BEATLES

The finality of what's happened is just starting to sink in. Artie asked to meet me this afternoon downstairs in the *Skiving Scholar*.

~~~

The Skiving Scholar *was a smoggy bunker of existential dread. The downstairs was windowless and oppressive, with brown carpets on not just the floor and the walls but, unbelievably, the ceiling. Only the bleakest of students could be found there during daylight hours.*

~~~

I sat there with a pint, chain-smoking as he babbled at me that he wasn't sure he'd made the right decision and, how he's 'got so much on his mind' and how he's even considering leaving uni. I had nothing to say. I didn't get angry. I didn't cry. I was in control. I just corked it all up to deal with later. He looked upset, though, which gave me strength. I fed off his pain and guilt like a mosquito, and it kept my tears at bay. He told me he needed time to think, and he knew it was selfish, but would I consider getting back with him next term if that's what he decided? Unbelievably, even though every cell in my body was screaming a resounding 'yes', I looked right at him for the first time since we'd got there.

'I can't, Artie. I couldn't bear three weeks over Christmas with that potential false hope. I'm not just going to wait around for you. If you're ending it, it's over.'

The truth is that if he did come back in January and tell me he'd missed me and wanted to get back with me, I'd be with him quicker than Sonic. The problem is that I then took it too far. I just wanted the upper hand.

'I think we both know this is over.'

'Oh, greeb, I'm so sorry. I'm not sure I've done the right thing.'

'You have. You know you have. I could see this coming. You've wanted to end it for a while. It's normal to feel regret when breaking up with someone. It doesn't mean you've made the wrong decision.'

'You're right, Claire. Thank you.'

How I didn't punch myself in the face at this point, I'll never know. I'll almost certainly never be able to look myself in the eye again.

We walked back to the flat in silence. The whole time, I was just trying not to cry. We stopped at my door, and he turned to face me. He put his hands on my shoulders and held me at arm's reach, looking straight into my eyes. It was like he was taking me in for the last time. The tumour in my throat was growing.

'Aww, Claire. I really am sorry.'

As soon as I turned my back, I burst into tears, and I cried every tear in my body. I felt like I was being water-boarded by my own tears. A few hours later, I thought, 'fuck this' and went on a massive night out with Lou. We ended up dancing in Dance Academy. It was great until I bumped into Mike on the way home. He'd been with Artie all day and said he was PLEASED it was all over now cos we had both been miserable! WHAT!? I asked if we were still friends.

'No, sorry, Claire. I can't be friends with both of you, and my loyalty is to Artie.'

Great.

~~~

FEAR AND LOATHING IN PLYMOUTH

FRIDAY 19TH DECEMBER 2003 1.15AM
LISTENING TO BACK ON THE CHAIN GANG BY THE PRETENDERS

I'm such a cliché. I haven't eaten or slept since Artie dumped me.

```
Text from Artie: See ya, greeb. Have a
good Christmas. I'm not sure I'm ready
to give up on us. Can we see what hap-
pens after the holidays?

Text to Artie: U know I want that, but
I'm really not sure u do. But sure…
we can see.
```

But I know it's bullshit. He just can't be the bad guy, thinking it's kinder to say that but he's just keeping me hanging. I know we won't get back together. He'll go back to Bath, get fucked up with his mates and live his perfect single life with those beautiful stoners. And he'll never look back.

Urgh, it hurts so much. He's gone. I can't imagine ever feeling happy again. I am completely heartbroken. I can feel my world crumbling around me when I think of him and realise he's not mine anymore. I felt like I had the best thing in the world, and with the snap of his fingers, it was gone. God, I loved him so much. More than I've ever loved anyone. I feel like my heart has been smashed into shards of glass that cut me every time it beats.

~~~

Yikes.

~~~

I've just chain-smoked my way through the entire Red Dwarf box set, series I to VIII. Nothing helps, though.

~~~

Heartbreak can push some people to entire tubs of Häagen Dazs, drugs and alcohol, depression or the arms of a wrong-un. Personally, when I have to deal with truly distressing times, I choose to bask in the warm glow of Red Dwarf. During the pandemic, my husband and I were quick to indulge in this nostalgic comfort. It allows me to turn off and chuckle stupidly at the word 'Smeg'. I will always find solace in the reassuring, timeless humour of Red Dwarf.

~~~

Bruce came into my room earlier to find me in a terrible state of hibernation and the repetitive… it's cold outside, there's no kind of atmosphere…

'Fucking hell, Claire. Get it together. Open a window, at least. Jesus, mate.'

~~~

…*I'm all alone, more or less… let me fly far away from here…*

~~~

'C'mon buddy. Turn that shit off. Let's go out for a Chinese - my treat.'

'I'm not hungry.'

'How can you let it get to you? You can't have liked him that much - it wasn't that long…'

He was trying to help and snap me out of it, but…

'FUCK OFF BRUCE YOU DON'T UNDERSTAND!'

'Fine. Suit yourself.'

I'm heading back to Edinburgh, and I don't want to go. OBVIOUSLY, I want to see my family, but I hate who I am there and how I'm viewed. I'm cool (ish)… (er?) here. Ok - Maybe not 'cool', but at least I'm not universally hated.

~~~

I thought I knew what it was to be hated, but I hadn't pinned a target on my back in the form of a published 'The Diary of a Teenage Dirtbag' yet. Edinburgh just LOVED that.

~~~

Ellie and Lou came and got me and forced me to the Chinese with them. I ate what I could, forced a smile when appropriate, but it was all very superficial. Bruce hasn't got much patience for me at the moment. I wish I could just snap out of it but I can't!

~~~

FRIDAY 19TH DECEMBER 2003 10.30AM
(PLYMOUTH TO EDINBURGH TRAIN RIDE)

LISTENING TO DON'T WORRY BABY BY THE BEACH BOYS

Fuck me, this is a long train ride. There's nothing like getting dumped and spending the rest of eternity on a train, watching the passage of time. Pfff. All I can see is the grey sea and the grey sky, through my grey fucking tears. My mum is going to freak out when she sees me. I've lost weight, my skin is ashy and terrible, my eyes swollen, and my smile elusive.

Oh god. It's definitely over, isn't it? I've never felt so devastated - so much so that it has a colour; a deep burgundy. I just can't believe it. We'll never kiss again. He'll never hold my hand and give it a little squeeze as he smiles at me… sigh… I can circle around it a thousand times, but the bottom line is that Artie Callaghan never loved me back.

FIVE
NOEL 2003

SUNDAY 21ST DECEMBER 2003 1.48AM
LISTENING TO COME AS YOU ARE BY NIRVANA

Arriving in Edinburgh was such a relief. I can't describe how full of love I was to see my family. I had a really long dinner with Chloe and the parentals who all seemed very excited to see me. Which is nice.

Then I popped over to Next Door Andy's (who has changed a million times for the better). He actually called ME and asked if I wanted to go round for a couple of drinks! We went to *Scruffy Murphys* and then to *Berties*, and I actually got ID'd for the first time as a legal 18-year-old - HAHAHA IN YOUR FACE BERTIES!

~~~

Next Door Andy was an idiot; a reckless and cocky, but lovable idiot. I had a very predictable coup de coeur when cool as fuck fourteen-year-old Andy moved in next door to Celine Dion obsessed me in 1998. But Andy became so much more than just a childhood crush; he's my pal. We navigated the peaks and troughs of adolescence together, and Andy was a comforting presence throughout. Albeit brutally honest—like a sibling or, dare I say it, a best friend. He would never admit to such a friendship, of course, and in many ways, it wasn't true; he could be mean, and I sometimes sensed that he was embarrassed by me when with his boys. It stung, but I don't think I would change a thing - he gave me a friendship that no one else could, and I adored him. For all his faults, he was wonderfully witty and self-deprecating. He was emotionally far more intelligent than anyone would have guessed behind his drunken bravado, and whilst he teased me to no end, he was fiercely protective of me, and we both knew that whatever was said, we'd always be there for each other. We had some beautiful moments, just the two of us on his roof, where we would sit, perfectly content in the comfortable silence of friendship.

~~~

I bumped into Charlie Harper in *Berties*. I was so excited to see him that I babbled excitedly for about 20 mins. Then I suddenly remembered the last time we'd seen each other. Urgh - sucking face behind Maggie's back before he ended up shagging 'Man Shoes'. A life low.

Next Door Andy and I then danced 'til closing in Espionage, and I called Artie on the way home… eek! But it was ok. Next Door Andy was quite drunk and hilarious, and I probably sounded pretty cheery down the phone, which is good.

I spent today cleaning and tidying up my room and then saw my beautiful Maggie. I went round to hers, had dinner with her parents, then sat and chatted for hours, smoking out of her bedroom window. She is having the best time in Brighton - will definitely have to visit next term. LOVE HER! I can't believe how pumped I am to be back in Eddy.

~~~

MONDAY 22ND DECEMBER 2003 2.15AM
LISTENING TO AUTOMATIC BY LESS THAN JAKE

Urrghhhh. I just called Artie again. It's obvious that it was a mistake. SHIT. I'd been out with Maggie, and I ended up drinking too much as I was stuck sitting between William Macleod and FUCKING Gretchen. How it happened, I have no idea. I think we were all trying to prove how much we don't mind and how mature we are, and then boom… sat in an amicable little row. What a nightmare. I couldn't believe it. I don't care how grown-up and mature I try to convince myself I am, I bloomin' well hate them.

~~~

I could talk about William and Gretchen forever; hell, I wrote an entire book about them. But that was so 2020, and I've almost put out this particular bellyfire now. William was everything to me. My first love, my first heartbreak, my first everything. And like a lot of first loves, it turned sour, and we nearly destroyed each other. And Gretchen? I won't even go there. Let's just say I've never hated anyone more in my life.

~~~

So anyway, I just drank through it, and now I'm pissed, and I drunk-dialled Artie.

'I wondered if you've had a chance to think about us? You said you needed time to see if you've made the right decision. Have you decided?'

'I dunno Claire, it's only been a few days…'

I wish he'd properly dumped me. I wish he hadn't kept the door ajar. This tiny slither of hope will be the undoing of me for sure.

~~~

FEAR AND LOATHING IN PLYMOUTH

TUESDAY 23RD DECEMBER 2003 2.32AM
LISTENING TO PLACE YOUR HANDS BY REEF

Well, today's been interesting. I went shopping with my darling Maggilicious and bought myself the BEST black and white polka dot Irregular Choice heels. FUN. We then went to *The Watershed* and met Charlie. It was sweet and familiar and comfortable - just like old times. Charlie and I looked at each other knowingly when Maggie went to the toilet. The message was clear... she never needs to know about us. I won't tell a soul, and neither will Charlie. Hopefully, the guilt will subside with time.

It all went a bit downhill from then.

Maggie and I went to *Rev* and EVERYONE from St Felix's was there. Grumpy Arseface Toby was there (still grumpy and with a face still like an arse). It was so weird seeing everyone, and if I'm honest, I didn't give a flying Jimmy about any of them.

~~~

Feeling a bit Scottish now again, are we?

~~~

But it was so nice to see Mish tonight... PSYCHE! The RUDE FUCK. I haven't seen or spoken to him in five months. We had years of friendship, we worked together, we spoke every day for two years. We had our 'affair' that left me humiliated, ostracised and heartbroken. School finished, and he cut me out of his life. Extinguished me. He ignored my calls and texts until I got the message... or not, as the case may be.

But I saw him tonight (and I was pissed), and all my emotions bubbled up, and I ran over and gave him a huge hug.

~~~

Jesus. Have some self-respect Claire. This guy is poison.

~~~

He peeled me off him like I was contaminated and said all of … ummm… THREE WORDS to me.

'What you doing?'

I was trying to work out if he meant, 'What the fuck are you doing touching me?' or 'What are you up to now? How's Uni?' but he squeezed my shoulder (in a faux-sympatico way) and turned and walked off. Wow. Real nice. FUCK HIM. There's A LOT of stuff I would do differently in my life if I got a second chance, but top of the list is definitely hugging Mish tonight.

~~~

FRIDAY 26TH DECEMBER 2003 2.25AM
LISTENING TO YOU MAKE MY DREAMS BY HALL & OATS

Jeeez. Edinburgh is bloody brilliant. What a cracking Christmas day (ha). I spoke to Lou and Bruce, which was lovely, Maggie came round, and then I went for a walk with Next Door Andy, who was fuming. His dad gave him an old chess set, but there were two pieces missing, and his step-mum gave him a £5 HMV voucher. Yikes.

Next Door Andy and I went out to *Subway* on Lothian Road last night. I'd had a Christmas Eve dinner with my family and then headed out with him about midnight. We danced all night on an empty dance floor and owned it. I'd have bottled how I felt with him if I could. Who says you can't have an entirely platonic friendship with guys?!

I got to bed about 6am, and as my dancing high wore off, I felt the tears arrive as I thought of Artie, and I texted him. I want him back so badly.

```
25/12/03 06:02 Merry Christmas. I miss
you.
```

~~~

SATURDAY 27TH DECEMBER 2003 2AM
LISTENING TO HEY JULIE BY FOUNTAINS OF WAYNE

Hmmmm. I want to go back to Plymouth now. I miss my life there. Don't get me wrong. I've loved seeing my family but I miss living with Bruce and Ellie and Lou and Mark. They make my life easier. No drama, no fuss. Just love and support. ARGH, I'm not saying my family don't love and support me... OBVIOUSLY, they do. I'm ready to go back, that's all.

~~~

FRIDAY 2ND JANUARY 2004 2.35AM
LISTENING TO HURRICANE BY BOB DYLAN

Next Door Andy and I just watched The Hurricane. WHAT. A. FILM. How have we not seen it before? Epic. Nice one, Denzel.

~~~

Next Door Andy and I remember very little from our formative years, but we both have a multicoloured, HD memory of sobbing our way through The Hurricane.

~~~

I have decided I need to be one of life's good guys. I hate myself for writing this, and I know I'll never be able to read it back as I'll cringe to the brink of death, but... well... I want to make things better. I am going to do everything in my power to create happiness. Cringe away future me, but the sentiment is strong and ultimately much better than the so far... I love this guy... my heart is broken... I am drunk... I am stoned... I love someone else... I am heartbroken again. I am still drunk.

Yawn.

Get a life, Claire and do something with yourself.

~~~

You're wrong, teenage Claire. Maybe I'm getting soft as I hit middle age, or maybe I'm all cringed out from everything else you've written that you somehow don't think I'll mind, but I think this is rather sweet.

~~~

I hosted a big dinner on Monday night, which was great. I couldn't be arsed to go out afterwards, so everyone left about midnight, and I called Artie. We spoke for hours. He was absolutely fucked, but talking to him makes me feel complete. He called the next morning and then again last night to wish me a Happy New Year. Dare I dream? Can I allow myself to believe we could still work? The 'what ifs' are driving me insane.

~~~

SUNDAY 4TH JANUARY 2004 3.45AM
LISTENING TO THIS LOVE BY MAROON 5

AHHH, I have just had THE BEST NIGHT with Maggie, Next Door Andy, Big Sam and Clyde. Next Door Andy is DA MAN - I love that guy. We danced all night in *Subway* again, and I was bursting with love for them. What more can a girl ask for? Not much, I tell you, not much.

~~~

Clydie has an enormous heart and an even bigger beard. There are few people less superficial than Clyde. This can be both a blessing and a curse, for he undoubtedly feels too much, but with that comes an unwavering love and loyalty for his friends and family. From the day I met Clydie, I have had an overwhelming desire to smother him with merriment. He doesn't need it at all, of course. He's a big boy who laughs and jokes and lads (yes - a verb in this instance) about like the rest of them. But there is sometimes an uninvited blue-ness that has no place being there.

I don't want to make him sound sad. Some of my most hilarious and joyful Edinburgh-based times have been thanks to this guy. If Clydie was anything like Next Door Andy and I (with our slight tendency for narcissism), he would have been devastated to see that he was cut from 'The Diary of a Teenage Dirtbag'. But Clydie being Clydie felt nothing but happiness for me (I think!).

Clydie was Next Door Andy's best man, and he will always be one of mine.

~~~

WEDNESDAY 7TH JANUARY 2004 00:15AM
LISTENING TO ARE YOU GONNA BE MY GIRL BY JET

I went to the library on George IV Bridge today - ACHIEVEMENT! I should have gone a bit more this holiday. Next term, I'll work. One dud term is allowed, right? I haven't failed anything, and I've handed everything in, but the background commitment may have been… somewhat lacking. Bloody boys. But I've got four years and two terms to make up for it. It'll be ffiiiiiiiiinnnnnnnnnee.

Yesterday was such an incredible day. I met Herbie for a walk and a coffee, and we went to see the Degas exhibition. I wish I was studying art. I haven't painted in months… We went out with all the A-level French lot, and I got home feeling pretty content. It was a great day and night. No drama, no drugs, no heartbreak, and I'm not drunk. Winner.

I've just got off the phone from Artie. He called when I got back from la bibliothèque, and we had our first sober chat since the start of the holidays (the first time he's been sober). I love him so much. Talking to him felt so right, and I had so much to tell him. It's torture, really. I spend every night lying in bed fantasising about all the ways he might ask me back. The worst part is that deep down, I know it won't happen.

Next Door Andy and I hung out at his tonight, wallowing in

our respective heartbreak. He just got dumped too. He is NOT USED TO IT, which is quite funny really. Misery loves company and all that, though. We sat on his roof like we'd always done, wrapped in a very musty Harris Tweed blanket and sank some beers. I looked at him and questioned if I could ever fall for him. I seem to manage falling in love with everyone these days. Why not one of my oldest friends who knows the secret unfiltered parts? That's a good reason why. What we have is sacred - I've got to keep it safe.

'Why the fuck are you staring at me like that? Have you fallen in love with me again?'

And he's a prick.

'Again? Fuck off.'

I lit a cigarette as he opened a couple more beers.

'We'll find love though, Andy. We're normal, loveable people. We'll be fine.'

'Aye, right.' He snorted. 'I'm not worried about me. It's the weirdos on the fringes of society like you that need to worry.'

'Sounds like flirting talk if ever I heard it.'

'You fucking wish, pal.' And with that he put his arm around me and gave me a little squeeze. It was freezing, but that gesture felt like warm brotherly love, and I made a mental note to never let Next Door Andy get away from me.

~~~

FRIDAY 9TH JANUARY 2004
LISTENING TO SOMEWHERE ONLY WE KNOW BY KEANE

Pfff, it was quite a stressy day. Had a driving lesson this morning (last one hopefully!). Then I went back to St Felix's to talk about Medical School applications. It was weird as fuck going back. It just made me think of Mish and William and Gretchen. I could almost smell them when I arrived. Urgh.

I met Herbert in town late afternoon for a pint, then got home to discover that I'd lost my train tickets back to Plymouth. I had no choice but to tell my mum, who took it surprisingly ok.

I've got my driving test tomorrow - Fingers crossed, I'm not doomed to walk alone for the rest of my life.

~~~

SATURDAY 10TH JANUARY 2004 00.43AM
LISTENING TO TAKE ME OUT FRANZ FERDINAND

I PASSED MY MOTHER FUCKING DRIVING TEST!
Finally. Third time's a charm bitches.
I'm a driver now! YEEEEHHAAAAWWWW.

SIX
BIG DICK DAVE

MONDAY 12TH JANUARY 2004 2.45AM
LISTENING TO MY SWEET PRINCE BY PLACEBO

Ahh… I'm back in Plymouth, and it feels goooooooood and the best part is I've still not had to deal with the trauma of seeing Artie, and I'm far too excited to see everyone. I went out tonight with Bruce, Ellie, Lou, Mark, and Tommo, Rich and Trigger from upstairs. I'm so much more relaxed here than in Edinburgh. It's like my Edinburgh is still haunted with the echoes from all those bitches. Even if all is good, I can feel it in the air.

Right. Bed. I have some work to do tomorrow and a big Tesco shop. I'm going to have to be far more careful with money this term (and/or get a job).

~~~

WEDNESDAY 14TH JANUARY 2004 2AM
LISTENING TO THE REASON BY HOOBASTANK

Well, Artie can fuck right off out of my face. Texts from yesterday:

```
To Artie: Do u fancy hanging out to-
morrow? Just as friends or whatever.
It doesn't have to be a 'thing'.
```

> From Artie: Sounds good! I'll give u a call in the morning and we'll sort something out.

So I've been psyching myself up all day whilst staring at my phone and nothing. Then FINALLY:

> 7pm From Artie: Hey Greeb, Mike and I are going for a drink if you want to join?
>
> To Artie: Sure. When / where?

Aaaaand nothing. Two hours of climbing the walls, waiting for him to reply. If it were anyone else, I would think they were doing it on purpose, but Artie's not like that. He's just got his head in the clouds… of dope.

> 9pm Text to Mike: Are you heading out anytime soon cos I might just go out with the flat?
>
> From Mike: We decided to stay in in the end. Catch ya laterz x

Thanks for letting me know you fuckers. So I went out with Bruce and Big Dick Dave. Bruce has spent a long time trying to convince me that I should 'give it a go' with Big Dick Dave in virtue of his massive shlong.

We danced in *Walkabout* and I had to admit BDD was not too shabby to look at. He came back to ours and talked AT Bruce and I for hours before eventually going home. Christ does his chat reek. A BEAUTIFUL man (who probably has a big dick) but his chat reminds me of Skater Chris' smelly, bullshitty, just plain annoying chat. There is no physique in the world that would make me ignore that chat. I just want Artie!

THURSDAY 15TH JANUARY 2004 11.40PM
LISTENING TO TASTE IN MEN BY PLACEBO

Yesterday was amazing! I went for lunch at Wetherspoons with Ellie, Lou, Bruce and Mark. Lou and I then went for a tour round Plymouth Gin Distillery and invested in a litre bottle of the navy strength for the flat. Then I went to the *Union* with Rich, Tommo and Trigger. We were having fun hustling idiots at pool (made £20 tonight!) when my stomach dropped as I saw Artie and Mike walk in. My brain was madly flitting between 'stay calm, stay cool' and 'FUUUUUUUUCCCCCCCCKKKKK'. So I went over and chatted and smiled and laughed and could not have demonstrated more of a 'cool cool cool... everything's cool with me' vibe if I'd actually been cool.

~~~

The pool hustle... I remember it well, and I'm embarrassingly proud of it. In true 'misspent youth' fashion, I was a fairly accomplished pool player at eighteen. I didn't look the part, though (which only worked in my favour).

Plymouth was full of boneheads who took one look at this giggling, blonde teenager and foolishly underestimated just how much time I had spent in a pub. Naturally, I took full financial advantage. I leaned into the ditsy, slightly tipsy act, and they flocked to me like moths to a flame.

I was devilishly cunning (of course), always watching my opponents play before flicking my hair and making my move (like a freakin' lioness). Before they knew it, they were challenging me to a play-off for a fiver. In hindsight, this little hustle probably funded my entire first year at university as I would often 'make' £10-£20 each time.

Twenty quid in 2004? That covered a pack of Marlboro Lights, a night out, a Jake's tuna, chips, and cheese melt, and even left me with a fiver for the piggy bank.

Take that suckers.

~~~

I then went out with Lou and Ellie to *C103* tonight and what a night of dreams! We danced for about four hours solid. Epic. I was stood in the corridor between the 'R&B room' and the 'cheese room' having a fag when this mega cute guy came and leant against the wall next to me. We just looked at each other and smiled for ages before he finally spoke. His voice was smooth and northern with a sing-song quality that made me smile.

'Hi.'

'Well, hello.'

'Are you an RnB or a cheese girl?'

'Definitely both, but cheese tonight.'

Then he made some kinda cheese pun, which was quite funny, but I can't remember it, and it would definitely do him a disservice if I tried to guess. He came and danced in the cheese room for a bit with us, and we shared a cheeky snog. Joe, that was it. Lovely northern Joe. He asked for my number, but I was too wankered and forgot until I got home. Fate will bring us back together if it's meant to be…

I met Artie in *The Scholar* today for a catch-up, and it was lovely, but it's clear that we'll never get back together. Can we be friends if I'm still madly in love with him?

'Are you ok with everything, Claire?'

'Of course. Everything is fine!' I choked (with what might as well have been my last breath).

I grimaced at him in an attempt to smile, and Artie accepted it and smiled back with apparent relief. FUCK. Maybe he can still change his mind?

~~~

SUNDAY 18TH JANUARY 2004 3.15AM
LISTENING TO AMERICAN IDIOT BY GREEN DAY

Tonight was certainly very interesting. I played pool and danced in the *Union* with the lads. Then I busted Mark's girlfriend being a massive slag, snogging and dry-humping some rando against the wall. Gross. Kate and I were on the pints, and we got totally creamed.

~~~

What a disgusting word. Bleurgh. Did I mean drunk? God, I hope I meant drunk.

~~~

Despite the aforementioned creamed-ness*, I still managed to beat Artie at pool - woohoo!

~~~

*Now that's just being ridiculous.

~~~

Then I put a thong on my head…

~~~

Good. All the greats put thongs on their heads.

~~~

…and won a Guinness T-shirt downing a pint.

It was just Rich and I at the end of the night, and we went for a long walk up to the Hoe, shared a spliff, and I laughed SO HARD I thought I was going to wet myself. He's such a great guy.

Artie has asked for a rematch tomorrow - yay!

~~~

WEDNESDAY 21ST JANUARY 2004 11.30AM
LISTENING TO COMFORTABLY NUMB BY THE SCISSOR SISTERS

I was going to have an early night last night, but it went a bit wrong. I was in *Roundabout* with Bruce, Lou, Ellie and the upstairs gang when Big Dick Dave arrived and sat with us. He was looking HOT. He was also not giving shit chat like last time. He was actually quite charming…

Anyway, we lost him and went to *Walkabout*. On our way there, Bruce had his arm around my shoulders, and he put his head against mine.

'I know just how we're going to get you over Artie.'

'Let me guess. Does it have a big dick?'

He gave me the seediest smile and mimed thrusting someone from behind and holding their hips. Then he did his gross orgasm face. It makes me smile every time. Silly Bruce…

'IT does… Big Dick Dave thinks you're fit, by the way, Claire. I think he likes you… And I know he was a bit of a twat the other night, but he's a nice guy. I would. Plus, his hair smells like candy floss…'

'Like nuzzling Daddy's beard…'

'What the fuck? I didn't have you down as a daddy-issues kinda girl!'

'Haha! No! Candy Floss in French is barbe a papa … literal translation is daddy's beard.'

'You're a weirdo dude.'

Anyway, when we got to *Walkabout*, BDD was already there. He kept putting his hand on the small of my back and it felt cute and protective. We were chatting for ages, then danced when *Don't Stop Me Now* came on and pulled. It felt brilliant. We went back to mine and chatted and pulled again. His chat was good! Was it because I was drunk? Am I desperate now? Am I blinded by his beauty?

'I really like you, Claire. I don't want to scare you off, but I want you to know. Bruce told me about your ex. I'd never treat you like that. Can I ask… what do you think of me?'

I felt like I was holding all the cards, and I smiled at him and pressed myself against him.

'I think… You're all right… which is better than if you'd asked me a week ago.'

'What? Why? Never mind… 'all right' friends or 'all right' prospective?'

'All right prospective.'

Who'd have thought it? I like Big Dick Dave. Do I need to stop calling him that? What if we end up married and with kids, and I have kicked it all off calling him Big Dick Dave? Ha. Fuck that. No way I'm marrying him. I like him, but he's not Artie.

Bruce showed me a text BDD had sent this morning.

```
Cracking night bud. Your house mate
is such a lil fittie. Keep plugging me
please mate!
```

Love it.

~~~

MONDAY 26TH JAN 2004 3.30AM
LISTENING TO CALL ON ME BY ERIC PRYDZ

Boy do I need to start going to bed at a reasonable time. Right. The weekend. I went to the cinema on Friday with Big Dick Dave, and he came back to mine. We just pulled and fooled around, but PG all the way - I'm getting the hang of this 'not being a total slag' thing.

Stayed in last night cos I had so much work to do, and also, Jiminy Cricket was in my ear telling me to chill the fuck out. So

I wrote an essay on statins, and the whole time, I wondered if I will ever know what I'm talking about. Medicine is impossibly vast and never-ending. I feel the same about it as some people do when they think of themselves in the universe: overwhelmed and insignificant.

Tonight I played pool in the *Union* with Artie, Mike, Laura and their lot. They were all doing lines in the toilet and Laura couldn't understand why I didn't want any. I just don't.

Pete Bond was there with Robin Mills, and I had a bit of a drugs rant to them.

'Legality and safety aside, don't ever do coke, Claire. You're just on the cusp of being insufferable as it is with booze alone. You don't need coke. Coke is for those that need a social boost, and let's be honest, you do not need that.'

'Haha. I wasn't tempted, but if I ever am, I'll remember your wise words, buddy.'

~~~

Of course it was Pete! I have never forgotten these words. It is true. I would be a total nightmare on coke (legality and safety aside, of course).

~~~

Being around Artie hurts so much. I shouldn't have even gone out. I should have been in bed, fresh for work tomorrow. No matter what I do, I am still completely in love with him. I hate having to be friends with him; I hate it with a passion. I went to bed, and all I could think about was walking through the topiary in black tie with him on that frosty night in Torquay.

SEVEN
LOVELY NORTHERN JOE

THURSDAY 29TH JANUARY 2004 2AM
LISTENING TO TAKE YOUR MAMA BY SCISSOR SISTERS

Oh, Big Dick Dave, you really are just a pretty face. He told me he'd met the Foo Fighters in a pub in Manchester, and I was like, 'Nope! I'm out.' IT WAS EXACTLY LIKE SKATER CHRIS AND THE CHILIS. How has that not come up before?! Is this the new thing? The 'lie du jour' appears to be "I met this massive world-famous band in my local shit hole". So Dave is out but…

I saw Joe again last night… Lovely Northern Joe from the night of dreams in *C103*. I thought he wouldn't actually be cute and that I'd just been drunk, but I saw him last night and thought *ouch! Damn boy, you are h-o-o-o-o-ot!*

So we chatted and danced and pulled again. He came back to mine, and we talked all night. He made me laugh so much and I realised after he left about 6am that I hadn't once thought about Artie.

~~~

THURSDAY 29TH JANUARY 2004 7.14PM
LISTENING TO PIANO MAN BY BILLY JOEL

Oh My God. Have I met the man of my dreams? Or is he just Artie's opposite? Lovely Northern Joe Friedrich invited me round to his today (having only left mine a few hours earlier). I went round after lunch, and we sat in his room all afternoon and listened to music. Then he played the piano and sang Billy Joel. I've found my very own Piano Man. TAKE ME JOE!!!

I'm not entirely sure how we got on to the next 'activity' (!?) or whose idea it was, but we did the most bizarre thing and sat for an hour and drew each other. It didn't feel weird at the time, but writing it now feels a little odd. He's such an amazing artist. This guy man - it's too much. BUT we didn't kiss all afternoon. I got a bit worried when I got home that he wasn't interested after all.

```
Text to Joe: Oops, I forgot to kiss
you... hopefully, next time! Thanks
for a cracking, fun-filled afternoon.
Claire xxx
```

Confident little madam, aren't we?

```
Text from Joe (2mins later): I'll just
have to kiss you twice next time to
make up for it. Thanks for a great af-
ternoon. J x
```

What a belter! I can't stop smiling. I came into the kitchen, and Bruce and Ellie were making some food. Bruce told me I looked smug, and it was putting him off his lunch.

~~~

LOVELY NORTHERN JOE

TUESDAY 3RD FEBRUARY 2004 1.30AM
LISTENING TO NOVACAINE BY GREEN DAY

Standard carnage weekend.

Friday: I started with G&Ts with Bruce and Lou at the flat, Terminators at *The Scholar* followed by yet another crazy night of dancing and Snakebites in the *Union*. I was wearing my pink and white 'tartan' beret, and I felt invincible. Bruce told me it (le beret) was ridiculous, but I love it. Rich and I were the last to leave again, and we went back to Tommo's flat, where we shared a spliff. I got myself into the most delicious state of giggles I've been in, in a long time. Is half a spliff every month ok?

Joe came round on Saturday night, and we watched *Identity*. After about two hours of pulling, we were both getting so carried away, and my top was riding up, and I had my hands under his T-shirt... ummm. He took it off, and I kept thinking about him singing and playing the piano. Before I knew it, we were having sex. He goes on for ages and it was brilliant. GREAT sex. Unfortunately, he was a bit loud when he came, and it made me wince. It was a fairly high-pitched 'oh yeah'. Urgh - I really didn't like it. Even thinking about it now is making me shudder. I REALLY like him though!

~~~

THURSDAY 5TH FEBRUARY 2004 1.30AM
LISTENING TO THE LONGEST TIME BY BILLY JOEL

Joe came to *Walkabout* all by himself (without knowing any of my friends) just to see me last night, and he officially asked me out. I said no...

AS IF! YESSSSSSSSS! We then went back to his, and he played the piano, and I was 100% seduced, like putty in his hands. Anyway, we had a wonderful night and I was awoken this morning with breakfast in bed. I like him so much and so far no faults to report.

~~~

FRIDAY 6TH FEBRUARY 2004 2AM
LISTENING TO SHE WILL BE LOVED BY MAROON 5

Joe came round for dinner, and it was a bit hectic in the kitchen as Bruce had a girl round (can't even remember her name, but she was totally forgettable), and Lou had invited Rich (only as mates, apparently). So Lou, Rich, Mark, Ellie, Bruce, Bruce's bimbo, Joe and I were all squeezed around the table.

Ellie had been pretty emotional and hormonal all day. We were all tiptoeing around as she kept flitting between crying with laughter and crazy <don't-fuck-with-me-or-I'll-eat-you> maniac. We started eating, and I can't remember why, but Mark playfully hit Ellie on the shoulder. So she hit him harder (but still playfully) back. Then he hit her one more time (probably harder than he should have done), and Ellie completely lost her shit. She started punching him and screaming and swearing at him. She went hell-red. It took ages to register that Ellie was completely short circuiting as she's normally so calm and composed. I don't think I'd even heard her swear until tonight. Bruce and Lou had to wrench her off Mark, and she stormed out the kitchen. We just sat there in stunned silence. What was that!?

~~~

This is a perfect example of how I have managed to naively upset people with these books. Ellie was, and still is, a perfectly reasonable person. Have I documented two years' worth of completely vanilla behaviour on her part? No. Did I even attempt to understand the reason why she was acting abnormally on this day other than 'hormones'? I did not. She was upset, and I did the most patriarchal millennial thing and said she was 'crazy from her girl-mones'. Sorry, Ellie.

~~~

GREAT impression for Joe too. Wonderful. Please come round for dinner and meet my house mates and see how mad they all are… hahaha… nothing to see here… "We're all mad here!".

~~~

SATURDAY 7TH FEBRUARY 2004 3.30AM
LISTENING TO LAURA BY SCISSOR SISTERS

I'm totally confused. I'm really liking Joe, but I bumped into Artie tonight, and to be honest, I felt like my heart stopped the second I saw him. I don't want anyone to know how much I'm hurting cos it'll just belittle how much I like Joe.

Artie doesn't have anything I want in a guy. He makes me angry, he's lazy, doesn't work, loves drugs, has different hours to me, not musical, but let's face it, I probably still love him. I can't believe I just wrote that! JOE!! HELLO?! Boyfriend calling Claire!

```
3.45am Text to Artie: This is going
to sound weird but I think I need
to hear you say "I don't want to
ever get back with you."

3.50am Text from Artie: I don't think
it would work between us.
```

What the fuck did I think was going to happen?! I feel so guilty. The false hope has been completely annihilated. I KNOW I'M GOING OUT WITH JOE, but I'm… crushed… crestfallen… heartbroken… thwarted… ashamed… chagrined. FUUUUUCCKKKKKKK.

MONDAY 9TH FEBRUARY 2004 3AM
LISTENING TO HAMMER TO FALL BY QUEEN

Everything seems to be ok after my little Friday night Artie relapse. Joe cooked a curry for me last night and then back to mine for a bit of rumpy pumpy (snigger). We chatted for hours and I reckon I could cuddle him forever. There is just one teeny tiny ickle problem.

~~~

What in the tabloids is going on with all this rumpy pumpy / teeny tiny ickle - ness?

~~~

He's just a bit too vocal when he cums. It makes me cringe so much. "Ahh yes. Ooohh yes. I'm cumming, I'm cumming. I'M CUMMING!"

<shudder>

Talk about spoiling the moment. I just want to smack him in the face and burst into fits of giggles from sheer embarrassment. This can't be a thing. I can't let it. He's perfect in every other way!

EIGHT
CHLOE

SUNDAY 15TH FEB 2004 1.45AM
LISTENING TO PICK UP BY BONOBO

Wednesday was Joe's 20th and he went out with his house mates. He was fucked, and I was NOT feeling it, so I left and didn't text him, and he didn't message me, and I wasn't even bothered. This doesn't feel like a good sign.

Chloe, (my sister), arrived yesterday to spend some of half term with me (which is cool).

~~~

I have, up until this point, avoided too much chatter about any of my living relatives. It's dangerous territory, but growing up, my sister felt like my ally. It's not always easy being a big sister, for there comes a point in time when you have to weather 'the transition'. I can only imagine this is something that you also have to do as a parent. You essentially go from 'the boss' to 'not the boss' when you have a sudden realisation that they know more / are cleverer / are cooler / are more likeable / are actually in control of everything / don't need you. In my sister's case, it was all of the above. I remember it well. It was June or July in 1994, and we were watching Saturday morning TV. I asked (told) her to get the remote and… <<shudder>> she looked at me with those piercing independent baby blues.

'No. You get it.'
Gasp.

I spent the rest of the 90s adjusting to this new power dynamic but I "forgave" her because she was so funny and was really the only person who saw behind the mask for years. I don't want to explain how brilliant she is because
 I don't need to and
  I'm her big sister, and it would be terribly off-brand of me to do so.

~~~

Kate invited Chlo and I round for a roast last night, and Joe did NOT love the idea cos Artie would obviously be there. I just love spending time with him, and we get on so well… I DON'T UNDERSTAND. Fuck, I shouldn't be with Joe, really. If Artie asked me back, I wouldn't hesitate.

We then went to the *Union* with Joe tonight, and lo and behold, who was there but Artie and Mike. We sat with them and I couldn't help getting on with Artie. Joe's really shy and not that chatty when he's out. I'm sure that me getting on with Artie didn't escape Joe's attention and… oh god, I'm ashamed to even write this down… I think me being with Joe was making Artie a little jealous, so I was basically trying to play them both. God, I'm awful.

~~~

WEDNESDAY 18TH FEBRUARY 2004 2.30AM
LISTENING TO MY OWN WORST ENEMY BY LIT

I FUCKING HATE ARTIE!

~~~

Standard.

~~~

I can't believe I thought I still loved him. I HATE him! Last night was Chlo's last night, so I had arranged for everyone to come round before finishing up in *Wonky Legs*. I was at the bar with Joe and Chloe when Artie arrived and proceeded to lecture us about trying E. He told me that I shouldn't be so closed-minded and he was only giving me 'advice'.

'You don't need to get hooked, Claire. You could just look at it as a unique experience.'

'Fuck off, Artie. Such shit chat from you.'

Joe was so drunk, so I figured I should take him home, but Chloe wanted to stay, so Kate said she'd look after her and bring her back later. I was just so angry that Artie was trying to push it. He knows I'm not keen. Drugs'll always be a big part of his life. We could never be together, there'd always be a mismatch.

THEN Chloe told me this morning he spent the rest of the night telling her how amazing E was, and when she basically said "no thanks", he said, "I don't want to be condescending, but you're only fifteen and still have an immature outlook on life". He is fucking dead to me.

```
MSN Chat with Artie (via Mike)

Woody: hello Claire…

Me: hello Mike

W: Artie just got back and he wants
to know whats pissed you off so much.

Me: Him promoting E to my fifteen year
old sister! I'm so angry it's unbe-
lievable. He can speak to me himself.

W: I WASN'T DOING THAT!!!! I cant re-
```

member much. I had a huge fight with Baz... but I wasnt pushing nothing. No harm meant!

Me: Im not interested

W: Thats fine but Im not sure it warrants this.

Me: Yes it fucking does!! If you can't remember what u sed then uv no fucking idea what it warrants! You crossed the line Artie.

W: How? All I said was what it felt like... Dude... I didn't want this anyway... I thought...

Me: "E's amazing. Everyone should try it just for the experience" and when she said she wasnt interested u sed "I dont mean to be condescending but ur only 15 and still have an immature outlook on life."

W: Well I never thought it would have implications. Sorry youre pissed off, I just cant see why a drunken conversation would get this big...

Me: Because it's my little sister and drunken or not, it was totally out of order. You've clearly no idea how angry I am at you.

W: Ok well I'm sorry. I wasn't doing it on purpose. I never go out to piss anyone off.

Me: No one ever does. Oh, and keep your opinions about Joe to yourself. You don't know him... calling him 'boring' just makes you sound petty.

W: I dont care who u go out with and don't believe everything you hear. You are my ex so I'm not going to be his best bud. Sorry about that.

Me: I do believe what I hear when it's Chlo's word against yours. I don't want u to be best buds, just reserve judgement... u urself hate it when ppl judge u.

W: Yeah ok. Well at least un-bar me from MSN... I think that's a bit much.

~~~

There is only a small subsection of the population that fully understands how shocking it was to be barred on MSN; such a powerful snub.

~~~

It wasn't easy knowing u had now got someone else... and I kinda forgot your sister was your sister, if that makes sense. I was just talking for ages with her.

Me: Cry me a fucking river Artie! Let's not forget who broke up with who and how much more that hurt than "it wasn't easy knowing you were with someone else". I thought we had smthg cool but obviously not. You have made it so easy for me to get over you thanks to your drugs obsession. So thanks, I guess. I'll unblock u.

~~~

'I hate you but let's be reasonable; not enough to warrant an MSN bar...'

~~~

W: Ok then thanks.

Me: Artie, I hope u dont think what Im going to say is immature but its probably best if we stop being friends. I dont think u understand how much I liked u and even though I really like Joe, it still hurts when I see u. I tried to be friends and I'm not trying to be spiteful but that's just the way I feel.

W: Ok. I'm sorry. I had no idea u felt like that so I'm sorry and I understand. I'm sorry if I've been a bit of a prick. I never wanted to hurt you. I understand that u don't want to be friends and I can only hope that one day that might change.

CHLOE

THURSDAY 19TH FEBRUARY 2004 11.30PM
LISTENING TO CRYIN' BY AEROSMITH

Right. An early night - that'll do me some good. Joe came round last night after he'd been out with his house mates. He was shit-faced and basically couldn't cum. I was so exhausted I just gave up. I'm finding it quite disconcerting... although I guess it means I don't have to listen to... urgh... I can't even write it. I'm not sure we're that well-suited. I like him but I'm not sure we click. Artie had so many flaws but it felt so right. Fuck. This has gone on way too long. Enough Claire.

Dream situation right now: Joe breaks up with me, Artie tells me he loves me and asks me back if he gives up drugs all together.

~~~

MONDAY 23RD FEBRUARY 2004 1.30AM
LISTENING TO SWEET CHILD O' MINE BY GUNS N' ROSES

I had the best Saturday. Lunch with Joe at the flat, *Roundabout* for Rugby with Kate and Pete Bond, Chinese with the flat, back to the flat for films with Joe - sex and orgasms all round. Amazing. I still have the niggle that our relationship is quite superficial. I've never opened up to him about anything, and he's never really told me anything of any significance. We're just floating about in parallel lines and occasionally shagging.

I've spent pretty much all of today and tonight working. Phew, I finally feel like I'm getting the hang of it, although I still don't feel like I've got a scoobie about anything.

I've also dyed my hair pink, which feels like something I should have done a very long time ago.

~~~

SUNDAY 29TH FEBRUARY 2004 3.50AM
LISTENING TO I MISS YOU BY BLINK 182

BOOOO. On the train leaving Brighton and I am mega sad about it. I've just spent the weekend with Maggie, and I have had such a banging time. She's living with Maria from school, and I met all their arty Brighton girls - so cool. I wish I was someone's arty pal. I wish I was Artie's pal... fuck me... how do I circle back to him regardless?! What am I doing studying medicine?! It's like some kind of sick joke and it's only a matter of time until I'm found out.

I've missed Maggie so much. I arrived on Thursday, and we twirled around in our little best friend bubble, ran across the street like Phoebe from friends and danced in underground seaside clubs. Epic.

Being away from Plymouth has also made me miss Joe. Good sign, right?

~~~

MONDAY 1ST MARCH 2004 1.30AM
LISTENING TO WE DIDN'T START THE FIRE BY BILLY JOEL

Hellish journey. Everything kept going wrong. I didn't get back to Plymouth till half 11, and Joe came to pick me up at the station. I was so pleased to see him. I really want things to work between us. All I need is more depth (emotionally not physically) and quieter orgasms.

~~~

That's what all the girls say...

~~~

I can't believe I've wasted so much brain energy on Artie. Not just brain energy… this diary is nearly full, and all it says is 'I love Artie' 10,000 times. If only I'd written medical words rather than god knows many Artie-related diary words… should I stop writing a diary? No, I'd probably explode. I'm already too quick to share. If I didn't offload here, my friends wouldn't put up with my inane babbling for very long. Like now… what am I even writing about? Bugger all.

~~~

WEDNESDAY 3RD MARCH 2004 1AM
LISTENING TO ALETHEUO - TRUTHSPEAKING BY DJ KRUSH, ANGELINA ESPARZA

Last night was CRAZY! I went to the beer festival at the *Union* in the afternoon with Rich, Tommo and Trigger, and we all got fucked. Then back to Rich's for drinking games and then *C103*, where we were the only people there so went to *Destiny's* and got even more drunk. We were all dancing like twats when the mother of all foam parties descended on us. The foam filled the club and was nipple height - completely nuts. Then back to mine and shared a pizza. I put some DJ Krush on and lit a cigarette when Rich looked at me rather aggressively.

'You can be a right twat sometimes, Claire.'

It stopped me dead. What? Was that Rich? Tommo looked as surprised as me.

'Easy, mate. What's got into you?'

I found my words enough to stutter, 'Sorry what?! What the fuck is that supposed to mean?!'

'Oh, you know.' My god, he was talking like a grade A psychopath, calm and composed as he sautéed bits of your brain. 'You think you're so cool, hanging out like you're one of the lads, smoking and listening to drum and bass.'

Ouch. No one has spoken to me like that since school. I just thought it was them, but hearing the similar rhetoric again made me doubt myself - was it me? I don't think I think I'm cool. Do I? I sat in silence for what was probably a minute but felt like hours. I felt every mean word from the last ten years sweep over me again. Was my entire university life an illusion? Did everyone secretly hate me? FUUUUUUUCK.

Tommo was the first to speak.

'Not cool, man. You're pissed, let's go home. Cheers for pizza, Claire.'

Rich started laughing. 'Oh, come on guys - I was only yanking her chain. You didn't think I was being serious, did you, Claire Bear?'

I fucking did, and there it was... *Claire Bear*... previously only used by Mish and Charlie when they were trying to convince me that I was the crazy one. I wanted to cry, but I did the only thing I felt I could. I laughed.

'Haha, of course not! you fucker!'

The relief from Tommo and Trigger's laughter filled the room and the corridor as they left. As soon as they were out the door, my eyes filled with tears. I pulled an old spliff out of my top drawer, exploded out of my window and filled my lungs.

'Hey, greeb.'

Oh god. I turned to look at the love of my life, leaning over his balcony and staring at me with his kind eyes. He looked glorious in the streetlight, and I felt a deep ache in the centre of my chest.

'Hey, Artie.'

'Mind if I join you?'

I passed him my keys, and 2 minutes later, we were side by side, out my window, sharing his old spliff. We didn't talk much, and neither of us mentioned Joe.

'Do you think I think I'm cool?'

'Woah, that's a bit of a head fuck right now, greeb. For what it's worth and whatever that even means, I do not think you think that.'

His sincerity nearly broke me, and I almost kissed him, but the enormity of it felt like too much. I felt like he might even have kissed me back tonight. But then what? I love him. FUCK.

I reckon I've aged about ten years off the back of last night. I've got to stop partying this hard. I went to bed after sunrise on a Tuesday night and then just rocked up to a lecture a couple of hours later. No idea what it was on. Something horrendous like the complement system. I lasted about 20 mins and thought - nope, this is not for me. Hopefully, it's one of those things I'll never really need to know about.

~~~

Jan 2023

It is ABSOLUTELY one of those things I never needed to know about. Pff... the complement system... total rubbish... probably. I'm pretty sure I haven't killed anyone because I don't know about the complement system.

~~~

June 2023

Believe it or not, I needed to know about it today. I looked it up - no biggie. I wouldn't have remembered it for 20 years without use, anyway. But it turns out, the complement system is a thing that makes sense once you're 37 years old.

~~~

THURSDAY 4TH MARCH 2004
LISTENING TO I WANT IT ALL BY QUEEN

Hold me back, I'm SUPER pissed off with Bruce.

Joe came round last night, and we were messing around and started having sex... and kept having sex... on and on and on and on! It was going on for AGES! I'm not in the habit of timing but I started trying to look at the time. He just wasn't cumming, and I felt like I was getting cramp in my legs. I was moving around in every position, and nothing. Is it me? We eventually just stopped, and neither of us said anything. We were just lying there in silence, staring at my ceiling. I felt so insulted and so unsexy. Then he just kissed me on the forehead, got dressed and left. It's been bothering me for a while now, so I went into Bruce's room.

'All right, mate. Sounded like a bit of a sesh in there. You ok?'

'Kinda. Not really. Do you ever have a problem cumming?'

'Haha no! Only when they're munting!'

~~~

This conversation is definitely not going to help.

~~~

'Joe can't cum sometimes, and even when he does, it feels like a massive effort and takes ages. Do you think it's me? Am I munting?!'

'You're fine, Claire. It's not you. Everyone's different. Was he drinking? Being drunk can do it FAW SHAW.'

'Yeah, maybe. Although I don't think he was drunk tonight.'

'Dunno then, mate. It sounds like it's him, though. Not you.'

Hopefully, Bruce is right, and it's not me.

Bruce and I went to the *Union* tonight with the flat and the upstairs boys. Bruce was pretty drunk but nothing major, and we were play fighting in the pool room. We were just having little digs at each other, and I made some comment about him shaving his chest hair when, out of the blue, he shouted at me.

'Well, you can't even make your boyfriend cum!'

In front of everyone! They all just stopped and stared at us. I was so shocked, and he just kept laughing. MOTHERFUCKER! I am so angry with him. I could have punched him. It's a miracle I didn't, actually. It was so uncalled for and he's totally crossed the line. I confided in him about something I felt really insecure about, and he made a joke of it in front of all our friends. Wanker!

~~~

SUNDAY 7TH MARCH 2004 3.30AM
LISTENING TO WAKE ME UP WHEN SEPTEMBER ENDS BY GREEN DAY

Bruce apologised, and we're ok now.

I saw Joe again tonight, and sex was completely fine. I left his about 11ish as I'd told Rich I'd join him for a quick pool hustle, but I was too late. I was walking back home when I bumped into Mike and Artie. Mike was quite chatty about what they'd done tonight (no prizes for guessing what… yup, you guessed it. It was drugs), but Artie just nodded at me and walked ahead. Ouch. What's happened since the start of the week?

Got home, had a long shower, cleaned the bathroom, and I've just done a few hours work. Well done me.

~~~

SUNDAY 14TH MARCH 2004 3AM
LISTENING TO I'M LOST WITHOUT YOU BY BLINK 182

I went to the *Union* with Rich tonight, and Joe was there with his house mates, but I hardly spoke to him - I really should end it. I was at the bar when I saw Mike and Artie. We were having a polite chit-chat, and suddenly, some bimbo arrived, and Artie put his arm around her and kissed her on her head. BARF! How I didn't just vaporise there and then, I'll never know.

'This is Charlie.'

What a smug, smiley, bitch, whore fuck!

'Hi, Charlie. It's so nice to meet you.'

Breathe. Breathe. Breeeeeeaaaathe.

I excused myself and went to go and DIE somewhere. But it's cool. I'm with Lovely Joe. How could he? I thought he didn't want a relationship! OMG and she's so pretty. FUCK. Then I bumped into a few of Artie's friends, and they all started telling me what a snob Charlie was and that none of them liked her. That helps a bit. Oof what would Artie say knowing his mates were bitching about his new gf to his ex... apparently she's told him he has to 'stop dressing like a teenager'. Then G-man said something like, 'For what it's worth, Claire, I know Artie doesn't want to get back with you, but I think you were perfect for him, and you were really good together.' Mike and Laura then confirmed the unanimous disliking for Charlie. In yaw face bitch!

~~~

THURSDAY 18TH MARCH 2004 00.40AM
LISTENING TO HAPPY ALONE BY KINGS OF LEON

I am sooooo tired. Talk about burning the candle at both ends. Joe came round on Monday night, and we watched a few films, and I fell asleep then woke up to a note from Joe.

```
Sleep well angel. I've gone home as I
have a lot of work to do. Xxx
```

I felt weirdly put out. It felt like if he wasn't going to get a shag, there was no point in staying.

Tuesday night was the medics' pub golf. Soo drunk and messy. I ended up in *Roundabout* with Kate, Frank, Robin and

Pete Bond. I fell down nearly a whole flight of stairs, holding two pints. I was sat at the bottom (with a broken bottom), and I'd barely spilt a drop.

What.

A.

Hero.

I spent most of today feeling tired and depressed and hungover. I'm such a fat, alcoholic waster of an arse. How did this happen?

~~~

FRIDAY 19TH MARCH 2004 2AM
LISTENING TO TAKE ME TO THE CLOUDS ABOVE BY LMC VS U2

I've just had the best day with Pete Bond. We went for a huge walk around Plymouth and didn't stop chatting. Then to the *Union* for a couple of pints and pool. Earned enough money for dinner at *Cuba* and then back to the *Union* for drinking and dancing.

~~~

'Dinner' at Cuba consisted of a large portion of curly fries and their signature drink, a Dr. Pepper - Amaretti and Coke. Yum.

~~~

Pete Bond dances in a wild, carefree (totally embarrassing!) way that I wish I could do. I've grown so fond of him so quickly. I hope I'm friends with him forever. What is it about ginger guys and personalities?

~~~

SUNDAY 21ST MARCH 2004 3.30AM
LISTENING TO ONLY THE GOOD DIE YOUNG BY BILLY JOEL

I spent the night with Joe tonight. He cooked and played the piano - it was sawwwweeeeet. He's a sexy mother fucker when he plays the piano. I'm just not sure I've got 'the feeling'. I think it's coming, though… We've been together for a while now, and I'm surprised I haven't thought that I love him - it normally takes me a second. But maybe that's a good thing. Maybe I shouldn't go a million miles an hour and have drama, passion and all the associated shit. Joe and I don't fight, he's hot, he's good to me… WHY DON'T I LOVE HIM? It's slightly concerning that I keep feeling the need to reassure and convince myself that I do in fact want to be with him. Maybe this is love, and everything else until now has been lust?

~~~

TUESDAY 30TH MARCH 2004 2AM
LISTENING TO SWING SWING BY THE ALL-AMERICAN REJECTS

Jeez. So much has happened since the last time I wrote. I haven't seen Joe much cos he's pissing me off quite a lot. He came round last Monday - ABSOLUTELY steaming. I was watching 24 with Lou and Rich and he made such a tit of himself and we were all just trying to concentrate. Then he left muttering something about 'what's the point'. This was not the first time he's tapped out when he realised sex wasn't on the menu.

Saturday was England vs France 6 Nations final. We all watched it in the flat upstairs. You had to drink 2 fingers for a mention, try, conversion, successful penalty… any score basically for 'your player' (We all took a name out of the hat). You also had to drink whenever the commentator mentioned your player.

I got the French scrum-half, Yachvilli, who happened to score every try, conversion and penalty. His name came up every other second. DISASTER!

So VERY drunk and we were all on the way to *Dance Academy*. Rich was giving me a piggyback when he tripped and sent me flying head first over the top of him. I was out cold for a few seconds, but other than a big bump on my head and a bit of a headache, I felt ok when I came round so we still went out.

~~~

Jesus.

~~~

I felt really sick when we got to *Dance Academy*, but I wasn't sure if it was Yachvili's fault or my minor head injury. I thought I'd just shake it off on the dance floor, but that made it worse. I only just made it to the toilet. I felt awful so I went home with Lou and she called Joe to ask if he could stay with me. I was fine, but she said she'd feel happier if I wasn't alone. So he came round and realised no sex. Next thing I knew, I woke in the night with THE WORST headache of my life and no Joe. BASTARD.

I've had a banging headache since, but at least it's stopped me going out, and I've chilled out a bit. NOTHING from Joe. Fuck him.

~~~

31ST MARCH 2004 6PM
LISTENING TO STREET LIFE BY RANDY CRAWFORD

I just ended it with Joe, and I feel weirdly awful about it. He made it so easy for me, though… too easy. Part of me wonders if he was trying to get me to dump him?

Artie and I spoke on MSN tonight, and I know this is sick and wrong because I've just been in a relationship with someone else for two months, but I OBVIOUSLY still love him.

~~~

1ST APRIL 2004 11AM
LISTENING TO TOO MUCH LOVE WILL KILL YOU BY QUEEN

Rich and I stayed up all night finishing up our work for the end of term and ended up sharing a bed cos it was 6am by the time we finished. I'm going to miss spending all my time with him over Easter.

NINE
EASTER 2004

3RD APRIL 2004 6.40PM
LISTENING TO DOWN BY BLINK 182

I'm back in Edinburgh, which is great. I seriously needed a time-out. I miss Rich, though. Just as a friend, but I miss him. We were chatting earlier…

'I told Lou how I felt about her yesterday.'

Of course, I felt wracked with jealousy. Once a psycho, always a psycho. Do I want Rich? No. Do I want anyone else to have him? Course not.

'Lou? How do you feel?'

'I told her I really liked her, and she said she felt the same!'

'Yay! I'm so pleased for you, Rich.'

Except not 'yay'. What's wrong with me? I guess I should be happy for them, but I feel crushed. We're never going to be as close now if they're together. That's another friendship I'm going to have to say goodbye to. Or two friendships really.

~~~

4TH APRIL 2004 MIDNIGHT
LISTENING TO HISTORY OF A BORING TOWN BY LESS THAN JAKE

Last night was Caarrrraaaazzyyy. It was Stripey's birthday and I got completely rat-arsed with Maggie, Herbie and the A-level French boys. Everyone came back to mine afterwards, and we played poker all night. I won, then vommed. Fucking hell. WHY AM I SUCH A FUCKING REPROBATE?!

I've been feeling really rough all day and spent the day at Next Door Andy's. We watched film after film after film, drinking tea and grunting at each other. I've missed the effortlessness of being with him.

I spoke to Lou tonight, who seemed really giddy and excited about Rich. It's cute, but the selfish part of me feels like I'm going to lose both of their friendships. I wish I could care more about other people rather than only ever having my own interests at heart.

~~~

MONDAY 12TH APRIL 2004 4.30PM
LISTENING TO FIVE COLOURS IN HER HAIR BY MCFLY

Well, this is weird. I HAVE to make a note of this. I'm sat in my childhood bedroom with none other than William Macleod. Weird. We saw each other in *Gaia* last night, and both kinda said it would be nice to catch up. So here he is. I've missed him. I've missed his silliness. I think I'm over all the mess too - which is great. Are we going to finally be friends now? Surely not. But… it's William…

TEN
FINN

THURSDAY 22ND APRIL 2004 2PM
LISTENING TO HIGHWAY TO HELL BY AC/DC

Finn Ellwyn-Cox, you bloody Claire magnet.

~~~

Ah, Finn. Charming, confident, and effortlessly entitled Finn, who took the predictable route from Eton to Exeter University, as every true posh boy does. From the moment we met (Frankenstein's, Edinburgh Fringe, circa 2000), I played the role of his little bit of rough. Over the years, I kept falling for him, seduced by stolen weekends and fleeting nights.

The night before my medical school interview, I should have been revising and getting an early night. Instead, I was with him because, with Finn, restraint was never really an option.

A part of me always thought we might end up together. But, inevitably, his boarding school bravado and my distinct lack of finishing school etiquette would have put an end to that soon enough. He'd also have insisted our future children go to boarding school. No thanks, pal.

~~~

I'm back in Plymouth, and I feel like all the fun has left my life. I've been working loads, and after spending all day geekin' in my room

FEAR AND LOATHING IN PLYMOUTH

yesterday, I could feel my feet itching like mad (metaphorically). I couldn't be arsed with another night in Plymouth, so I did the most spontaneous thing I could think of (and afford) and booked a train ticket to Exeter to see Finn.

I arrived, and we went out with his house mates and got pretty smashed, then back to his and... of course, we had sex. I am so predictable. Is he like my fuck buddy now? Friends with benefits? Yuck - I hate that concept, but Finn and I have been sleeping together on and off for a couple of years now...

So anyway, the sex felt perfunctory. No romance, no seduction... quite literally in and out. He didn't even need to try, and when he was done, he just rolled over with his back firmly turned to me. I tried to get him to roll over and give me a cuddle, but it was like hugging an erection. Too hard to be asleep... too warm to be dead. Motherfucker.

I was so upset and felt so used. I decided to leave and get back to Plymouth. I called Rich for him to check the train times from his laptop. I was in floods of tears by this stage, thanks to a tasty little combination of booze, humiliation and cum on my trousers.

~~~

This is uncomfortably graphic.

~~~

I ordered a taxi and halfway to the station, I realised I'd left my wallet at Finn's. FUUUUUUCCKKK. I turned around and got his house mate to open up while I snuck back in (this time desperate not to wake Finn). I was scrabbling around in the dark and whacked my head on the desk... FUUUUCKKK... feeling around on the floor... used condom... oh my FUCKING Christ - what am I doing here?! I finally got on the 4.04am train. I must have looked a right state with my bloated, mascara face.

Rich came and met me at the station and took me back to his

where he made me a pot of tea and a tuna melt. He is so so so sweet.

'What are you doing, man? Sounds like this guy treats you like shit, and you just take it. You should demand more.'

I looked at him with my bleary eyes and REALLY looked at him, his strawberry blonde hair, his kind green Irish eyes and thought, *What about you, Rich? Would you treat me well?* He probably would. Quiet, lovely, unassuming Rich, always there for me, invisibly holding me up in the background. Picking me up at the station at 5am and making me tea. Never asking for anything in return. Is Rich my guy? Have I stupidly been falling for the charming, charismatic Finns who pretend to sleep once they've finished fucking me? Or falling in love with the guy who chose drugs over me cos he brought me a mango one morning? Rich is funny, and looking at him, appearing genuinely concerned tonight, made me think, 'he's not bad looking actually…' maybe… maybe…

Finn called first thing this morning as I was finally going to sleep.

'What the fuck, Claire. Where are you?'

'I'm back in Plymouth. You made it clear that I wasn't welcome. Straight to sleep and then completely ignoring me.'

'What are you talking about? I DID go straight to sleep. I was exhausted.'

'Oh.'

I realised at this point that I may have overreacted slightly.

'Harry said he let you back in to get your wallet or something at 4am?! Claire - that is so dangerous! I was really worried about you this morning.'

'Yeah well… I felt humiliated by you and felt like I had no choice but to go home… sorry.'

'Oh, babe. I would never want to humiliate you. I'm sorry. I was just pissed and really tired. Why don't I come and see you in Plymouth this weekend?'

'Oh. Ok. Yeah - that sounds nice.'

Backbone like a strawberry lace me.

~~~

FRIDAY 23RD APRIL 2004 2AM
LISTENING TO TALIHINA SKY BY KINGS OF LEON

Well, I feel like a complete wank for leaving yesterday. Finn and I spent hours on the phone tonight, and he told me that he would love to be my boyfriend. He says he's always wanted to but that he wouldn't do long distance. Fair enough. What I would do for that. Although, in a way, what we have is special in its own way. Almost un-ruinable.

~~~

MONDAY 25TH APRIL 2004 1.50AM
LISTENING TO YEAH! BY USHER, LIL JON, LUDACRIS

What a weekend.

Friday: As soon as I'd finished those damn lectures, I went to the *Union* beer garden with Rich and the boys, soaked up some sun and then to *Roundabout*. We were all fairly cooked and then watched Kill Bill 2 at mine.

Saturday: Another GLORIOUS day. I went to the Hoe with the boys, and we played rounders for six hours. Back home to pick up some supplies and then back for a sunset BBQ. Finn text about 8ish.

```
I'm on the train beautiful - I can't
wait to see you. x
```

YESSSSSSS! I did not think he would actually come. I raced home - showered, shaved, changed clothes, changed bed, tidied room, and then walked to the station to meet him. He scooped me up, and we had a really romantic / film-style kiss at the station. We went back to mine and watched films and fooled around all night. This guy man. I can't resist him. My chest feels funny and like I need to take a deep breath to suppress the urge to burst into... flames? Song? Tears? Laughter? All of the above. He left early this morning and gave me the biggest, lingering kiss and whispered 'bye beautiful'... ahhhhh shudder!

I went back to the Hoe today for another day of rounders in the sun. I am getting Baaa...rown!

Lou got back late today and told me, "I'm not really feeling it with Rich". After all that! I know I had a weird, selfish jealousy about them, but I was gutted for him when she told me. They've only been official for about a week. She's going to break his heart, and although I love Lou, I hate her for hurting Rich.

OMG, I'm so achy. Twelve hours of rounders'll do that to a girl. Every muscle in my body feels bruised. I can't walk, laugh, sit or stand without excruciating pain coursing through my veins. THE AGONY! How pathetic... rounders... basically the sport for people who can't play sport. It's not even a sport. It's a game... like chess and here I am rendered BORDERLINE PARALYSED.

~~~

WEDNESDAY 27TH APRIL 2004 1.30AM
LISTENING TO SWEETNESS BY JIMMY EAT WORLD

Everything is a mess, and I have this inexplicable melancholy... like a tortured artist. Maybe if I actually was an artist, I'd release... whatever this is... through the medium of paint... like some obnoxious creative type. Instead, I don't know what to do with myself, and I feel like something horrible and out of my control is about to happen.

I have soooo much work to do, and I am procrastinating the bejeezus out of it.

Bruce got dumped by G, and I spent hours tonight mopping up his big man tears. I love that he can confide in me, but I can't help but find that I soak up some of his depression. I'm an emotion-sponge. Lou still hasn't got round to ending it with Rich. I wish she hadn't told me…

I haven't heard from Finn since he came down at the weekend. I probably shouldn't read too much into it, but I can't help reliving every single detail of his stay… what underwear was I wearing? … did my makeup make me look like a tart?... Did I smell?... Was I too clingy / too needy / too annoying / too drunk / too quiet / too slutty? Did I kiss him too much / not enough? Did he fake orgasm? Was he thinking about someone else? AHHHH!

I saw Artie today with that beautiful-bitch-whore-Charlie. Urgh. Mr Commitment-phobe seems very happy with his nearly long-term girlfriend!

I just want someone to cradle my face, stare into my eyes and love me…

~~~

MONDAY 3RD MAY 2004 6.30AM
LISTENING TO INNER CITY LIFE BY GOLDIE

So completely fucked right now. The only thing I have a tangible grip on are the words on this page. Everything else is a hazy, messed-up blur of total stupidity.

Met Rich in the *Union* beer garden at 4pm today and Trigger came and joined us. Artie and Mike then arrived and sat down with us. The fluttering I get when I see Artie is definitely abating.

Finally. Still would though.

We teamed up and smashed the pub quiz, winning a crate of beer, which we polished off sans problème.

Rich and I went back to Mike and Artie's and smoked one, two … maybe more spliffs. Then Rich came back to mine, and we spent ages doing one of those internet compatibility quizzes. Rich and I got 85% (only 70% with Lou), Trigger and I: 60% and Artie 95%! I obviously had Artie on the brain, so I MSN'd him.

>   Me: Hey. You still up?
>
>   Artie: hey greeb. I am indeed. Not ready to give up the night?
>
>   Me: Never. Do you fancy a walk? Keep the night alive?
>
>   Artie: Sure thing. See you downstairs in 5?

So we walked. I never wanted the night to end. We smoked the last spliff, and we were walking back as the sun was coming up.

'It's been a fun night, Claire, I'm glad we're cool. You know I never wanted to hurt you.'

'I know.'

I was pretty giggly, and he gave me the BEST hug. I still love him, but I'm completely fucked now. Bad Sunday Claire. Naughty Claire. Work tomorrow… today… in a couple of hours… FUUUUCCCCKKKK.

ELEVEN
LILY

THURSDAY 6TH MAY 2004 00.45AM
LISTENING TO TONIGHT, TONIGHT BY THE SMASHING PUMPKINS

I went to *C103* with Rich and Trigger, but I lost them early doors. I also lost all my baccie - MERDE.

The music was banging, however, so I decided to hang about for a bit. I figured I'd eventually bump into someone I knew. They were playing loads of old-school punk rock in the rock room, and I was drawn to it…

First stop: find a fag and feel less naked and aimless.

There was a girl perched on the edge of the DJ booth. She was shimmering in a haze of cigarette smoke, and I couldn't take my eyes off her. She was EVEN HOTTER than Avril Lavigne.

~~~

Lily had an intimidating, angular allure. When I was near her, I flitted between desperately wanting to be her and an overriding urge to run and hide from her.

Her jaw and cheekbones were Grace Jones-esque; and her nose: delicate with a neon-pink, plastic hoop. She had pouty, French, 'angry' lips, enormous eyes (that out of context would have looked 'buggy') and dark choppy, asymmetrical, hair. She was the coolest thing I had ever seen. Her hip bones stuck out of her ripped black jeans, and her belly button was pierced to match her nose. Lily was a slightly gothic, punk rock goddess.

~~~

'I'm so sorry to ask, I know it's a massive pain in the arse, but is there any chance I could nick a rollie.'

'Can you roll?'

'Impeccably.'

'That's a pretty bold statement for someone with a big turquoise necklace.'

'Wow. That's surprisingly cutting. I guess my necklace and I are going to have to prove you wrong. I'm Claire, by the way.'

After about an hour of flirty, passive-aggressive chat we were dancing but like they slow dance when it's either a 1950's high school dance or an under-12s disco. We were facing each other but at a safe arm's length apart, and she had her tiny wrists draped on my shoulders. I (very awkwardly) had my hands around her waist. It was ELECTRIC! Was I being 'the man'?

Then some guy walked past with similar hair to Artie and, I'm sure, the same hoodie. I was staring so hard that we ended up making eye contact. He looked at me and my I'm-having-a-slow-dance-with-Lily dancing and wiggled his tongue between his V-shaped fingers.

'Fucking dykes!'

Lily reared up. It was like she'd been turned on.

'FUCK OFF YOU UGLY CUNT!' she screamed.

She took two large strides up to him and pressed her middle finger up against his nose. Ha! He looked terrified… crazy bitch. I looked at her and wanted nothing more than to kiss her. So I did! AND SHE KISSED ME BACK! We then pulled and danced until closing. It was like nothing else. Is this my epiphany? All this time I'm looking for 'Mr Right' and here she is!

```
Text to Lily: thanks for an epic night.
I'm kinda new to this but I'd love to
see you again... ?

From Lily: you didn't seem that new!
You approached me after all. I loved
it too, sweet. And I'd love to see you
again. L x
```

~~~

SATURDAY 8TH MAY 2004 2.30AM
LISTENING TO NOCTUARY BY BONOBO

I met Lily, her house mates and her brother for drinks in *Ride* after I'd finally finished my essay from hell on communication skills. Sooooooo boring. I don't know why they insist on teaching this shite. You can either talk to people or you can't. You don't need to invent a whole bloody science around it.

~~~

How dare I have such disdain for (arguably) THE most important aspect within medicine. Shame on me. I teach communication skills at the university, and to put it simply, medicine would not exist without it. I'm displaying such revolting arrogance and disregard for my craft... urgh...

~~~

She was wearing an impossibly short grey T-shirt dress, ripped fishnet stockings and Dr Martens. She looked amazing. We had a few pints, and the others all wanted to head to the quay club. I couldn't be fucked, and I REALLY wanted to kiss Lily again. We were all hovering outside Ride and I finally managed to get her by herself.

'I'm not sure I can really afford to go out now. Do you want to come back to mine and watch a film instead?'

She ran her hand down my back and around my waist.

'Sure, sweet. Sounds good.'

I'm not sure about the 'sweet' thing…

We went back to mine, but I was essentially sober, and I felt soooo nervous. Am I a lesbian now? I thought about, in theory, what might have to happen next (after kissing) and found myself grimacing at the thought. That doesn't feel very lesbian-y of me…

~~~

Beautifully articulated by Rosamund Pike in Saltburn: "I was a lesbian for a while, you know, but it was all just too wet for me in the end. Men are so lovely and dry." Dec 2023

~~~

We were watching a film, and she started kissing my neck and then my lips. I was half totally into it, but my brain was working overtime. Stupid brain. Too stupid most of the time and then won't dumb down when I want it to. We started pulling, and I had absolutely no idea what I was supposed to do with my hands? Touch her boobs? Felt weird. Her arse - also weird. More intimate? Nope - not sure I want to. She rolled on top of me and sat up, straddling me. She pulled off her dress and I noticed an enormous tattoo of a pigeon on her side.

'Nice tat. It's…ummm… unusual… why a pigeon?'

'I value the ordinary.'

And in that moment Lily sealed her fate. Value the ordinary? So much so that you get a huge tattoo of a pigeon on yourself? Nope. I'm out. Pretty sure I'm not into girls. Lily was hot. Anyone could see and appreciate that - doesn't mean I would.

I value the extraordinary.

TWELVE
THE SISTERHOOD

TUESDAY 11TH MAY 2004 00.45AM
LISTENING TO FIT BUT YOU KNOW IT BY THE STREETS

The strangest thing has happened. I think I have GIRL friends. I went out with Three Legged Frank, Robin Mills, Pete Bond, Next Door Kate, Connie and the other medic girls ('Mad Dog', Suzie and Beth) on Sunday night. I can't believe how alike we all are. Girls aren't so bad after all. Have I found my people?

~~~

My experience of girls up until this point had been overwhelmingly negative. School did not gift me lifelong girlfriends but instead left me with an aggressive undercurrent of defensiveness when it came to women. Maggie was the exception, not the rule. If I had learnt one thing during my formative years, it was that women mustn't, under any circumstance, be trusted.

I went to University, a coiled spring, my armour was up and ready for whatever my 'University Gretchen' would throw at me. I spent the first few months in Plymouth, keeping women at arm's length, waiting for 'her' to reveal herself. I kept all female interactions polite and superficial. I found comfort, instead, in the simpler and less intimidating male friendships. "Any moment now, and the mean girls will pounce", I thought. But they never did. Wom-

en were… normal. Pleasant even. My first group of 'girlfriends' were Kate, Connie, 'Mad Dog', Beth and Suzie, and they gave me everything I had ever wanted. I wonder if my pathological search for love was an attempt to compensate for my lack of girlfriends.

I get it now. I get 'sisterhood'. I thought I was destined to be one of those women who is invariably hated by other women and who only has 'guy friends'. But the 'medic girls' made me realise that it wasn't me that was the problem, it was them… back in Edinburgh… the mean girls. The meanest girls. I WAS capable of female friendships! I wasn't broken!

Years went by, and I started to breathe, shedding my teenage shield and relaxing in a world where I didn't need to protect myself from fifty per cent of the population. It took time, though, to change such an ingrained belief; I had to relearn how to be friends with women.

Do I still get a little sweaty in all-girl environments, hen dos, baby showers, etc? A little, yes, but do I love women now? Also yes. Would I send my children to an all-girls school if it was the only school left in the world? That's a hard no.

~~~

So anyway, we did the quiz at the *Union* and drank far too much. Lovely Northern Joe was sitting at another table with his house mates, and I couldn't stop looking at him. He is GORGEOUS! Why exactly did we break up? We ended up chatting afterwards and I felt completely different towards him. I felt giddy and nervous. We talked all night, and then he came back to mine and watched a film. We cuddled all night, and I eventually went for it and kissed him. AHHH, I'm so happy! I think Lovely Northern Joe and I are getting back together! Woop Woop!

~~~

FEAR AND LOATHING IN PLYMOUTH

SUNDAY 16TH MAY 2004 1.30AM
LISTENING TO... THE SOUND OF MACHINES BEEPING

I'm sat having my break on my first shift as an auxiliary nurse. 8pm until 8am - Urg, it's awful, but I needed some money, and a weekend night shift pays £8 per hour, and I only needed to do a few days training. AND if I was an annoying, earnest, keen bean, I would say that it's good experience for the course. But I'm not, so I won't.

I'm so sunburnt from today, and this brand new-starched-to-fuck-uniform is rubbing and owww... but oh god, I've just realised what a disgusting person I am for having even written that down, given that I'm working on the burns unit...

I feel so useless here. Obviously, it'll get better with time (is it obvious?), but I don't feel confident about anything. I'm definitely more of a burden. With everything I've been asked to do, I have to bother at least two people in order to find out how to even do it or where to find the thing I need to do it with, or what the thing that I need looks like.

~~~

3.45am

Urg, I want to go to bed. What was I thinking?! I should be in an art college. I've been wiping arses for nearly eight hours tonight. Not that I actually mind, which is weird. It's the least I can do for these poor people, but I would still rather be in bed ready for a day of painting.

Moving swiftly on to the more enthralling topic of last night. It was our last ever PBL session and Three Legged Frank had made cocktails for Mad Dog's birthday.

~~~

Oh, my wonderful Doglet. 'Mad Dog' is without a doubt the least likely person to earn herself the title of 'Mad Dog'. She is petite, porcelain-skinned and beautifully restrained. She is THE example of how introversy is better than its opposite (me). We have complemented each other superbly for two decades. We have been each other's sidekicks, and I couldn't imagine my life without her. For every word I vomit into anyone's open ears, she thinks and selects hers in her head before speaking a perfectly crafted selection. She may not be loud, but she is not quiet in a meek or timid way; she is a powerhouse with razor-sharp wit and outrageous humour that you would be unwise to underestimate. She is my maid of honour, my daughter's godmother and, dare I say it… my best friend.

The title of 'Mad Dog' came from Pete Bond (the self-appointed coach of the medic girls football team). She arrived on day one, looking like a fragile English rose, but nooo… let her loose on the pitch, and she was just like a frenzied mad dog.

~~~

We finished our PBL session, sat outside in the sunshine drinking Frank's cocktails, and all took a few mins reading our group feedback. Out of 8 of them, they all wrote the same positive for me.

```
'Thanks for all your amazing dia-
grams!'
```

```
'Your drawings are brilliant, Claire!'
```

And so it went on. Is that all I offer to the group? Good drawings?

'Quick, doctor! This patient's arrested!'

'Sorry, no. I'm not the real doctor - I just do excellent anatomical diagrams…'

We spent the rest of the afternoon drinking snakey-bs in the *Union* beer garden, then went to meet everyone for Mad Dog's birthday in Wetherspoons. We had a few more drinks, then dinner at *The Crystal Dragon*. Suzie's boyfriend bet me £5 to eat the stained, cut-out, decorative potato flowers - £5 per platter!

Everyone's got a price, man.

~~~

They tasted absolutely TERRIBLE; like arse, but... chu-ching - £20. Onwards for cocktails and dancing in *Bar Rumba*, but I still felt squeamish, so I drank water for the rest of the night. I went home with Robin at about 1ish to watch Red Dwarf. I felt awful, so I threw him out just before throwing out my stomach contents. I was sick all night. I'm too old for this shit. I guess it could have been the potato flowers, but it could also have been the copious amounts of booze.

I haven't spoken to Joe for a while too. We're back together, but it is soooooo casual, I'm not sure either of us have really noticed...

Right. Better get back. Those heart rates aren't going to take themselves.

~~~

FRIDAY 21ST MAY 2004 1.30AM
LISTENING TO COME WITH ME BY SPECIAL D

It's so weird that it's always about 1.30am that I choose to write.

Monday: Went to see *Butterfly Effect* with Bruce, Mark, Trigger and Tommo - it's so fucked up. No Rich now he's in love with Lou. We never see them now. It's sad. I went from spending so much of my free time with Rich and now... Poof, he's gone.

Tuesday: Massive drunken BBQ on the Hoe with all the medics. Mad Dog went for a swim with Three-Legged Frank and Kate - they are mental. I wish I'd gone in too. I'm such a pussy.

Wednesday: Back to the Hoe for another blazing day in the sun with the flat, Bruce's gf - G, Rich, Trigger and Tommo. Then to *C103* where I finally met up with... (checks notes)... my boyfriend. Sorry - who? Joe came back to mine, and it was actually so nice. I've missed him. It was like we got back together on paper but then just continued living our totally separate lives. It feels safer that way. Safer than falling in love and then inevitably spending the whole summer heartbroken. Also: the sex thing seems to have 'normalised'. No weird noises and no endless sessions.

So all should be good, but, man alive, am I irritable. G is sooooooooo annoying, and Bruce is like her fucking lap dog. He is totally infatuated with her. I DON'T UNDERSTAND! She is a TOTAL IDIOT! The second she opens her mouth, I smile but start screaming inside. Lou bloody loves her too, and seems to turn into her when she's around. Urgh. Not that I ever see her anymore now that she and Rich are the ultimate couple-y couple. I miss him. I miss her!

~~~

SUNDAY 23RD MAY 2004 1.32AM
LISTENING TO LOOK WHAT HAPPENED BY LESS THAN JAKE

I.SAW. LESS. THAN. FUCKING. JAKE. TO. FUCKING. NIGHT.

Robin Mills messaged last week and asked if I'd realised they were playing in Plymouth... errr no, I had not. SO anyway, we miraculously managed to get tix. They were amazing. I obviously thought of William Macleod all night. Goddamnit. Less Than Jake and your year's worth of associations. I was also surprised to see that it was just us and tiny little emo tweens, so we just walked right up to the front, within touching distance of Less Than Jake.

~~~

WEDNESDAY 26TH MAY 2004 1.52AM
LISTENING TO NO ONE KNOWS BY QUEENS OF THE STONE AGE

I've been so hungover all day. Every one of my cells is dying… "pop" … "pop"… the sound of Apoptosis… programmed cell death… by BOOZE. URRGH, I hate myself for making a medic joke. I've spent the day either lying on my bed, bathroom floor, or bedroom floor. WHY DO I KEEP DOING THIS TO MYSELF?! I have no energy to write, but I just want to say that I HATE the whole Rich and Lou bollocks. I miss them so much. They're both as bad as each other with how they've just cut me out now they're together. I never see them. I miss how close Rich and I used to be. I feel like a complete stranger around him now that he's turned into a ball-and-chain-under-the-thumb-fuck. Right, I've got my SSU* to do now. I'll at least get the plan down, and I'll write it tomorrow. Really should have just done that rather than writing more shit in my diary that no one (not even I!) will ever read again.

~~~

*Specialist Study Unit: A three week specialist placement culminating in a presentation and 2000-word essay on an aspect of this specialist area.

~~~

```
Toilet paper

Shampoo

Hair Dye

Leg Tan

Essay
```

THE SISTERHOOD

```
Mark's card

Lou pressie and card

Charge camera battery

Lose 5kg
```

THIRTEEN

MUMPS

FRIDAY 4TH JUNE 2004 2.30PM
LISTENING TO HERE WITHOUT YOU BY 3 DOORS DOWN

Boom - new diary. I haven't written in ages, but I had to really knuckle down and stop fannying about having fun for the end of term. So I got all my work in, miraculously managed 100% attendance, and my exams are all done. They didn't go too badly. I'll definitely have to up my game next year, though. Slightly wild first year is probably ok. I'd hate to look back and think I didn't enjoy my time at university. Although, I'd equally hate to look back, having failed, to see a trail of stale fags, booze, destruction and empty notebooks.

Right. So, in the interest of the start of summer and a new diary baby, I'll summarise what's going on.

I'm still with Lovely Northern Joe, although it has to be one of the most ridiculous relationships ever. We live a ten-minute walk from each other and have fuck all to do now that uni is over, yet we never see each other. I just can't seem to make time for him. There's always something else I'd rather be doing. A relationship expert would no doubt say that it's not very good, but to be honest, this is one of the best relationships I've ever been in.

He treats me well, he's hot, and the sex is good. We get on, and there's never any fighting or intensity. We give each other tonnes of space, and I'm just happy with it. There's no reason to break up with him, so I'm just not going to. I'm not sure what's going to happen over the summer, though…

Moving on, I quit smoking. I was lying in bed on Monday night, and I thought, "I'm going to stop. You can't smoke forever, and if I stop now, I'll hopefully get away with it". The first night was a little odd. I'd managed about 19hrs, and we were sat in the flat having dinner when I burst into tears for no reason (well, there was a reason). Anyway - well done me.

I'm going home in a week. Wow, that's weird. First year is over already. I've bloody loved it and I would do the whole thing all over again if I could: JP the sexy South African, *Zanzibar*, White Russians in *Voodoo Lounge* (RIP), Artie and Mike, My 18th, Friday nights at *The Union*, Terminators in the *Skiving Scholar*, my flat, Rich and the upstairs boys, the medic girls, Three Legged Frank, Robin Mills and Pete Bond, *C103*, *Dance Academy*, Tuna and Chip melts in *Jake's*, Monday night *Wonky Legs*, Pound a pint at the *Roundabout*, Dancing in *Walkabout*, BBQs on the Hoe, Big Dick Dave, Lily's Pigeon, Lovely Northern Joe…

~~~

THURSDAY 10TH JUNE 2004 7.40PM
LISTENING TO EASY MONEY BY BILLY JOEL

I've got mumps. Fucking brilliant. I woke up this morning, went to the bathroom, and I was staring at myself in the mirror for ages. I couldn't work it out, but I looked really weird and lopsided. I shrugged, thinking I'd slept funny and went into the kitchen. Lou came in, and we were both staring at each other. She looked so weird and we were both laughing at each other. I had a glass of orange juice, and OH MY FUCKING CHRIST THE PAIN!

'Hold up', I said, getting the old clinical medicine book out, 'we've all got mumps.'

The upstairs boys all have it too. Oh well, we feel fine. We just look like hamsters. I'm going home in two days, and it's going to be so weird being away from here.

~~~

SUNDAY 13TH JUNE 2004 10.33PM
LISTENING TO DIAMONDS ON THE SOLES OF HER SHOES BY PAUL SIMON

I'm back in Edinburgh and bedridden with mumps. Everyone else is feeling better, and I feel AWFUL. My parents came to pick me up, and we went out for dinner, but I couldn't eat anything. It hurt so much. We drove back yesterday, and I slept on and off in the back seat, wrapped up in my duvet. I feel so sick and shivery.

I miss the uni gang, though. Most of us are going to Rich's in Coventry over the summer - which'll be ace! Right, going to take some paracetamol and get some sleep. I'll hopefully feel better in the morning.

Also: Joe who? I'm not even sure I need to address it. I reckon we'll just naturally drift apart over the summer.

~~~

SUNDAY 20TH JUNE 2004 11.45PM
LISTENING TO FREE BY DONOVAN FRANKENREITER

Wow. Well, quite a lot has happened. I ended up being admitted to hospital. I woke up the morning after my last entry with intractable vomiting. My brain felt like it was going to explode, and on a few occasions, I couldn't make it back to my bed from the bathroom or vice versa and was sick on my bedroom floor.

Mum called for a GP to visit, and they admitted me. I then spent five days in hospital with meningitis and pancreatitis off the back of mumps. I've never felt so ill in my life, and it just felt never-ending. I finally stopped vomiting on day 5, but the nausea was still unbearable that I couldn't move. I woke up the next day, and there was an almost miraculous recovery. I finally felt more normal. I begged to go home. I just needed some blood tests repeated in a few days. So I'm back in my own bed and I feel tired and lonely but so relieved I don't feel sick anymore. On the plus side, I am super thin.

~~~

TUESDAY 22ND JUNE 2004 00:17
LISTENING TO I'M NOT OK (I PROMISE) BY MY CHEMICAL ROMANCE

Joe called today.

'You've been in hospital?! Claire, baby, I didn't know! Why didn't you tell me?'

'Sorry, Joe. I wasn't with it most of the time. I didn't really tell anyone.'

'What can I do? I'm going to look at flights and come and see you as soon as I can.'

'Oh. Ok. That's really sweet, but you really don't have to. They'll be so expensive.'

I'm really not sure that I want him to come and visit. We didn't see much of each other when we lived within touching distance. It seems like madness for him to fly up to Scotland. Am I happy with him? Not no but not yes either. There are only a few occasions in my life where I think I was truly loved up and happy. Probably at some point with William Macleod, but all the badness eclipsed it. Definitely with Gael at Mattie's house Summer 2001 when we'd had sex all night, and I was having a fag out the window, and the sun was rising, and he was watching me from the other end of the bed, smiling. I can still remember how happy I felt. The other times were with Artie, in particular, when he got me a mango just cos I'd mentioned, "I'd bloody love a mango", when we were watching Apocalypse Now. Does this mean I don't love Joe? Probably. We've been together on and off for six months, and at no point have I wanted to say I love you. Status quo (the state of being, not the band) is not a reason to stay with someone.

~~~

WEDNESDAY 23RD JUNE 2004 00:12AM
LISTENING TO WHAT'CHA KNOW ABOUT BY DONOVAN FRANKENREITER

Joe is coming to Edinburgh for five days. I feel really guilty that I'm not super excited.

~~~

MONDAY 28TH JUNE 2004 11.23AM
LISTENING TO ARMAND VAN HELDEN MY MY MY

I've been in Coventry at Rich's since Friday, and what a barrel of laughs it's been. It was just Rich and I until Sunday, and we just hung out with some of his schoolmates. He played cricket, and we went to the pub. It's been chilled and SO NICE with it being the two of us again. Trigger arrived Sunday night, and he's just developed mumps after 3 weeks of incubation since he saw us. Bad luck. Lou's arriving soon and although I'm excited to see her, I'm gutted I'm going to have to share Rich again. Not that it's sharing… more like… handing him back in his entirety.

~~~

MUMPS

THURSDAY 1ST JULY 2004 00:05 AM
LISTENING TO 1985 BY BOWLING FOR SOUP

I got back from Coventry yesterday after some very disappointing days. We didn't leave Rich's from Saturday night to Wednesday morning. I was going completely mad. No one wanted to go out. There were just seven of us festering on his estate with the TV endlessly wittering away in the background and the constant trickle of cheap lager. Our friendship's shine from university has definitely worn off. Plus, Trigger's mumps turned into orchitis, so he left early as he was terrified he was going to lose a bollock (not that there is any more chance of that happening with us rather than at home, but hey, his balls: his call).

So yeah, it was shit, BUT I have discovered the most EXTRAORDINARY thing. To this day, I always thought that when having sex, its duration was largely dictated (DICKtated) by how long the guy lasts until they cum. Now and again, I believe it possible for them to cum and stay hard enough to keep going for a second time, but this is mega rare. BUT FUCKING RICHARD JAMES MONROE CAN CUM, STAY HARD AND CARRY ON AND ORGASM 4-5 TIMES BEFORE HE HAS TO STOP! Lou has confirmed this. Ladies and gentlemen: the male multiple orgasm. All this time, Rich, one of my best friends, has won at sex. No wonder I never see them anymore. I'm speechless.

I'm a bit worried about Joe getting here (completely unrelated to the above revelation!). What if he irritates me, and then it's ruined?

I finally saw Next Door Andy, Big Sam and Clyde today - I've missed them. Next Door Andy almost looked relieved when I told them of my little trip to the hospital.

'Oh, you've been ill!'

'Yes, I've been ill! May I remind you that that is a BAD thing!'

'Sure, sure, but Big Sam and I saw you get back from Plymouth with your parents, and you looked like shit when you got out the car that we were like *Wo! Check out Claire! Uni's not been kind to her!*'

'Because I was ill!'

'Yeah, and you looked massively fat and weird.'

'Because I had mumps! Fucking hell, guys!'

'Exactly! Phew.'

'Phew?! Are you joking?! Me being ill is better than getting fat.'

'Obviously not...'

Honestly.

FOURTEEN
JOE IN EDINBURGH

SATURDAY 3RD JULY 2004 1.45AM
LISTENING TO F.U.R.B. (FU RIGHT BACK) BY FRANKEE

I was thinking about Artie today. I really was completely and utterly consumed with love for him. It'll probably leave a mark. I had a long on-off dream, when I was in my sick, delirious state that Artie and I got back together. It made me so powerfully happy. God, I'm an awful person. What the fuck am I doing with Joe? Here I am with a devoted boyfriend like Joe, and I can't stop banging on about my ex. Get a fucking grip, Claire.

I went to *City* last night with Next Door Andy, Big Sam, Clyde and their other mates. I spent so long flirting with Si that when he asked, 'So, how's your love life?' I just said, 'Fine, thank you!'

I didn't have the guts to mention Joe and just kept right on flirting. I'm convinced I would never cheat, but why am I doing this to him? He deserves so much more respect.

~~~

FRIDAY 9TH JULY 2004 8AM
LISTENING TO I HEAR TALK BY BUCKS FIZZ

I've just dropped Joe off at the airport. Aaaaaaaaaand breathe. I'm so relieved it's over. Visiting me in Edinburgh is basically like the kiss of death to any boyfriend. No one has survived unscathed, and Joe is no exception. I reckon even Artie would have succumbed. Gael was immediately put in 'ick corner'. Skater Chris... erm, I can't actually remember? Oh yes - he was CHEATING ON HIS GIRLFRIEND WITH ME! THE PRICK! And poor Joe has been tossed onto the reject pile comme les autres.

He was here for four days, and I thought I was going to have to rip my skin off with irritation. I even stopped playing music as I couldn't bear the 'tsis tsis tsis...' noise he made whilst miming the drums.

Monday night: we went for a drink with Maggie MacFarlane, Herbert and co. It was fine but he honestly might as well not have been there. Everyone made an effort for a bit but then gave up. After we got home, he started being all touchy-feely, but it was making my skin crawl. I didn't want to kiss him, and I definitely didn't want to have sex with him. He'd been so quiet all night. I get that he's shy, and the others can be a bit overwhelming at times, but this is not the man of my dreams! It's not his fault at all. He's always been like that, but seeing him sit there silently made me realise it wasn't right. I need someone to match my energy. I need an extrovert.

~~~

Wrong. I fell in love with and married an introvert.

~~~

The next day, we walked around Edinburgh and went to the cinema to see *Shrek 2* with Maggie. It was ok but being with Maggie made me so aware of how little Joe had to say. I mean, he spoke, but he never really said anything. We're clearly not compatible. How have I never noticed this? I guess we never really spent time together sober or not having sex. Bloody hell, Claire. A six-month relationship of nothing-ness. We went out that night with Herbie et al.

~~~

Et al? Like I'd been reading medical journals?? Pull the other one.

~~~

When Joe went to the toilet, Maggie told me she didn't want to be left alone with him. She said he was boring and they had nothing to say to each other and it was really awkward.

~~~

I wish I'd said something. I wish I'd stood up for Joe. I was so easily influenced by what everyone else thought. I guess that's part of being young and still learning to form your own thoughts and opinions. One nod from Maggie and Joe was out. Joe wasn't boring, and he didn't deserve the whispering. He was probably intimidated by a very confident group of people who, aged eighteen, somehow appeared to have it all figured out. No one had, of course, but the Edinburgh youth faked confidence better than anyone I knew. We were loud and brash and untouchable. I learnt in my early teens that showing weakness was not an option. Attack was the only form of, not just defence but, survival. Dog eat dog, so to speak. Joe had a far more mature friendship group where everyone was just… nice. As everyone in Edinburgh got louder, Joe retreated, and I interpreted this as being boring. Sorry, Joe.

~~~

I couldn't get what everyone had said about Joe out of my head. I felt so irritated by everything he said after that. It's like he's not even making an effort with my friends anymore.

On Wednesday, I had dinner with everyone at home. We got drunk and then went to *City*. Joe started dancing with me…

nooooo! That's it. I couldn't take it anymore. He was holding my hips and grinding his groin against me.

'I'm looking forward to having sex with you tonight, baby. You're looking so hot...'

I squirmed. The creep.

'Look. Joe. I'm sorry, but since you've got here, I've really not been in the mood to have sex. I'm really sorry, I don't know what it is.'

(I do.)

He practically pushed me away and then spent the next hour being really piss-faced with me. I'm not really sure what I thought I was going to achieve, but hey, out came the words.

'Do you not think we're different, Joe? Do you really feel we actually get on? Really? I don't get on with your friends, and you clearly don't like mine. We've been together six months and have barely spent any time together. It's just such a weird relationship!'

'This sounds like a dumping chat, Claire.'

It does, doesn't it? But sadly, he still had two days in Edinburgh, and I wasn't sure how it would pan out if I dumped him.

'No. It's not. Sorry. I'm drunk. It's been a weird night.'

He walked off after that, and I turned around to bump into FUCKING MISH.

'Hey.'

'Hey.'

~~~

Ah, Claire. Nooooo. Not 'hey'. Oh, how I wish I'd said something better. Something meaner; tougher even.

~~~

'How's it going? How are you finding medicine? I'm loving Plymouth, and the course is great.'

'Me too. It's felt so good to get away from Edinburgh if you know what I mean. I'm really pleased to see you've got a nice boyfriend. I always knew you would.'

'Hmmm… yeah. And what about you? Are you and Lyla still together?'

'Listen, it's been great seeing you, but I was actually just leaving. See ya around.'

'Ditto. See ya.'

I watched him walk back to Grumpy Arseface Toby, who was watching from a distance and Andy 'lads lads lads' Burns, who gave me a wink and a two-fingered salute. Edinburgh makes me feel so weird and makes me forget who I *think* I really am when I'm away.

~~~

How many of these random encounters were there where I gushed pleasantries to a man who treated me like total garbage?

"And I never saw Mish again - August 2003" - from The Diary of a Teenage Dirtbag.

APART FROM THE THOUSANDS OF TIMES WHEN I BUMPED INTO HIM DRUNK, AND I WAS SWEET AS PIE AND THEN FORGOT ALL ABOUT IT!

~~~

Joe and I didn't really talk much for the next few days. We went to the cinema and for walks so we didn't really need to engage with each other. I think we both know it's over, and we don't really need to say it out loud.

~~~

TUESDAY 13TH JULY 2004 1.45AM
LISTENING TO PLANET TELEX BY RADIOHEAD

I am fucking raging. Chloe got back from a party tonight and hasn't stopped crying. One of her best friends got off with her boyfriend, and she walked in on them. She really liked him too, and all she's saying is crap like 'I'm not surprised he got with her… she's so much skinnier / prettier / funnier than me…'

FUCK. OFF.

I wish she could see what I can see.

~~~

THURSDAY 15TH JULY 2004 4AM
LISTENING TO I DON'T WANNA KNOW BY MARIO WINANS FT. P.DIDDY AND ENYA

I went out with Next Door Andy, Big Sam, Clydey and their boys tonight. It was such a laugh. We drank next door for a few hours, and they snorted their excruciating bottle caps of whisky. Then, we walked into town. I then spent the rest of the night bouncing on the dancefloor in a four-way hug with Andy, Sam and Clyde. It was perfect. I got home and went on MSN to see that William Macleod was online.

```
Me: Hey Stranger.

W: Hey. You're up late. You need to
stop booty-calling me…

Me: Ha ha. Been out with Andy. What
about you?

W: Can't sleep
```

Me: Got stuff on your mind?

W: Not really

Me: Oh ok. You alright?

W: I'm fine. I don't care about things as much as you think I do.

Me: What's that supposed to mean? You used to care about things A LOT.

W: Yeah well, things change. I don't really care about anything or anyone that much now. It's better that way.

Me: Jesus. That's a bit bleak. What about me? You cared about me. You can't not care about anything! That's just NOTHINGNESS.

W: I never REALLY loved you. I just thought I did at the time. But that wasn't love. What we had wasn't love.

Me: Fuck this. I'm not having this conversation now. How do you always manage to get under my skin?! I'm out.

W: I'm just being honest.

If William never really loved me, then I don't really know what love is anymore. No. There's no way. I hope that's not true. I am lying in bed now thinking about it, and it's making me cry. Fucking William. How can he keep doing this to me?! He's ruined my idea of love. He's ruined EVERYTHING. No. I can't let him. If he wants to shut himself off from any emotion and spend the rest of his life as a robotic, empty vessel, then be my guest. He can survive, and I'll live. He had such a huge heart - what happened? There is, of course, the very real possibility that he's just saying that cos he likes to get under my skin. Man, I'm drunk. Poo and bed.

FIFTEEN
SUMMER 04

SATURDAY 17TH JULY 2004 00:00
LISTENING TO BEND IN THE ROAD DONOVAN FRANKENREITER

I've arrived safely in the South of France and I am UPSET by how much weight I've put on this year. I look awful in a bikini, and that makes me so sad.

~~~

SUNDAY 18TH JULY 2004 2AM
LISTENING TO SULK BY RADIOHEAD

Beautiful day and the tan's coming along nicely but man, am I bored, and I am craving fags BIG TIME. I'm an adult. My parents clearly know I smoke, but I still can't quite bring myself to do it in front of them. Gahhh. I was supposed to see Sexy Laurent and Marie (who, incidentally, are still together! WHAAAAATT?!?!?) tonight, but it was late, and I was tired.

~~~

MONDAY 19TH JULY 2004
LISTENING TO IT'S THE END OF THE WORLD AS WE KNOW IT BY R.E.M

I've been so piss-faced all day. EVERYONE IS SO ANNOYING. It's like my entire extended family have made a pact to drive me insane. I want to scream the second I see someone so much as open their mouth.

~~~

All right there, you massive teenager.

~~~

Also, something slightly awkward happened earlier:

> Text from Joe: Hey, baby. Sorry, I've not been in touch since Edinburgh. I think I was waiting to hear from you, then realised how silly that is! How are you? Are you in France yet? Miss you xxx

Oops! Slight hiccough in that it appears I am still Lovely Northern Joe's girlfriend. Although, if I had thought he was my boyfriend, I would have been mega fucked off to not hear a peep in ten days. I think I'm still in love with Artie. Which is ridiculous as he never even knew I loved him, and it was quite a long time ago now… This unhealthy obsession needs to end. I'm still having elaborate and detailed dreams about us getting back together in some kind of dystopian future.

~~~

SATURDAY 23RD JULY 2004 1PM
LISTENING TO 2+2=5 BY RADIOHEAD

The South of France is starting to get to me now. It's all very well having nothing to do, developing a stunning tan surrounded by my whole family, but I'm going MAD.

~~~

You spoiled brat. It is amazing that I simultaneously had insight into how ungrateful I was being but scoffed at my fortune nonetheless.

~~~

I'm just getting sucked down into a family/boredom/irritation vortex. Urrrghhhhh.

~~~

SATURDAY 24TH JULY 2004 3AM
LISTENING TO IF YOU COULD READ MY MIND BY GORDON LIGHTFOOT

What a wonderful night I just had with Sexy Laurent… without Marie, which was a bit of a relief. She understandably does not like me. We went for a drink in Villefranche, and she left early cos she was working early tomorrow. Although she was blatantly pretty unhappy about the whole thing - not that I blame her. Sexy Laurent has dumped her for me on more than one occasion in the past. I would HATE me if I were her. Actually, considering the facts, she's fairly pleasant with me.

 ANYWAY. We went for a drink and chatted and laughed and then went for a dance (there was some live music in the street with people dancing). I had a feeling I could have pulled him but stayed well away - I could very easily be wrong, and it would have been a super shitty thing to do - even for me. He's in a long-term 'in love' relationship, and I have no place interfering. It has taken my mind off Artie, though!

~~~

SUNDAY 25TH JULY 2004 00.30
LISTENING TO EVERY LITTLE THING SHE DOES IS MAGIC BY THE POLICE

I've decided to stop fannying about wasting my time and being bored when I can finally catch up on all the work I didn't do properly this year. I'm going to start by going through all the clinical skills examinations as they, at least, feel useful and like something I might use if I ever become a doctor.

Today: Cranial Nerves and Peripheral Nervous System: Completed it. Boom.

~~~

MONDAY 26TH JULY 2004 00.20
LISTENING TO (NICE DREAM) BY RADIOHEAD

Well, Sexy Laurent can fuck right off. I text him about 8pm and asked how his day was and if he was doing anything tonight.

```
Text from Sexy Laurent: Bof la journée.
Ce soir je la passe avec Marie. Je te
laisse, j'ai plu de crédit. Peut-être
à demain.
```

Fuck that. She's blatantly said something cos "no credit", "maybe tomorrow" is clearly bollocks. If he wants to suffocate under her thumb, then be my guest. I'm not texting him again.

~~~

Good for him.

~~~

I just feel so rejected.

~~~

Good.

~~~

WEDNESDAY 28TH JULY 2004 00.20AM
LISTENING TO WE'RE NOT GOING TO TAKE IT BY TWISTED SISTER

I discovered HATE at first sight today. Sexy Laurent messaged and asked if I fancied joining them for a coffee this afternoon. I went to the village square and Marie was there with her crimped blonde slag of a friend, Monique. I went in for 'la bise' and she turned her head away and muttered 'conne'. SORRY WHAT?! I pretended like I hadn't heard and introduced myself. She laughed and said she knew EXACTLY who I was. What a nob. I then spent the next hour building up an insane amount of steam. Sexy Laurent acted like he didn't notice as they giggled and whispered together. What are they? Fucking twelve? I felt like I was at school again. I then heard Monique say, 'She's fat' (in English!) and pointed at me.

I'm out. I just got up and left. I'm not putting up with this shit.

SIXTEEN
NICO

FRIDAY 30TH JULY 2004 6.25PM
LISTENING TO PARADISE CITY BY GUNS N ROSES

I've just got on the train to St Jacut - yippee! Take me to my happy place!

~~~

SUNDAY 1ST AUGUST 2004 6AM
LISTENING TO ME GUSTAS TU BY MANU CHAO

I am completely fucked. I've just had my first night here for summer 2004 and let me tell you, it has not disappointed. 'The other' Claire and I smoked weed and drank Ricard before heading out and seeing everyone at the bar, five Teq Pafs, two more spliffs at La Banche beach and back to the bar.

~~~

'The other' Claire had lived all over the world, and I was transfixed by her. She was a few years older than me, dry (not alcoholically) and witty with auburn hair, olive skin and a killer smattering of freckles. She drank and smoked to excess, and when Marc wasn't around to scratch my itch, I went a little nuts with Claire.

A 'Teq Paf' is a large tequila served in a tumbler with an equal

measure of tonic. A beer mat is placed over the top of the glass and you slam the glass to make it fizz before knocking it back.
  Wait… that word 'slam'… Is this the same as a tequila slammer?
  <researches>
  Holy Moly - it is. THIS WHOLE TIME!

~~~

Marc finally arrived, and I wanted to explode with happiness when I saw him. I had actual tears in my eyes when I ran to him and hugged him tighter than I've ever hugged anyone. We sat down with some rum and went through our year. He's got a new girlfriend and… wait for it… 'Elle est complètement folle!'

We all went back to Nicolas'. Marc and I were sitting on the floor, playing caps, when Nico came and sat next to me. He put his arm around my back in a friendly way, but it felt so good that I leaned into him and pulled him.

~~~

What? In the middle of a game!?

~~~

He's got lovely big billowy lips… I think it's the size of him that I'm attracted to. He's like a bear. I've always liked him, but (I hate myself for saying this) I've always just thought he was 'too nice'. Urgh. Yup - hate myself. Nico's got a tangle of curly dark brown hair that I LOVE. Hold up. Is that my thing? Hair? I think back to all my exes and… oh my god, that's it! I'd always thought that none of them had anything in common, but they do… HAIR… lots of it.

Marc then gave me a lift home, and we just sat in his car at the port, shared a spliff and listened to 'Steal My Kisses', which I always think of as our song. Bloody love that guy. I'd do anything for him.

~~~

MONDAY 2ND AUGUST 2004
LISTENING TO TIMES LIKE THESE BY JACK JOHNSON

I spent the day on the boat with Marc - we felt dreadful, it was so hot. We just smoked throughout the day, and he was sick over the side of the boat. It's a bloody miracle that I wasn't too.

There was then an apéro at Viking God Max's tonight. I haven't seen him since last summer, but Marc told me it didn't matter if I went. He greeted me in a very casual way. Too cool to ever have felt anything but also convivial enough to show he didn't give a shite. It was ALMOST like he didn't recognise me. Man, he's a twat. A sexy twat though, and as the night wore on, I really wanted to get with him. IT'S THE BLOODY HAIR!

Nico arrived before I made a tit of myself. We sat outside and he had his arm around my shoulders. He's never really liked Max and seemed to know what I'd been thinking as he started telling me that he never really understood what I saw in Max (les cheveux Nico…). He told me he thought I was better than Max and much preferred me when I hadn't been drinking or smoking and that people like Max would never see that. He reminded me how Viking God Max had treated me like shit and asked why I put up with it? Good question. So I did the only thing that drunk Claire is capable of doing, and I pulled Nico again. I'm so bloody fickle. I'm just chasing the lust dragon…

Marc and I went and sat on the beach till sunrise, chatting away. We promised we'd always stay in each other's lives. I can't imagine a world without him if I'm honest. So stoned, though. After this summer, no more weed. Nico's the first person who has challenged the booze and drugs like that without sounding snobby or condescending… it has made me think.

~~~

THURSDAY 5TH AUGUST 2004 5AM
LISTENING TO BONGO BONG BY MANU CHAO

Just got back from a massive bonfire on the Châtelet beach, and Chloe's still not back. Oh, wait. That's her now… tut tut tut. 'The other' Claire and I spent most of the night together dancing around the fire. I'm not sure we're particularly good influences on each other. It's like we're playing party-chicken. Nico and I had a little kiss at the start of the night, but I think he left early, as I didn't see him after that.

~~~

MONDAY 9TH AUGUST 2004 5AM
LISTENING TO THREE LITTLE BIRDS BY BOB MARLEY & THE WAILERS

We went camping on the island on Friday night, and I couldn't get Nico out of my mind. How weird. I've known him for years, but feel like I'm only just seeing him now. How did I never notice him before? We stayed up all night and sat round the fire with the others. I sat in between his legs with my back nestled in nicely to his warmth. He smells so good too.

    We spent the rest of the weekend walking around and hanging out at his. He's so sweet and makes me feel so looked after. I stayed at his last night and it was so nice just being in a bed with him. I was a good girl, though, and we just kissed and cuddled.

    Oops! I've just seen a missed call from Joe. 4am in the UK. He must be pissed. Shit! I never actually ended it, but we haven't spoken for three weeks. Surely, that means it's over, right?

~~~

TUESDAY 10TH AUGUST 2004 4.30AM
LISTENING TO JE NE T'AIME PLUS BY MANU CHAO

Well, the Nico thing lasted a REAAAALLLY long time... NAWT. He ended it because I was apparently drunk all the time with Marc or Claire. WAKER. Or wanker even. Damn. That's pretty sobering... misspelling wanker cos I'm drunk describing someone who says I'm drunk all the time. Fuck. The worst part is I know he's right. I've lost the plot this summer. St Jacut just does stuff to me, man... I'm gutted there won't be a 'summer romance' this year. I thought it might be possible with Nico but now that's done, I'm not 'allowed' someone else. One fling per summer - fine. Two? Slug. hahahaha! I mean SLUT! Not a slug yet... I want to feel the all-consuming passion. That fragile new love. Will I forever just be chasing the summer I had with Gael?

I'm going to Jersey to visit Bruce on Saturday, and Mark (Wolverhampton Mark with a K) is coming too, which will be fun. As for Joe - I'm confused and unsure what to do. It's not clear if it's over or if I actually need to end it.

God, I'm fucked. Right bed.

~~~

WEDNESDAY 11TH AUGUST 2004 2AM
LISTENING TO AMOR PA'MI BY SERGENT GARCIA

Today has been so flat. I don't know what I'm doing. I'm just drifting around with Marc and Claire, wasting my life. I am such a fucking bum. How long can I realistically continue like this until I ruin my life... ruin my brain. There must be a point of no return when making these lifestyle choices. This isn't cool anymore. I'm eighteen years old, and I got dumped for drinking too much by a twenty-two-year-old. Fucking check yourself, Claire. You aren't Kate Moss, you fucking embarrassment.

NICO

I spent the day on the beach with 'the other' Claire. We played Tarot, smoked and grunted at each other.

When I get back to Plymouth, I'm starting again. I'm going to work. I'm going to cook and eat properly, drink less, stop smoking, maybe even... wait for it... do some exercise! Look out future, I'm coming for ya. I refuse to be sat on that beach in my 30s and 40s with Claire, a haggard and stoned med school dropout, as I silently pass her a spliff from between my shakey, yellowed fingers.

Marc and I entered the pool competition tonight and got to the final. Point proved - we are living, breathing examples of a misspent youth, smashing leathery, alcoholic Frenchmen at pool at our age - it says something, that's all.

Marc and I were sat outside *Le Dauphin* around midnight as all the old boys were leaving when Gael and Ewen Le Pervert arrived. I felt my heart stop. I'll always feel something when I see Gael, BUT Ewen... I haven't seen him since THAT night. They both said *salut*, and I floated up and out of my body to watch myself casually give Ewen Le Pervert la bise.

We sat down, Ewen next to me and Gael next to Marc. Time felt like it was moving in slow motion, and like, if it had been raining, the raindrops would have just hung in mid-air. I know I'm sounding really dramatic but I cannot stress enough what an effect Ewen had on me. How dare he pitch up and brazenly sit next to me after what he did? How dare he pretend like everything is normal. How dare he!? But also, I feel floored by the shame of it all. Shame that I allowed myself to get into that position; that I was drunk at the time. And the overwhelming shame that I let him get away with it; that I didn't tell a soul. And STILL allowing him to sit next to me, colluding with his denial and his pretence. Fucking bastard.

I was vaguely aware of them talking about a catamaran when

Ewen placed his hand on my thigh under the table. My whole body froze, and I felt like his hand was branding me. My entire world became just his hand. He kept talking and looking ahead at the other two when he dug his fingers in and grabbed a fistful of flesh. His action was clear. This was not an attempt at seduction but an act of violence. I thought I was being electrocuted. I have no idea how long he squeezed for, but when he let go, I did a silent gasp, realising that I'd been holding my breath. I kept my eyes ahead and tried to remember how to breathe. Do I hold it in longer than out? Do I breathe quicker or slower than this? How deeply do I inhale? Is this normal? Marc caught my eye and raised his eyebrows, silently checking in. I nodded in the most reassuring way that I could.

'I'm fine.'

And that was it. Another 'nothing *actually* happened' moment that will stay with me forever. I'm looking at my thigh now, and I can see his finger marks.

~~~

Yeesh. That is obscene, and just like the initial 'incident', I barely remember it. I cannot imagine that there once existed a version of myself that would sit there silently and 'allow' this to happen. How was he so confident that I wouldn't raise the alarm? Why didn't I scream? Punch? Kick? Anything? I froze. I choked. Whatever the expression, my body and brain were disconnected. This is maybe what allowed me to so easily forget? I have a slight pet peeve when 'young' patients so routinely tell me that they 'disassociate'. I'm not saying it's not true, but it's as common as eczema these days (how old do I sound now?!). I ask myself if this really is what is happening, but now I wonder, with all these examples of forgotten youth, did we all 'disassociate' throughout our teens and early twenties and then forget that too?

SEVENTEEN
JERSEY BOYZ

SUNDAY 15TH AUGUST 2004 7PM
LISTENING TO TOMORROW MORNING BY JACK JOHNSON

I'm on the Seacat on the way back to France from Jersey. I had the best weekend with Bruce and Wolves Mark - I'm gutted to leave, although I'll be moving in with them and Ellie and Lou in a month, so that's GREAT! I JUST LOVE THEM SO MUCH!

I arrived on Friday, and the three of us headed to the beach. We had a lovely dinner with the O'Neil 'rentals and then headed to their local pub and got 'twisted' as Bruce would say. When we got back, Bruce and I stayed up chatting, and then I slept in his bed. We were so giggly and pissed as puddings. It was friendly but cuddly (nothing untoward, as we'd periodically do this back in Plymouth anyway). We're just each other's safety blankets. THEN he pressed his hard-on against my thigh (but only for a few seconds).

'Sorry Claire!!! It's John… Jooooooohhhhhhnnn made me do it.'

What is this fascination with naming your dick? I haven't named my vagina. Is it some way to absolve yourself from taking responsibility for your actions? 'It wasn't me - my wang did it.' My vagina is my own and has not got a mind of herself. Itself? Own your penis' men!

Saturday: Bruce was working so Mark and I hiked over the sand dunes and spent the day on the beach.

~~~

Is 'hiking' really the correct word here?

~~~

We had another delicious dinner with the O'Neils, then went clubbing with Bruce's Jersey boys. What a shite night. Bruce was in a bad mood and made Mark, and I feel like a burden. Bruce then pissed me off by saying loads of stuff like 'I have NO IDEA what happened last night.' and 'YOU made me drink so much!'

Hmmm mmmmm sure, Bruce. Whatever. I didn't make him drink anything! He's a grown man who drank his own drinks. But also, fuck you for treating me like that and then acting embarrassed that you might have shown some attraction rather than embarrassment that you were a drunken sex pest.

Bruce, Mark and some of Bruce's friends were talking in the taxi last night about how all girls are mind fucks. Bruce was very animated about this.

'Totally. I haven't met a single girl in my life that isn't a mind fuck.'

'Fuck off, Bruce. Have you ever thought that girls are the way they are because of how they are treated by men?! Besides - I'm not a mind fuck.'

He spat his beer out laughing and pointed so aggressively at me.

'YOU, Claire, are the biggest mind fuck of them all! I love you, but you can't claim to be all sweetness and light, babe.'

Everyone thought this was proper funny, in particular the group of fucking meatheads I'd met about three seconds earlier.

Not cool, Bruce. It almost made me feel a bit tearful because part of me knew he was right. William, Gael and Joe - fair enough. But then, now I think about it - Mish, Finn, Skater Chris, Ewen Le Pervert, Viking God Max and JP, the sexy South African… well. Nuff said. It's not always me. But then it's always the girls, isn't it? We're always the crazy bitches while guys cavort about drinking beers in the backs of cabs, pressing their erections on their friends, then wildly stating that all girls are mind fucks. I'm pissed off now. I wish I'd said something.

Anyway, we got some mini golf on the go today, which was a laugh, and now I'm on my way back to St Jac.

~~~

18TH AUGUST 2004 2AM
LISTENING TO CLANDESTINO BY MANU CHAO

I just got a voicemail from Joe.

'Hello, stranger. Long time no see. Speak soon.'

His voice pisses me off. What does he think is going on? We've been apart for two months, and I've called him once. This is the first proper contact from him. I'd hoped the end of the relationship was obvious to both parties. We've both got a functioning phone. I mean, come on!

Urgh. I need to turn the light off. Chloe is getting piss-faced with me. FINE.

EIGHTEEN
MARC

THURSDAY 19TH AUGUST 2004 2.15AM
LISTENING TO YOU SHOOK ME ALL NIGHT LONG BY AC/DC

I am so fat. FUUCCCCCKKKKK. I'm just this big, disgusting, monstrous blob… with eyes… and some greasy tufts of hair. I'm going on a diet. Or I'm just going to stop eating. This is so depressing.

~~~

No! This again? See The Diary of a Teenage Dirtbag for my feelings on this. How do I stop this from affecting my children? How do I protect them from this and teach them to love themselves? How was this so important for so long? How much of my brain was taken up trying to achieve a weight that was just under my natural weight? It was maybe 5kg over at most, but I worked so hard at it. If I'm honest, it was part of the reason I smoked. I restricted and chose alcohol calories over food calories for years. My drive to enjoy myself eventually won, and my love of food and life eventually led to a love of my body. But it took too long, and I mourn for my young adult brain space wasted on boys and dieting.

~~~

MARC

SATURDAY 21ST AUGUST 2004 2.38AM
LISTENING TO EASY SKANKING BY BOB MARKEY & THE WAILERS

Last night was certainly one for the books. I started with a few Ricards at mine with Marc, François and Ben. It was deliciously old school, and I can just feel my whole body relax when I'm around them. Went to the bar, kept drinking, and then to Les Belges' house. Everyone was getting royally pissed with their insane Belgian beers.

Marc and I then spent the rest of the night joined at the hip. He's like the best girlfriend I never had (we can pee together, etc). Then we went to Nico's (there were about twenty of us) and started this crazy dream (oops - I didn't mean 'dream', I meant 'game', but I'm talking to Chloe about coffee and weird dreams). So anyway, we started this crazy game. We were drinking warm boxed, white wine from a 5-litre 'cubie' - sooo vomitative. Basically, when one person downed their drink, everyone else had to follow. Stupid really. Ben, Guillome, Jean-Charles, François etc were all sick. Ben fell through Nico's hedge into the neighbour's garden and then couldn't get back - hilarious. Then a bunch of us went to the Rougeret beach for a fire. I just sat chatting to Marc and we spoke about his childhood again. I think he finds it helpful to talk about it… I wish he hadn't cracked the rum open, though… bleurgh.
I went back to his. We were SO DRUNK… TOTALLY FRIDGED. Marc knocked over EVERYTHING, and we had some saucisson and then dodgem-ed up to bed.

I woke up this morning to the LOUDEST drum and bass ever. He'd clearly forgotten I was there as he'd maxed his music and gone downstairs.

~~~

Ahh yes. This was the morning. I spoke of this morning as a Marc-related memory in Teenage Dirtbag. I spoke of the messy, booze-related spiral that Marc and I were in. It was so dangerous. I wrote very frankly of what took place with Marc growing up. This was partly my story and my errors. What I regret was writing about his childhood trauma. This was not my story to tell. I had never anticipated, however, that it would be read by anyone who knew Marc or that anyone in France would even hear about it. It was just some background on a person that no one knew. I saw Marc in 2022 for the first time in over a decade.

'I heard you wrote a book! That's amazing - congratulations! What is it about?'

(FUUUUUUUCCCCKKKKKKK!)

'Erm. It's my teenage diaries with my adult commentary.'

'Wow. I bet there are some good stories to tell… and some recognisable faces. Is it going to be translated into French?'

<Profusely sweating>

'Non.'

~~~

I headed downstairs and found him dancing naked in the kitchen - clearly still fucked. We sat in his garden and had a coffee. He didn't even bother getting dressed, and we realised we were clearly both still drunk, so thought it would be funny to have another Ricard. Pissed as puddings and giggling like two little tickled girls, we headed to the café. We kept finding bits of chorizo everywhere. WHAT HAPPENED LAST NIGHT?

We got to his car, and he'd scraped it all down the driver's side. I can't believe he'd driven / I'd let him etc. The driver's door was completely jammed shut.

'Merde. Mais bon. C'est pas grave. On y va ma Claire.'

And off we went. We played a few hilarious games of pool, reminisced and pieced together the night before. I do love him so much I could cry.

MARC

~~~

Une folie à deux.

~~~

MONDAY 23RD AUGUST 2004 2PM
LISTENING TO LOS DESAPARECIDOS BY SERGENT GARCIA

I went to Les Fennecs Festival yesterday, but I felt really lonely. I spent most of the night feeling like a third wheel with Marc and his gf. All week, it's been 'Claire and Marco' but now, despite how difficult she can be, he adores her and I have no place being here with them. I'm happy for him, but I'm also a complete 'mind fuck' after all, and I miss not sharing him. I'm not his. I just want to belong. Fuck. I feel lonely. I want my 'someone'. *Can… anybody… find me… somebody… to love?* Pff. I can't be arsed writing anymore. What's the point? Who am I talking to? It's not like I write anything of any value or interest. It's just a pointless stream of consciousness. WHY AM I STILL WRITING?!?!

PUT.
THE.
PEN.
DOWN.
YOU.
FUCKING.
LOSER.

~~~

WEDNESDAY 25TH AUGUST 2004 7PM
LISTENING TO BLACK STAR BY RADIOHEAD

Well, I was my drunkest ever last night.

~~~

Jesus. Please stop.

~~~

Marc, Ben, François and I cooked at mine then headed out. Usual usual blah blah then ended up back at Jules' house playing strip poker with Marc, Viking God Max and the other drug boys. I was wasted, then ended up upset (can't remember why) and staying in Marc's bed.

~~~

Where's your self-respect, Claire?! There's a good reason we erase these memories. I don't want to remember this! Or worse even, not remember it but know it happened and that other people might remember it. I have always been incredibly quick to judge the drunk, crying girl playing strip poker at a party.
 'I'm glad I've never been like that. How embarrassing for her...'
 Hmmm...

~~~

I'm going to miss Marc so much. It's cruel really that we only really get to spend a few weeks a year together. He's one of the greatest people I have ever met. I would do absolutely anything for him. I hope we're this close forever. Urgh, my back and kidneys hurt so much, I'm so hungover.

~~~

MARC

FRIDAY 27TH AUGUST 2004 11.15AM
LISTENING TO THE WHOLE OF THE MOON BY THE WATERBOYS

I'm sitting on the plane at Dinard airport, having just left St Jacut. I feel ripped apart. Marc and I spent the whole of the last week together. It's all a blur but there's a lump in my throat when I think of how happy we make each other. No one knows me like he does. I've never let anyone in like Marc. Warts and all. He is the best friend I've ever had and the pain I feel on leaving is too much to bear. I will do everything in my power to ensure that he is always in my life. My big brother… see ya next year, buddy. Wahhhhhhhhhh. Stop the plane. I don't want to leave. The world stops spinning when I'm in St Jacut. I don't want to face reality. Shit - the fucking medical degree I've completely ignored for the last few months (and my health).

Fly me back to Neverland!

NINETEEN
SHAGOPOLY

SUNDAY 29TH AUGUST 2004 2.45AM
LISTENING TO SUNRISE BY NORA JONES

I'M SINGLE! I rang Lovely Northern Joe after I got home.

'Hey, Joe. Listen, we probably just need to have a talk about things.'

'I know what you're going to say, and it's cool. I know we drifted. I know I drifted. In fact, I've met someone else. I knew we were done.'

'Oh, right! Great. I'm happy for you. I guess that's that, then. No hard feelings?'

'None at all. You're a great girl, Claire and I hope you meet someone who makes you happy.'

'Thanks. You too, big guy.'

HOW FUCKING GREAT IS THAT!? PHEW.

~~~

WEDNESDAY 1ST SEPTEMBER 2004 1AM
LISTENING JESUS OF SUBURBIA BY GREEN DAY

Maggie had a big dinner at hers last night, and we played 'Shagopoly', which is basically a cross between spin the bottle, strip poker and Monopoly. If I could put as much effort into my degree as I did compiling the rules of Shagopoly, I'd get a bloody distinction.

Anyway, the twist was I ended up 'having' to pull Herbert. I'm not going to lie, I didn't hate it. Probably just because I'm a crazy bitch, and I feel like I can mentally tick off what I spent a lot of last year wanting to do.

~~~

Mystery solved. Two months after the release of TDOATD, my parents brought me a red and white 1999 Kickers shoe box that I had hidden behind my wardrobe in my childhood bedroom.

'There it is!'

It was stuffed full of cards, letters and photos from my adolescence. I sat, working my way through it for what felt like a whole day, wishing some of this had been available to me pre-publication. I eventually emerged from a (now familiar) nostalgic funk, feeling like I always do when I am reminded of that period and so many forgotten memories; unsettled, sad and embarrassed. Then, tucked neatly in an envelope alongside a letter from Maggie, was a black and white photo of me snogging Herbert. Not just snogging but cupping his face in my hands. Surely not… but it was undoubtedly me and undoubtedly him. WHAT THE FUCK WAS THIS?

I had only just, the weekend before, enjoyed a delightful lunch with Herbert and his family. Everyone told me how much they had enjoyed the book, and Herbert's wife was able to look past my previous infatuation with her husband.

'I loved it, Claire, and I think your portrayal of Herbert is exactly how I would have imagined him then. Your mention of the boys and his sister was also terribly sweet. Well done you.'

'Aww, thank you. Yes, it was a weird time, but at least we were

able to get over it and remain friends. It's just a relief that we never kissed or anything...'

'Ha ha, yes, that would have been a little weird.'

And yet there it was, literally in black and white. I had no choice but to go full detective. Location? Uncertain. The letter and photo had no date, and the only reference in the letter was:

```
'I had no choice but to print it out
for you so you can remember this mo-
ment forever.'
```

Clearly not...

It didn't look like my house. My hair was longer than it had been when I was at school... that top... classic early to mid-noughties filth... bought around 2004. The only conclusion I could come to was that I had snogged Herbert during or after 2004. I couldn't ask him. I couldn't ask Maggie (any salvageable friendship had been burnt to the ground when I went to print and publicly assassinated Gretchen and, to a lesser extent, Maggie's character.)

I felt tortured by all the questions that this threw up. How do I not remember this? Have I forgotten EVERYTHING? Who am I?

But thanks to being part of a generation document. I have answers. Phew. It was only a game.

~~~

Ten days left in Edinburgh, and I can't wait to leave.

~~~

FRIDAY 3RD SEPTEMBER 2004 3AM
LISTENING TO PLAYING WITH THE BOYS BY KENNY LOGGINS

If only every night could be as easy as tonight. I had a wonderful night at Douglas Macdonald's. It was the usual lot: Maggie, Herbie, Al Winter, Hector Mckellen, Elliot Brown and David Moore.

~~~

These boys have, up until this point, been described as 'the A-level French boys' (half of whom had actually done A-Level French).
"Too many characters have led to the demise of many a good book."
(Source unknown and possibly made up.)
But this is definitely not 'a good book', and there are only so many times where it felt acceptable to blur Herbie, Maggie, and I's entourage.
These boys were old-fashioned, whimsical and peculiar as hell. They should have been bullied for their academic prowess, bizarre sense of humour and total sporting ineptitude. Yet, somehow, they were lucky enough to have found their people in childhood and, with that, an enviable security that comes with knowing (and liking) oneself at a young age. Thus, as a collective, bullying them was verboten. In fact, they developed a confidence that, in theory, should not have existed in these weird and lanky scholars. They taught me to embrace lunacy and shake off some of my insecurities.
Douglas was the son of two awkward hyper-academics who wore patchworked tweed and lived in a rickety old Edinburgh townhouse bursting with books and dust. This formidable level of brilliance was accompanied by an almost inevitable social clumsiness. And the Douglas Apple did not fall far from his tree. He was giraffe-tall with strawberry-blonde curtains and a colossal brain. Despite being made of pure, 100% intelligence, he was actually quite normal.
Al Winter is also half-French and grew up round the corner from me. We smiled through our Holy Communion together with all the other French families that halfheartedly jumped through religious hoops until their enfants became 'terrible' Scottish heathens and renounced their faith. Al and I then went to school together and shared a lot of friends. He was friends with Mish and the rugby boys, Charlie, Andy 'Lads Lads Lads' Burns and also Herbert and the eccentric eggheads. On paper, we were very similar, but in reality, we were two very different people who had a lot of enforced time together.
Al came to our wedding and wore fabulous tartan troos, ce-

menting the friendship in my mind with a very thoughtful gift. We had a dormitory-style set-up so we could have everyone to stay. I bunked Herbert McNash and Al Winter with Next Door Andy and the future Mrs Next Door Andy. ND Andy was awoken on Sunday morning, delighted with the spectacle of a naked Al Winter brushing his teeth and singing La Marseillaise.

~~~

I drove tonight. I was over it. By 'it', I mean drinking, and too much of 'it' at that. Plus, getting to Doug's is a right faff, but I mainly didn't want to drink. It was too much with Marc this summer, and Nico's words were still ringing in my ears.

We had such a fun night. Douglas cooked a weird dinner of pork and rice and potatoes with cream for dinner. I'd made chocolate mousse for dessert. Everyone else was pretty pissed, and we played some more games. Maggie licked chocolate mousse off my face... chin to eyebrow - I have never laughed so hard. I snogged Herbert again during another lengthy round of Shagopoly. Are we both encouraging this? Bit weird doing game-snogging sober, though, and I eventually convinced everyone to call it a night and gave Herbie and Al a lift home. They sang the whole way, and it filled my heart. When I got home, I started wondering if maybe I did like Herbie again. But maybe it was just that months of hanging out with idiots and druggies made me find Herbie's company rather refreshing. He was shit-faced, though, tonight, and I was obviously completely sober, so the mismatch was enough to stopper my thoughts for a bit. Should I be going for someone a bit more like him? My mum would say yes. OBVIOUSLY. Bloody Shagopoly has a lot to answer for.

I went out last night with Big Sam, Clyde and Next Door Andy - we were all off our faces (which contributed heavily to my abstinence tonight). I love them so much, although the drug chat is back, and Sam and Andy were pilled up to the eyeballs

- so annoying. Fucking pills. What's wrong with just going out without pills? I know it's not about me, but part of me thinks: is my company not good enough? Although, the answer is clearly: No. It's not. Never has been. Drugs always win over me…

~~~

SATURDAY 4TH SEPTEMBER 2004 2AM
LISTENING TO MUSHABOOM BY FEIST

Can't sleep. I'm thinking too much, and I'm all farty.

~~~

Oh, how lovely. That was definitely worth sitting up and putting the light on to scribble down this literary tit-bit.

~~~

I'm thinking about money and how I essentially have none. I'm thinking about all the stuff I need to buy for winter. Shoes, coat, smart clothes for placements… argghhh. I've just blown all my auxiliary money this summer… on what? Fucking fags, weed and tequila? Jesus. And I'm thinking of my new house, and work, and Herbie, and Marc, and France and fuck… Artie… still. My brain is so clogged with crap - it needs the brain equivalent of a toilet plunger. What is that? Vegetables? A book? A lobotomy?

~~~

SUNDAY 5TH SEPTEMBER 2004 2AM
LISTENING TO FALL LINE BY JACK JOHNSON

What the fuck is wrong with me?? I had another Herbert dream. We all know what happened last time I had a dream about Herbie. Aaaaaand it has predictably had the same effect. How am I so susceptible? One dream and I'll completely change how I feel about someone. We were both staying in a friend's big house and sharing a bed (in the dream). The room had beautiful wood panelling, a roll-top bath and a four-poster bed with titanium white sheets. There were floor-to-ceiling windows overlooking the grounds… The works. He'd been awake since sun-rise (cos Herbie's an insomniac) stroking my hair, and when I woke up, he kissed me and it was perfect. Then I ACTUALLY woke up and was like… ah fuck, this life again. Fortunately, the feeling has been dissipating throughout the day.

Why do I insist on having repeated unrealistic dreams about people I can't have? I guess the constant barrage of disappointment is just toughening me up and preparing me for life… man. God, I'm a wanker writing rubbish like that. An alternate viewpoint is that I am very lucky to remember all my dreams. We spend a third of our lives asleep, and I remember most of mine. Does that mean I get to live more than everyone else? And it's WAY better and more enchanting a world than real life. Yeah - sucks to be everyone else.

~~~

FRIDAY 10TH SEPTEMBER 2004 00.15AM
LISTENING TO LITHIUM BY NIRVANA

Just watched *City Slickers* with Next Door Andy. Boy, the 80s knew how to make movies.

~~~

Films. They're called films.

~~~

Saw William Macleod the other night. He's such a miserable fucker these days. He was so rude and scoffed at me (but somehow showing less emotion than a scoff) when I said I'd had a nice summer. Fuck you. Oh! I've just remembered that MSN chat about how he was dead inside or whatever. Shit, what was it - going to go back in my diary.

Just found it - July. Ha! It wasn't even that long ago! What a soulless, cold-blooded, emotionless, sad, sad wanker. Stop thinking about William - he will forever aggrieve me.

Right. Bed. Got a big day of packing tomorrow - I'm so excited! I'm ready to go back to Plymmy now.

Summer out.

TWENTY
AMITY PLACE

MONDAY 13TH SEPTEMBER 2004
LISTENING TO BREAKTHRU BY QUEEN

'Hi, I'm Claire Le Day. I'm a second-year medical student at Peninsula Medical School.'

And I'm back, baby. Bruce, Mark, Ellie, Lou and I have moved into Amity Place, which is just perfect. The place of friendship and amitié. I'm so happy to have friends like them. Mark and I have made a list of our goals for the year.

- Nail second year - no more faffing.
- Get fit, loving, funny, intelligent bf /gf
- Play Hockey (Mark) / Go to gym (Claire) every week.

~~~

Ha! And how did that go?
Spoiler alert - I did not go to the gym once in my second year.

~~~

- Eat Healthily
- Get Bruce over G and Mark over B (aka 'bitch shit fucker' said Mark)
- Give it up the bottom (Mark)

~~~

What? That got weird quick…

AMITY PLACE

TUESDAY 14TH SEPTEMBER 2004 00.30AM
LISTENING TO SLOW HANDS BY INTERPOL

DIET TIME YOU MEGA FATSO. Finn called to say he was going to visit next weekend. That gives me time… no booze, no food. Bruce and Mark are making me feel a bit left out, but hey, what am I going to do? It's cos of my lack of penis. Again.

I had a really drunken night last night with Pete Bond and Robin Mills. I fecking love those guys. We're already talking about living together next year when we go to Exeter for our third year. I think Pete and I would make a good couple. On paper. Like with Herbert. But then I fancy everyone. Or I at least have a seemingly endless capacity to find a fanciable quality in everyone. I just feel eternally lonely. I wish I wasn't so pathetic and desperate. It's a good thing no one can see the real me. I'm so wet and dislikeable.

~~~

WEDNESDAY 15TH SEPTEMBER 2004 1AM
LISTENING TO TURN THE PAGE BY THE STREETS

I'm devastated. Bruce has just upset me more than I ever thought he could. We were making lunch, and he made some sick joke about 'spreading', and I said he was a 'perv', then he said that if he didn't live with me, he'd either fancy me or hate me. I thought of him as one of my really good friends; definitely not on my 'fuck or hate list' (if I had one) (which I don't). I don't even think I can think of anyone that would deserve a spot on it. It's such a boy thing to have. Oh, no wait. The 2002 version of William was, without a doubt, a 'fuck or hate' situation… fuck AND hate?… back and forth… back and forth. Those were the days. NAWT.

I'll never forget hearing Gretchen and Maggie call me 'a short-term friend'. Everyone sees 'it' in the end. Mark thinks the only reason I'm upset is because I'm secretly in love with Bruce -

which is bollocks! I'd be just as upset if Mark said it. It just makes me feel like Bruce and I's entire friendship is fake and superficial and only cos we live together! FUCK HIM! I feel crushed. It was only two days ago that I said how grateful I was to have friends like him. Well, I take it back.

Right, I need to get some sleep. I'm working a twelve-hour shift at the hospital tomorrow, and I'm already going to have post-crying, puffy eyes. I'll probably not even be able to sleep for ruminating over this. I hope Bruce wakes up miraculously enlightened and overwhelmed with guilt. EVEN if it was true, what on earth does he gain from saying it!? FUCK HIM!

~~~

FRIDAY 17TH SEPTEMBER 2004 3.30AM
LISTENING TO STUPIDISCO BY JUNIOR JACK

The man of my dreams has just walked right out of my life. I met him in the *Union* tonight and I cannot describe how charming he was. I was instantly a giggling mess around him. I couldn't try to write some of the dialogue as I would never do the charisma justice. Irresistible Ian. And his smile… oh man. I genuinely thought there was a cartoon sparkle 'ding' when he grinned at me. We played pool all night and I feel like we chatted about our whole lives. He came back here, and he gave me a massage, and we pulled. If there was ever a point in your life when you had to gamble your heart and make a decision to spend the rest of your life with one person after one night, I'd have done it tonight.

Just as I was picturing our wedding day and future house and future children and…

'Sorry, Claire, I had better get going. Fancy one last fag outside with me before I go?'

'Sure.'

(Then outside...)

'I've had a great night with you tonight, but I think I need to be honest about something. I wish the timing was a bit better for us but my girlfriend of six months and I just broke up yesterday. I just don't really feel ready to take on anything too serious at the moment, and I wouldn't want to give you the wrong impression.'

But what about little Sebastian and baby Isla?! I've just ordered a new kitchen with a dark blue splashback like we talked about!

'That's cool. No pressure from me. I had a fun night too. If, say, in two months, however, you feel differently, you can always give me a call. Not that I'll be waiting by the phone!'

(I, 100%, will be.)

'I will. Can we be friends in the meantime?'

'Sure. Although I must warn you, I've got a lot of those already - you'll have to be very good.'

'Ha ha. I won't let you down.'

And we hugged goodbye, and I watched him disappear off into the mist (there wasn't any mist, but that was the vibe).

Goodbye, my love.

~~~

TUESDAY 21ST SEPTEMBER 2004 1PM
LISTENING TO MOVE YOUR FEET BY JUNIOR SENIOR

Last night was HILARIOUS. I Spent most of the afternoon in *Roundabout* with the medics. Got my SSU essay back and I NAILED it. Is this what my medical degree is going to be? A series of flukes until I finish, and I'm made to continue in the same vein but fake being a doctor instead of a student? Probably.

We all headed to *Destinys* for the foam party and I felt so swept up in love for Pete and Robin and the medic girls. We just bounced and slid around, pissed and soaking wet with the foam. Pete and I got ourselves all tangled up on the floor. He'd slipped and taken me down with him, and we then couldn't get back up again. I thought I was going to wet myself laughing. Beth and Mad Dog got themselves into a similar pickle. I think I've found my people, and I feel such a rush when I think of them. I refuse to let them be short-term friends. I want them in my life forever. Maybe the trick will be letting some of the ugly out for them to see. I surely can't expect people to be friends with a pretend version of me just cos I can be fun on a night out. That's not all I have. I have more depth, I'm sure of it.

I saw Sexy JP, the South African towards the end of the night. I was stood outside waiting for the others. We were both shivering and sopping wet.

'Hey, babe. Can I give you a little cuddle? For warmth of course. Survival purposes only.'

'Ha. JP, you sex pest. But yes, please.'

And what a cuddle. I'm so weak. We all headed to the *Union* and stayed until closing. The two of us spent the rest of the night together. He got up on stage and played some Ben Harper. Just when you think someone couldn't be more fanciable... Just before he got off the stage, he spoke into the mic and looked me right in the eye.

'Don't drink and drive or play music live.'

~~~

Bleurgh. What was wrong with me? This guy sounds awful!

~~~

This guy's amazing. He came back to mine, and we kissed and then fell asleep. HE'S SO BANGING HOT! The problem is he was so drunk. It's like bloody Groundhog Day again. Does he like me? Am I just a drunken bootie call? Oh god, I am...

I woke up to him kissing me on the cheek.

'See ya, beautiful. Cheers for a great night. I'll text you.'

Get a grip, Claire - people don't change. What do I think he's going to do now? Suddenly become the best boyfriend ever? Bollocks will he.

~~~

FRIDAY 24TH SEPTEMBER 2004 5AM
LISTENING BETWEEN LOVE & HATE BY THE STROKES

```
Text to JP: Great to see you the other
night. Are you about this wknd? X

Text from JP: Hey babe. Yeah, thanks
for the other night. It's always a
winner with you. But I don't think
we should take this further. I think
we're better as mates. I just get
drunk and get seduced by your womanly
ways. x

Text to JP: I seduced you?! Pull the
other one… But that's cool with me.
Catch ya laterz x
```

Pete Bond and I went out, just the two of us tonight. He's bloody brilliant, although he spends a lot of time pulling me up on things. I guess that's the sign of a good friendship. I think of all the people that can tell me that I'm being a twat, and it's all the good ones: Next Door Andy, Big Sam, Marc, François… Pete Bond. I wonder if he fancies me, but it's hard to tell as we're such good friends. I hope he doesn't.

Loving Ellie and Mark, too, at the moment. Our friendship feels quieter, stiller and yet no less powerful. It doesn't burn fast and bright but hopefully will stay lit longer.

Bruce can fuck off, though. I'm still upset with him. And Lou and Rich, they're still sickening. They see no one anymore. He's basically living with us at Amity Place, but there's no discernable amitié at all. They're just strangers through a wall now, and I have fulfilled my role as a short-term friend.

~~~

SUNDAY 26TH SEPTEMBER 2004 2AM
LISTENING TO TOO MUCH BRANDY BY THE STREETS

Last night was a little strange. My mum called and had a massive go at me for stealing or losing Chloe's boots. WHAT? Of course, I haven't. We're not even the same shoe size. Anyway, I was really upset and went out with Bruce and Mark to the *Union*. I'd been crying and looked like a baboon's swollen arse, so OBVIOUSLY, JP, Artie and Irresistible Ian were all there.

JP was looking fiiiiiine with a t-shirt that looked like it had been painted on. He came over straight away and said he'd been looking for me. He was clearly shit-faced.

'Are you ok? You look upset.'

'I'm fine, thanks, JP. Just been a weird night. You know… parents…'

'Still hot, though, babe. Even with those sexy puffy eyes of yours.'

'Errr… thanks.'

'I've missed you… wondered if you fancied a little late film sesh later?'

'I'm not doing this again. You'll only text me tomorrow to say, "Nah, you're all right, babe." Sorry JP.'

~~~

Is this the most self-respect I've demonstrated in my life? You bet it is.

~~~

I went and sat down with the boys after we got a drink, and Artie came over. I wish he hadn't seen me like this.

'Hi, greeb, you lil' legend. Long time no see. Any chance I could pinch a rollie?'

'Sure. How have you been? Did you have a good summer?'

We then spent the rest of the night talking. Why can't we just be together!? I love him. I'll probably always love him. We went back to his and shared a spliff with Mike. I've missed them, but it doesn't seem like anything will ever change with them. Artie and I fell asleep watching Life of Brian, and I woke up about 6.30am feeling tortured with self-loathing. I walked home and once again asked myself what I was doing with my life.

TWENTY-ONE

MILES

1ST OCTOBER 2004 3.50AM
LISTENING TO DATE RAPE BY SUBLIME

Miles is here and says he says he is DISGUSTED to see that he has not featured in my diary and INSISTS that I write something.

Miles is a proper-job, amazing friend, and I have no excuse (and no idea) why I haven't mentioned him before. I feckin' love this LEGEND of a man.

~~~

Miles had just started at the med school having previously done a degree in Bristol. All the freshers are assigned a 'buddy' on arrival, and Miles was paired up with yours truly. He displayed a plucky, preppy vibe which bordered on pomposity. He looked like every lead jock in 90s high school movies with his lean muscular build, blonde, short back and sides, and a rigid dress code of double collar rugby jerseys and stone-washed jeans.

Miles and I had a dazzling friendship where we spent all our days and nights together very quickly. But like all these flashes-in-the-pan friendships, I extinguished it pretty quickly with my childish self-centeredness that dominated everything at this age.

~~~

MILES

MONDAY 4TH OCTOBER 2004
LISTENING TO CREEPIN' IN BY NORA JONES AND DOLLY PARTON

Freshers week has been LIT! Miles is my new best friend. He's so funny and we get on so well. He stays at mine nearly every night, and we just talk until we fall asleep. His halls are rank and I think I just enjoy the company and comfort of having him around. It's completely platonic. He has a gf that he's been with for three years (since freshers week when they did their first degree). It's a shame that she's about three hours away and working, but he adores her, so I've never even entertained the thought of anything happening between us.

Bruce and Mark got back with their exes again last week (honestly!). Mark found out he'd been cheated on again, which is astonishing as they'd only been back together 48 hours, and he'd spent every night with her. I tried to quiz him on this, but he was too upset. Did she sneak out in the dead of night and have a quick street shag? Like a cat? Was it with a coursemate, and the geography chat was too much of a turn-on that they had to slip out between lectures and fuck in the toilets? I just don't understand how she squeezed it in... ha. That's what she said.

Bruce is no better. Him and G got back together after a long drunken phone call. She came round the next night, and we were all making dinner in the kitchen. Bruce was sitting at the table with me, and I was finishing up an essay (I find it easier doing these things when there's a bit of background noise/healthy level of distraction available.) ANYWAY... he was banging on about whatsherface off of Blue Crush. G stiffened and turned to him with a kitchen knife pointing at him.

'What you saying, babes?'

Now, THIS is why I don't work in my room. I turned to look at Bruce, and he was either clueless or enjoyed the challenge of her tone. I've never heard him articulate himself so clearly.

'I am saying that she is my IDEAL girl.'

(Yup. Definitely on purpose.)

'I can't believe you! So you would rather be with her than me? Do you actually fancy her even though you're supposed to be my boyfriend?'

Have you met Bruce? The surfing-obsessed beach bum? OF COURSE HE FANCIES... ahhh what IS her name? Kate something... who spends the whole film looking hot and surfer-y whilst surfing mega tubes... or whatever.

~~~

Bosworth. Kate Bosworth.

~~~

'Come on, G! This is nuts... you're not actually asking, are you?!'

She then started hurling stuff at him. Bits of bread. A tomato. A block of cheese... and then a plate before storming out. I was trying hard not to laugh, but then Bruce turned to me with a knowing look.

'See? All mind-fucks.'

Oh, fuck off, Bruce! We then went to the *Union* with Mark and Rich, etc, and I am not joking, Bruce was pulling some new bird within an hour of G storming out of ours. Ellie and Colin are going strong. Lou and Rich had their 6 monthiversary yesterday, and I am sick of being alone. It's so boring now. I then went to *Bar 38* to join the medics for the 3-legged Fresher's bar crawl. I was tied to Miles, and we got so pissed (and he dropped a Sambuca shot in my hair). We walked (fell) to *C103*, and I saw JP pull at least three separate girls. So gross. THEN I saw Lovely Northern Joe with his girlfriend. WHAT'S GOING ON? What are you trying to tell me, Universe!?

~~~

SATURDAY 9TH OCTOBER 2004 3PM
LISTENING TO LAST NIGHT BY THE STROKES

I have had a fucking mental week! Slacking a bit on the writing… I still managed to do all my work this week, although I definitely feel like both ends of my candle have been obliterated.

Tuesday: Got battered with Miles - *Roundabout*, *Varsity*, then *Walkabout*. He stayed over, and he told me his girlfriend fucking hates me cos she's never met me, and I'm apparently his first 'girl' friend.

I get that.

Hopefully, I can meet her when she visits next, and she'll see that I'm not a threat. Miles is a bit worried as she's said things about wanting to end it.

Wednesday: Ellie's boyf, Colin, had asked us if we'd do a bit of flyering for a Tim Westwood night coming up (for £20). Miles was helping me outside *Walkabout* when all of a sudden, I had a whole basin of ice water tipped onto me from a window above. I'd barely even caught my breath when I started getting pelted with eggs. There were at least fifty eggs raining on me from above. My ears were ringing, and I felt like I couldn't breathe. I could hear the shrieks of laughter above me. I felt so shocked and then felt the tears hit me. Miles walked back with me, but it took at least half an hour, and I was SO COLD. Colin says they'll be able to figure out who it was, and he'll 'fuck them up'.

Thursday: Huge one with Pete Bond, 3-legged Frank, Miles, Kate and Mad Dog. Pool in the *Union* (Pete is an excellent hustle buddy), *Cuba*, then *Deep*. We finished up in *Goodbodies* for breakfast about 4am.

Friday: Monster night again in *Union*. Then Pete, Robin Mills, Frank, Miles and I ended up at this party, but it was pure druggie and felt weird. I was looking for a toilet upstairs when this guy pressed himself against me and pushed me against the wall. He squeezed my breast really hard and went to pull me. I instantly freaked out and thought of Ewen Le Pervert, so I kneed him straight in the balls and ran away. My heart's still racing when I think about it. Is it just a matter of time until someone actually rapes me?! I don't think this dickhead would have tonight, but you never know… it's like dogs that 'get over-excited' and kill children. Ouff. It makes me feel a bit panicky when I think about it. I should probably be a bit more careful.

We left and went for another *Goodbodies* breakfast, which was fun, and actually, I'd kinda forgotten about boob-grope gate until just now.

TWENTY-TWO
THREE-LEGGED FRANK

SUNDAY 10TH OCTOBER 2004 6.15PM
LISTENING TO DREAMING OF YOU BY THE CORAL

Massive party at The Medic House last night. A bit of me wishes I was living with them: Mad Dog, Beth, Three-legged Frank, Pete Bond, Robin Mills, Connie and Suzie. JEALOUS! Frank and I got so stoned - I really fancy him. I was sick after Pete made me down a glass of warm white wine. I say 'made me'… he didn't 'make' me; we were playing a game I'd made up, and I fully scuppered myself with my own rules. Anyway, loads of fucked up shit happened, and I ended up sleeping in Frank's bed - lovely, sexy Frank. Nothing happened, though, as I ended up having a nightmare about Ewen Le Pervert, and Frank woke me up when I was supposedly tossing and turning and making funny noises. How embarrassing! I had a little silent cry afterwards - I couldn't tell if it was because I was mortified or if it was because I felt genuinely upset about the dream. Frank must think I'm mental now.

   I spent the whole day recovering at theirs, which was simply perfect. We all just ate crap and watched TV.

~~~

TUESDAY 19TH OCTOBER 2004 7.30PM
LISTENING TO LOVE IS ONLY A FEELING BY THE DARKNESS

I've spent the last week massively fancying Frank, and I decided to do something about it!

I set a date in my mind for Friday (medic booze cruise) and sat him down in the *Union* before we went.

'So. Basically Frank. You probably already know, but I want to say it...' (Man, I was squirmy.) '... I just want you to know that I like you.'

'Oh, Claire. Mate. I really like you too. Most guys would love to hear that, but the timing isn't great. My dad's really ill, and I don't want to get into any relationship at the moment. I just can't deal with anything else right now. Sorry mate. I love ya, really - I reckon we could be great friends, and like I said, a lot of guys would be so lucky to get a girl like you. You've not really got any annoying traits...'

He sure said 'mate' a lot...

'Thanks, Frank. Oh, course we can stay friends.' I winked and punched his arm. 'I was just trying my luck.'

He laughed, gave me a one-armed hug, and kissed my cheek. Harrumph. I think deep down, I know that he was just saying that stuff as an excuse which sucks balls.

I'm seriously piss-faced with Rich at the moment. Chloe's visiting and came on the medic booze cruise on Friday night. We had a great time, and after the cruise, we made our way back to the party at Rich and Tommo's house. The party was quietening down when we arrived, and Lou and Rich had just gone up to bed. So I went upstairs and knocked on his door.

'Hello, love birds! It's meeeee... sorry we're late. Can I tempt anyone with a lil' nightcap?'

Rich opened the door and screamed, 'WILL YOU JUST FUCK

OFF, CLAIRE! YOU'RE SO ANNOYING!' before slamming the door in my face. If there was ever any doubt left in my mind that he didn't like me… I keep seeing his face tonight. He HATED me. I feel crushed. I can hardly believe he was the person I spent all my time with last year. We were so close.

Short-term friend.

The more it keeps happening, the more I think Gretchen has a point. I have a *max* two year expiry date with friendships.

Anyway, Frank said he was coming round to watch a film tonight, and he's still not here. Please come. Please come. Please come.

~~~

WEDNESDAY 20TH OCTOBER 1.45AM
LISTENING TO CLUB FOOT BY KASABIAN

And he came. And just left. We watched One Flew Over The Cuckoo's Nest and just chilled out. I really do like him, but I think I'm going to have to be patient. Connie said she was sure he probably did fancy me. Surely, the fact that he came round is a good sign… right?

Pfff, I've not had sex for five months. That feels long. I know it's not, but it feels like everyone around me is getting some. Miles spent the whole of Monday complaining about how sore he was because of the amount of sex he'd had with his girlfriend over the weekend. Whereas I feel like I've simply embarked on my barren life journey that culminates in liver failure and dying alone in my 50s. I'll be repeating my third and fourth year at med school for the thirtieth time and living with freshers a third of my age cos I'll have exhausted all my two-year/short-term friendships. They'll find me dead and bloated, having drunkenly pulled a bookcase on top of myself. I can see the detective now, picking up some of the books off my fat body.

'Hey, guys. This Jane Doe has every copy of the Oxford Handbook of Clinical Medicine from 2003 to 2045. And there's an empty bottle of Sambuca. How suspicious... no one's drunk Sambuca since 2004.'

~~~

FRIDAY 22ND OCTOBER 2004 2AM
LISTENING TO NEXT EXIT BY INTERPOL

Last night was, without a doubt, one of the greatest EVER! It was the MedSoc "P" party. I went as a plant, and Ellie and I spent hours soaping my hair into punk-like spikes before spraying it green. I had green body paint and some brown fabric from a charity shop, which I safety pinned around me as a strapless mini dress. I won 'best costume' which came with a bottle of apple sourz (fun AND apt). We drank it in *Roundabout,* and then all headed off to *C103s*. Pete had made a sandwich board pool table, Miles, Frank and Robin were pilots (basically any excuse to be Maverick), Mad Dog looked insane as Princess Leia, and Kate came as a PE teacher. None of the effort mattered, though, as we were all covered in camo paint by the end of the night. It was soo messy, and Frank looked beautiful in his military get-up. I took 112 photos and spent most of the night dancing with Pete, Mad Dog, Kate, Frank and Miles.

I had the funniest walk back with Miles and Frank back to The Medic House. Miles was lying on the pavement, and Frank kept hurling himself into hedges and bushes to see if he was camouflaged.

'Hey, guys! GUYYSSSSSSS. Can you see me?!'

I was wetting myself laughing when the two of them started 'bollard surfing'. This lasted about five seconds, with Frank half-successfully balancing until Miles basically flung himself, head first, over the top of a bollard onto the pavement, splitting his forehead open. We eventually got back, and Frank and I patched Miles up the best we could before all sharing a spliff. I slept in Frank's bed again but still nothing. He's giving me such mixed signals! One second, we're inseparable, and next, he's cold as ice! I wish timing hadn't been the reason he'd given. It suggests that things will change with time and that it's not me. It feels so naive writing that down. Damn, I like him!

~~~

TUESDAY 26TH OCTOBER 2004 10PM
LISTENING TO ONCE IN A LIFETIME BY TALKING HEADS

It was Tim Westwood's gig at *Destiny's* last night and Ellie and Colin had VIP passes. I was allowed to invite someone else, so obvs, brought my main man, Miles. The friendship feels like what I have with Marc; raw, honest and invigorating. I can let it all hang out without any fear that Miles would judge me.

~~~

Let's give it a month and see how that went, huh?

~~~

Maggie's coming tomorrow - YAY! I just need to get all my work done and then the party gloves are off.

~~~

Are you sure you're still wearing your party gloves?

~~~

SUNDAY 31ST OCTOBER 2004 1AM
LISTENING TO PURE BY THE LIGHTNING SEEDS

Maggie and I have had an epic time together. I wish we'd had longer being this close when we were at school - life would have been so much easier. Summary of Maggie's stay:

Wednesday: 27th Oct - *C103s* with Kate and Miles. Maggie pulled Lovely Northern Joe's house mate - bleurgh! Mags then stayed at mine, and I stayed at Miles'. I had another fucking rapey nightmare!!! This is becoming a thing, and I don't know how to stop it. I spoke to Miles about it, and we had a friendly little cuddle. It was more out of comfort than anything else, but I feel the teensiest bit awkward about it now. What would his gf think? There was definitely no funny business, but it doesn't look good, does it? I guess she just doesn't need to know. But then it feels like a secret... Gah! I'm bricking it about meeting her.

Thursday: 28th Oct - It was £1 Vodka Red Bull night in *Roundabout*, and Maggie and I drank way too much Red Bull. I was lying awake with palpitations for hours, listening to the raindrops stampeding against the window. When I eventually fell asleep, I had these horrendous nightmares (plural!) about this virus that spread around the world and killed millions of people by basically turning their lungs to mush. It was terrifying.

~~~

Errrr... What?

~~~

Then I dreamt about being in a long-term and very sexual relationship with Connie before contracting Ebola and dying in her arms. So fucked up.

I still felt weird and twitchy when I woke up in the morning. I almost felt too scared to go downstairs. Every sound was exaggerated, and I was freaked out that something bad was going to happen.

Friday: 29th Oct - So tired. Maggie and I played some pool with Kate, Miles and Pete in the *Union*. But I couldn't do it anymore. Every cell in my body started screaming when I took a sip of a pint.

'DON'T DO IT! WHY WON'T YOU LEAVE US ALONE!? WHYYYYYYYYYY!?'

Maggie and Kate got back on it, but I tapped out, went home early, and left a key for Mags. She ended up going back to Lovely Northern Joe's at the end of the night and had sex with his house mate.

'Jeez Maggie… you didn't! I don't get it.'
'You don't have to get it. I got it…'
What a filthy little grin she has…
'Ha ha! How was it?'
'Not great. It hurt a bit cos he's got a short and very fat willy.'
'Paaaa haaaaaa haaaaa!'
'AND THEN he just stuck a finger up my arse!'
'WHAT?!'
'So I bolted out of there. Obviously.'
I nodded knowingly.
'Obviously.'

~~~

I don't know where to start with this. What would Gen Z say? They wouldn't like it. ONE BIT. We could have done with being a little bit less millennial in these situations.

~~~

Saturday: 30th Oct - Maggie and I spent the day chatting and walking around Plymouth before her train back to Brighton. I fricking LOVE her.

I was gutted to see Maggie go. I'd love to live with her one day. We talked about moving to London after Uni and getting a flat together. Oh, what debauchery that would entail! The stories we'd tell…!

~~~

I can still imagine this mythical future, but it is far and away from what actually happened. I write this at 1am in August 2024, and if this ever sees the light of day: Maggie, I'm sorry, and I miss you x

~~~

MONDAY 1ST NOVEMBER 2004 00.30AM
LISTENING TO WE BUILT THIS CITY BY STARSHIP

I spent most of today at the medic's house, and Frank and I watched about five *Studio Ghibli* films. We then had THE most pretentious argument about which was better; Princess Mononoke or Spirited Away. Frank said I was plebeian for thinking that Spirited Away was more moving, and I told him he was just trying to be obscure and interesting by not choosing Spirited Away. Plebeian… whatever next?

I stayed in Pete Bond's bed, and we chatted all night. We learnt the harmony for 'We Built This City' after discovering it was number 1 the week I was born. WHAT A TUNNNNNEEEEEE!

There was just one slightly weird thing the other night - I found myself feeling jealous when Pete was flirting with Mary Davies. Quieten down now, psycho Claire! What's wrong with me? I don't fancy him. I just want him to be mine forever! I wonder if everyone else is secretly mental, too? Thank god no one knows how much of a sociopath I really am on the inside. Reading my diary makes it hard to believe that I am able to function or, indeed, behave quite normally around other people.

~~~

I still find it totally astonishing that I turned into a 'normal' person who is (however implausibly) capable of considering other people's feelings. Once again, my memories have been altered, erased and gilded with time. Stupid and drunk? Sure, I remember that. But the extraordinary level of self-involvement that I displayed is pretty disappointing.

By working through my University diaries, I am systematically spoiling all the fond memories I have of being a student. I thought this was a time when I forged my real friendships, learnt grace and empathy, and, somewhere along the road, learned to be a doctor. Naturally, over time, my memories have become more charmed and poignant as all the selfish thoughts and actions I had, simply wafted away. But I just HAD to write them down. Look, Claire! Look at what a twat you were!

~~~

Right early start tomorrow for the beginning of SSUs - fuuuuuccccccck.

~~~

WEDNESDAY 3RD NOVEMBER 2004 00.15AM
LISTENING TO WHAT AM I TO YOU BY NORA JONES

I am TOTALLY FUCKED. Miles and I have just had a massive spliff, and I'm at the stage where I'm having to stop and re-read what I've written every three words to know what the devil I'm trying to say.

Haha, Miles is wankered. He's been sitting on my floor for what feels like hours, doodling. God, I'm stoned. On a Tuesday! What is it about Tuesdays? They're often the biggest night of the week for me. We've been listening to Kermit and Bigbird stoned. It's so good.

'Today's letter is… joint.'

'Errr, Big Bird. Joint is not a letter.'

'Today's letter is………………….. 3.'

'Ummm. Big Bird three is a number… like the number of joints I've smoked today.'

'Abcde…f…r…g…q…r…k…ft… I forgot what we were doing, Kramit.'

'Did you just call me Kramit? Hee hee, Kramit dee frog.'

OMG. I'm just sat here transcribing the audio. I am messed up.

'Hey Miles.'

'Ummm.'

'What you doing?'

'I dunno, man…'

Haha.

~~~

FRIDAY 5TH NOVEMBER 2004 3.30AM
LISTENING TO MOLLY'S CHAMBERS BY KINGS OF LEON

Went to Bar Footsie tonight with Lou, Ellie, Bruce, Rich, Trigger, Tommo and Mark. Rich and Lou seem to be normal with me again. Then I went to Miles', and we watched Momento and Touching the Void. He made some 'touching the void' poo-related joke, and we found it too funny. I'm turning into a four-year-old. Dragged myself home to sleep in my own bed tonight.

~~~

SATURDAY 6TH NOVEMBER 2004 2.45AM
LISTENING TO DROP THE PRESSURE BY MYLO

Miles got dumped by his girlfriend, so I was in get Miles drunk mode. We went to *The Fresher* with Rich and Tommo before Miles, and I peeled off for a quick Terminator at *The Scholar*. Then off to the *Union* for pints and pool. I felt my stomach drop when Pete, Robin and Frank arrived. 'No more fannying about' I thought. So I made a right tit of myself instead and took Frank aside for a chat. AGAIN.

'Franko… remember what I told you a couple of weeks ago?'
'Yeah…'
'Cos I was just wondering… you said not now cos of your dad (which is understandable, of course) but I just wanted to check… for my peace of mind… Is that a no for now, because of circumstances, but maybe one day? Or a definite no?'
'A definite no.'
Ah.

Well, that's a kick in the nuts. Why didn't he fucking say that in the first place! Miles and I went back to mine, smoked a spliff, and he then stayed over and had a little cry about his girlfriend. EX girlfriend! Although, I reckon they'll get back together.

~~~

(They got married and had three children.)

~~~

He's fallen asleep now, and I'm just sitting here feeling a bit bleak about everything. I wish I hadn't wasted so much thinking space on Frank. I feel devastated. What's wrong with me? Can he see the inner psychopath? Does he just find me unattractive? All of the above?

~~~

SUNDAY 7TH NOVEMBER 2004 2AM
LISTENING TO L.S.F. BY KASABIAN

I spent the day doing some work then went to 'The Medic House' to watch Scotland v Australia - we lost (obviously). Then went out to *The Crystal Dragon* for Robin's birthday meal, then *Cuba* - again. I am wrecked. AGAIN! I went back to mine with Miles and Frank, and we had a spliff, and all decided to stop. I've been banging on about it for ages, but the consensus was weed, and medical degrees shouldn't really mix. So that's that.

~~~

And that actually was that.

~~~

This week has been such a write-off. I STILL haven't written my SSU, and the presentation is on Thursday. Get your shit together, Claire.

To Do:
Forget about Frank
Smash SSU this week
Go to bank and change address
Call Scottish loans to sort out money they owe me
NO MORE SPLIFF

~~~

WEDNESDAY 10TH NOVEMBER 2004 3PM
LISTENING TO HUMBLE ME BY NORAH JONES

Bruce and I have pretty much made up. He's still struggling with the on/off-ness with G, though, and I don't really talk to him about it too much cos it invariably turns into a 'All women are fucked up' chat which sends me off on one. He's just been lounging about on my bed while I've been doing some work.

'Do you think I should give G another chance? She won't stop texting me and I DO love her.'

'Your call, buddy but if you're genuinely asking for my opinion, then no, I don't think you should. Although that's never stopped me in the past, so I can't talk.'

'Yeah. I just miss her. But she is MESSED-UP, man. She has more issues than a Rolling Stones magazine.'

'You did not just make that up!'

'Yeah, I did…'

'Bollocks Bruce! But I like it.'

TWENTY-THREE
PETE BOND

FRIDAY 12TH NOVEMBER 2004 3.30AM
LISTENING TO ONE LOVE BY BOB MARLEY & THE WAILERS

Miles and I are watching *Halloween* for the third time now - we are determined to watch it all the way through without falling asleep. I'm obviously not even watching as I'm writing. Pahaha! Not sure you can call this 'writing'!

Frank hosted a poker night tonight and the amount I had to fight to get an invite (because I am a girl) was RIDICULOUS. They made an 'exception' and 'allowed' me to play. Thanks to their gross underestimation of a woman's ability to play card games to a satisfactory level (and manipulate men into thinking they're airheads who don't know what they're doing), I won. In your face, you sexist fuckers. I think Frank was finding it a bit frustrating. Miles was too shit-faced to notice, Robin didn't have a clue what was going on, but Pete seemed to be rooting for me, which I loved. I kinda wish I fancied him. I mean, I do a bit, but not enough. We're each other's dates for the Christmas ball, which is cute.

~~~

SUNDAY 14TH NOVEMBER 2004 11.45PM
LISTENING TO SWING LIFE AWAY BY RISE AGAINST

It was the Medic's Varsity football game in Cardiff today, and it was AMAZING. I volunteered to be the mascot for the day (largely because it was freezing, and it meant I got to wear a very warm and fluffy bear suit). A lot of our year group from Exeter came too which was cool as we don't get to see them that much. I drank beer all day and shouted insults 'à la BASEketball'* at the other players… I was living the dream. I did not shower myself in glory, but it was so much fun!

~~~

*A niche reference to the 1998 goofy comedy about two bums who invent a game that blends these two American sports, which then, in turn, becomes a sensation. In BASEketball, trash-talking your opponents to distract and throw them off their game becomes an integral part of the sport. I loved BASEketball and watched it more times than I'd like to admit.

This was also the day (unbeknownst to me) that my husband, the love of my life and father of my children, first laid eyes on me. I shudder when I think of how I must have looked. A loud Scottish hooligan… in a bear costume and a Panama hat. It was a few years into our relationship when we realised we had both been at the Varsity game in Cardiff and might even have met! I watched his eyes flicker with recognition when I told him I'd been the mascot.

'Oh, that was you! I remember the bear…'
'What do you remember? Was it love at first sight?'
'Ermmm, not quite.'

~~~

We went out in Cardiff afterwards before getting on the coach back to Plymouth. I was absolutely squirming with jealousy, watching Pete and Mary Davies. All I've wanted to do for the last week is cuddle him. It's like I've forced myself to fancy him, and now I can't backtrack. Lindsay and Annika really fancy him too, but Mary... she's different... he definitely likes her. Anyway, this night in Cardiff got messy. Annika was all over Pete, and when he finally got rid of her, she pulled Robin. Mid-snog, she then burst into tears and ran away, saying she was in love with Pete (poor Robin). THEN Mary pulled Mikey, which I was horrified to discover made Pete mega jealous. I went back to theirs, and Pete spent hours banging on about how much he liked Mary and what should he do etc? I stayed in his bed but it's very much like a close friend and nothing more.

~~~

TUESDAY 16TH NOVEMBER 2004 3AM
LISTENING TO THE WINE SONG BY THE CAT EMPIRE

Bruce and I have just been out dancing, and it was excellent. Man, it is late, though, and I've got lectures, PBL and life sciences tomorrow. I'd planned to prep it all this evening but it didn't take much to blow that plan up. Bruce knocked on my door at about 6ish.

'Hey, mate. Do you wanna go for a drink? Just the two of us?'

I snapped my book shut and had my coat and shoes on before I could say 'Yup'. Anyway, we got pretty wrecked and danced like lunatics in *Wonky Legs*. We just got back and cooked Ellie's bacon - she's going to go apeshit. I am so TIRED. GO THE FUCK TO SLEEP THEN AND STOP WRITING SHITE.

~~~

PETE BOND

THURSDAY 18TH NOVEMBER 2004 2AM
LISTENING TO GOLDEN TOUCH BY RAZORLIGHT

I'm feeling pretty exhausted. I've pushed it too far, and I'm a wreck. One second, I'm high as a kite, the next, I'm on the brink of tears and one step away from rocking on the floor and scratching at my eyes. I need to go out. I can't bear just being stuck with me.

~~~

This inability to be content with my own company has continued to haunt me (albeit to a lesser extent as I get older). Having children, for one, has taught me to appreciate the quiet, peaceful moments associated with solitude, yet I am still plagued with unease and restlessness when alone for too long. The optimistic part of me chalks it up to me simply being an extrovert, a people person who thrives on connection. But a darker, more uncertain part makes me question: why do I find it so hard to trust my own thoughts and embrace my own company?

~~~

I'm confused about Pete, and I'm sick of being single. We get on so well, but do I really fancy him? We've talked about being together (only cos we spend so much together), but he laughs so hard at the idea (it's actually a little insulting). Is it really sooooooo hilarious that I might be a potential… ermmm… potential… something? Pete just talks about all the fit girls in the year below… ohh Lindsay… blah blah blah… Annika did this… Mary's so hot, do you think she likes me? Pfff. It's never me. What's wrong with me? Although Barry told Pete that Frank DID LIKE ME!

'It's a definite no' felt pretty conclusive, however. Do I trust MY OWN EARS or third-party gossip from Barry? Fucking hell, boys are so complicated. They've had us all believing that we're the head fucks when it's been them all along!

~~~

FRIDAY 19TH NOVEMBER 2004 3AM.
LISTENING TO EVIL BY INTERPOL

I tried to make Miles watch Love Actually tonight, but he left after about half a second.

'I thought I knew you, Claire! I can't believe you want to watch this. It's boring as fuck. I'm leaving.'

'Haha, ok, then. See ya.'

So it's still playing, and it's making me think of Pete Bond. Every time he tells me how jealous he is of Mary and Mikey it makes me want to vom. Anyway, Maggie and Herbert are arriving for my birthday tomorrow - YAY.

~~~

SATURDAY 20TH NOVEMBER - MY 19TH BIRTHDAY
LISTENING TO SOMEBODY TOLD ME BY THE KILLERS

```
Dearest Claire-Bear,

All I have to say is that you are a
massive jobby for making me drink one
of your Terminators!

I love you so much - you're the best-
est friend a girl could ever ask for.
I wish you the happiest birthday and I
hope that we spend the next 100 years
together. That is, if I haven't died
from lung cancer. I LOVE YOU. I DO!!!
Words can't express!

With all my heart,

Mags xxxxxxxxxxxxxxxx
```

~~~

Oh, this makes me feel very sad. Having spent so long absorbed in The Diary of a Teenage Dirtbag, I had forgotten about the good years Maggie and I had together as 'best friends' after school. I loved her so much, she was a wonderful friend in the end, and it pains me to think that I lost her.

~~~

SUNDAY 21ST NOVEMBER 2004 11.50PM
LISTENING TO THE LONG WAY HOME BY NORAH JONES

My birthday celebrations were a complete disaster. I had everyone round for drinks, and Kate had made an incredible cake of lips with a fag hanging out of it. Bruce, Ellie, Lou and Mark had spent all afternoon blowing up balloons. The medics (Pete, Robin, Connie, Mad Dog, Suzie, Beth, Frank) came with boxes of wine and gifts, and Maggie and Herbie were here with me, too. It was great, but I noticed that Miles was a total no-show (which is unlike him), and Rich, Trigger, Tommo etc, weren't there either. I couldn't help feeling a bit put out even though I was surrounded by wonderful friends. I wish I hadn't cared and that I'd just enjoyed what I did have rather than getting fixated on what I didn't- glass half full and all that.

```
Text to Miles 8.28pm: Hey, big guy.
Are you coming? IT'S MY BIRTHDAY MAN!
```

AND NOTHING. NO REPLY. NOTHING.

Lou said Rich and co were just going to see us at the *Union*. We live on the way. They could have popped in to say HB. Dickheads. Anyway, we went to the *Union* about 10ish and I saw Miles was there after all! I was annoyed that he hadn't come to my Bday and not texted and HE was the one completely ignoring me. What the fuck!? It's my birthday!

Anyway, I got over it and got drunk and had a fun night. I was walking home with Maggie, Herbie and Bruce when I got a text from Miles.

```
1.18am Text from Miles: You were out
of order tonight Claire.

1.20am To Miles: Excuse me?! YOU were
out of order!

1.21am From Miles: I have a girlfriend.
I don't think we can be friends any-
more.

1.22am To Miles: Fuck You! What the
fuck has that got to do with anything?

1.22am From Miles: What the fuck is
your problem?! Fuck YOU!
```

So I ignored the last text and stomped home. Pete, Robin, Mad Dog and Kate then came back to mine and I was angry-drinking and ranting about Miles when Pete piped up.

'To be fair to Miles, you were out of order.'
'I was not! He didn't come to my birthday.'
What planet was everyone on? Then Mags and Robin chipped in.
'Yeah, babe. I agree. It wasn't a good look for you. I can see why he's having to distance himself from you now.'
'What the fuck is everyone talking about!? HE'S THE ONE THAT DIDN'T COME TO MY BIRTHDAY AND THEN IGNORED ME!'
Pete stayed calm and walked me through what an absolute WANKER I am.

'Did you not see his girlfriend was there tonight? She'd come down at the last minute to surprise him for the weekend. I imagine that's why he didn't come here earlier. But he did technically make the effort to come to your birthday. With his girlfriend, no less! No wonder he kept you at arm's length - you were shit-faced, and she already doesn't like you. You were ranting and raving at the bar about "What cheek to show his face and then ignore me!" And he was on the dance floor having a loving dance with his girlfriend when you said, "fuck him!" And marched onto the dance floor and kicked him in the back of his knee AS HE WAS KISSING HER and stomped off.'

Ohhhh, that's not good.

I stared at everyone in silence, with my mouth agape. This was some kind of sick joke… surely? I hadn't kicked Miles. I hadn't even seen his girlfriend!

Oh God.

If I had kicked him when he was snogging his girlfriend…

Oh god.

'I don't remember doing this at all!'

'Well, you did, mate. We all saw. She was fuming and started shouting at him as you left the car crash behind you.'

And another friend bites the dust.

I've spent all day messaging Miles apologising but he isn't replying. What the fuck was I thinking? FUCK. WHAT A DISASTER! What else do I do that I don't remember? I'm not a blackout/mind-blank kinda person - am I?! I'm sure I usually remember everything. I just can't believe it. Have I lost Miles? HAVE I LOST MY MIND? I can't bear to lose him…

I'm not going to drink for a while. I can't believe I can't remember! Hurting Miles of all people… I feel awful. And Pete. I love him. Fuck. The feeling's not mutual (and why would it be now he has seen what a disgusting excuse for a human being I am?).

I need to get away from Plymouth. Away from Pete... and Frank... and Miles. It's all too much, and it's all my own doing. I just want to hide.

~~~

TUESDAY 23RD NOVEMBER 2004 2AM
LISTENING TO BRICK BY BEN FOLDS FIVE

There's nothing quite like Ben Folds for wallowing in self-pity. I've rogered it with Miles. I have not stopped texting him with all the ways I can think of saying sorry and I'm being met with nothing but radio silence. I think he's gone forever. The regret is crushing me. I can feel it pressing on my chest.

The other issue is Pete - I reallllly like him, and I just don't know what to do about it. I know, of course, that the answer is DO NOTHING, but once a self-sabotaging egotist, always a...

If I have to hear one more word about Mary, there is a 93% chance that I will die. Pfff, I have to be up in six hours and then spend all day with him again. It's torture... I'm so confused! I know he doesn't feel the same way but I can't not be with him! He's one of my best friends.

I want to go home.

~~~

SUNDAY 28TH NOVEMBER 2004 3AM.
LISTENING TO OBVIOUSLY BY MCFLY

It was the Medic Christmas ball on Friday night, and my heart is continuing to pine for Pete. Miles didn't even come to the ball...

I spent the whole night talking to other people about their love lives. Mad Dog about Matt (!), Mikey about Mad Dog, Connie about Chirpy, Barry about Connie, Pete about Mary, Annika about Pete and how 'no one understands what it's like to like someone who doesn't like you back' (sure, sure Annika, just you). And no one about me. I looked up at the end of the night and saw Pete dancing with Mary. He looked over at me and gave me a little wink and thumbs up, to which I returned with the biggest grin I could muster despite tasting sick in my mouth. I went back to the medic's house and stayed in Pete's bed. We sniggered and chatted all night and then had a little cuddle. MY HEART! It felt perfect and no one will ever be able to understand what we have.

Today was a completely different bag of potato chips. Pete was so cold with me. I'm so confused. Does he know I like him, and he's trying to put me off? Does he like me and doesn't know what to do with it? Was he just being drunk and friendly?

THEN Mad Dog, Pete and I were walking to *Roundabout* for the rugby, and he was joking about last night.

'I just wanted to get some sleep, and I nearly fell off the edge of the bed trying to get Claire off me!'

Pshhhhh… And in that moment, the sound of my heart fracturing echoed through Devon.

I laughed it off, but I felt so humiliated. It meant nothing to him. It felt like the worst possible thing he could have said. Mad Dog didn't laugh and looked at me knowingly. She was kind enough to say nothing, but I could tell that she knew exactly what was going on in my head… She's a mind reader…

~~~

She's a Consultant Psychiatrist now.

~~~

WEDNESDAY 1ST DECEMBER 2004
LISTENING TO LEAVE ME ALONE BY RAZORLIGHT

This Pete thing is eating away at me. I don't want to ruin our friendship, especially as we have to spend the next three and a bit years together, but if he does like me (which, if I had to guess, I reckon is 50/50), then he definitely wouldn't do anything. If I went for it, it would be a bit like going all in with a pair of 9s.

~~~

TUESDAY 7TH DECEMBER 2004
LISTENING TO DON'T MUG YOURSELF BY THE STREETS

I saw Miles today, and I cornered him outside his PBL room.

'Please, can we talk, Miles?'

'There's nothing to say, Claire. You've forced me to choose between you and my girlfriend, and that's no choice really.'

'What? No, I didn't!'

'You and Maggie spent your whole birthday night death-staring her and making snide comments. If I'm honest, you seemed jealous, and you really made it look like you fancied me. She's been saying this the whole time, and you kinda proved her right.'

'I do not fancy you! I just miss my friend! It sounds so stupid now but I was just put out that you'd not come to my birthday. There was nothing else to it. I didn't "death-stare" her! I didn't even know she was there!'

'I thought you didn't remember any of it…'

'Well… no… but…'

'Look, Claire. It's over. You showed your true colours, and I'm still picking up the pieces of my relationship. I don't even know if we'll survive, thanks to you. I don't want to be friends with you anymore. Ever again.'

~~~

You can't blame the man. I'm still haunted by how I behaved with Miles and his girlfriend. I bumped into Miles' girlfriend at a rave in a field in Cornwall a few years later, and I felt determined to right my wrong. I knew I couldn't undo what I'd done, but I would do what I could to have Miles' back. I owed him. Frank and Robin were living with Miles and had told me that as far as she was concerned, Miles had had an affair with me, and it was brought up at every opportunity. He wasn't even denying it anymore.

She saw me and, did an immediate 180 and started walking in the opposite direction.

'Wait. Please. Please just hear me out.'

'No offence, Claire, but I really don't want to talk to you.'

'I know. I totally understand, but I need you to know that Miles never cheated on you.'

She eyed me with suspicion, trying to read me.

'I know how it looked, and I can see why you wouldn't believe me, but honestly, I have nothing to gain from telling you this. I was just so drunk and annoyed that he hadn't come to my party. It's pathetic, really, but I wasn't jealous, and it really had nothing to do with you. I'm so so sorry about what I did to your relationship, but honestly, Miles never put a foot out of place.'

'Is this true, Claire?'

She started crying, but she was smiling at me. YES! I thought, I'm the good guy again.

'It's true.'

'But you guys spent so much time together. There must have been something?'

'No, not at all.'

And then the warm glow of righteousness made me take it too far. I thought we might even hug. MAYBE I can be friends with Miles again.

'We were close, but even when we shared a bed, it was 100% back-to-back and platonic.'

I watched her face drop.
Oh Shit.
'You guys shared a bed?'
Fuuuuuuuck.
'Ermm. But he never cheated on you!'
Too late. I watched her eyes fill with tears as she walked away.
I'm sorry, Miles.

~~~

WEDNESDAY 8TH DECEMBER 2004
LISTENING TO GLAMOROUS INDIE ROCK & ROLL BY THE KILLERS

Pete's being weird with me, and I can't quite tell why. He organised a boys' night out tonight, but we ended up bumping into them all in *C103*. King Pete had declared that they weren't even allowed to talk to girls! Robin had to neck a dirty pint for shrugging and saying 'sorry Claire' when I waved and said 'hey' when they arrived.

RIDICULOUS.

I HATE BOYS-ONLY ACTIVITIES SO SO SO SO MUCH! I HATE IT! I HATE IT! I HATE IT.

~~~

I still do. Always have. Always will.

Let me start with Stag Dos. I would fucking relish a Stag Do. I would have been in my element on my friend's stag dos, but I was firmly NFI'd.

'But you wouldn't enjoy it if you REALLY knew what happened on Stag Dos,' say the men who clearly don't know me AT ALL.

This bizarre tweenage 'girls=cooties' boy mentality will be the death of me.

My hen-do was (of course!) BRILLIANT. My sexism rant should not reflect badly on… can't think of a term that doesn't make me squirm. My… girls? Yeurch. Bitches? Better. Squad? Piss off Taylor

Swift. Anyway, 'they' gave me such an epic weekend in Bristol, and I LOVE YOU my... women? No. I'll get there.

BUT. Next Door Andy, Herbert, Pete Bond and Robin were among some of my friends who were not there and joined my husband for Rugby 7's in London. WHAT'S WITH THAT?!?

I have missed a lot of my good friends' send-offs for the simple reason that my genitalia is lacking. And by lacking, I absolutely don't mean 'not good enough', but 'physically less in mass'.

I want to go on a 'proper' stag do. I want a beer-fuelled, titty-showed vomit-fest that leaves me rocking anxiously on a Sunday evening train/plane home as I try to piece together the last 48 hours. Or at least I used to. I admit that with every year that passes, I find the idea of a stag do less and less appealing. Boy, would I be great on one, though...

~~~

I just need to go home. I need to get away from Pete and get some fucking perspective on things.

G got busted tonight. Turns out she's been shagging Tommo as well as Bruce since the summer. Tommo then apparently jumped to her defence cos she's been telling everyone that Bruce has hit her. WHAT? I don't believe it. Bruce can be a right nob, but he'd never be violent. Gah! She's just adding fuel to the 'all girls are mental' fire. She's apparently in hospital tonight after taking 'too many neurofen and Archers'. This feels like fourteen-year-old Gretchen all over again. And G is twenty!

~~~

WEDNESDAY 8TH DECEMBER 1.45AM
LISTENING TO THOSE SWEET WORDS BY NORAH JONES

I have done a list of all the things bursting out of my head. I wish I could turn myself off and plug myself in for a few days.

Work
- So overwhelming
- PPD (Personal Professional Development) portfolio to be handed in straight after Christmas
- SSU and AMK 1st week back after xmas - fuuuuuuucccccckkkk!
- Have to see Pete every day
- Barely hitting average grades in most things - totally unsurprising. Not working enough and too much play.
- Done no self-directed learning in clinical skills this term!
- Can't remember/cement any life sciences in my brain!
- Bottom line - I'm a medical student fraud and I shouldn't be here. It's only a matter of time until I'm found out.

Friends
- LOVE MAGGIE
- Pete - A bit in love with him - totally unreciprocated. Feel like he really doesn't care these days.
- Medics - LOVE them, especially Mad Dog, Robin, Suzie, Beth, Connie, Kate, and Frank.
- Miles - he's gone for good, and my heart aches every time I think about having lost him.
- Flatmates
- Ellie - so in love with Colin, I don't exist in her life anymore. I adore her, though.
- Mark - his gf takes priority over everything.

- Bruce - loveable rogue aka a bit of a dick sometimes.
- Lou - barely see her. NEVER see her without Rich, and I hate him!

Money
- Sheeeeeeeeeeeeeeeeeeet
- Pete somehow got paid for the last five HCA shifts I did, and I really needed that money! Trying to sort it, but it's such a faff.
- Have no food and no money
- Scottish loans fucked up AGAIN and owe me so much money
- I haven't bought a single xmas pressie

Love
- Ha. Pull the other one.

~~~

SATURDAY 11TH DECEMBER 2004 5AM
LISTENING TO VICE BY RAZORLIGHT

Guess what? I've had another disaster night. I went to the pub at 4pm with Pete, Robin, Kate, Mag Dog etc. We all got a bit pissed and headed to the *Union*. I spent ages talking to Mad Dog about Matt - I think he's being a bit of twat, but she's completely infatuated.

Then, Dakota (Northern Joe's gf from this year who he broke up with because she said 'no sex before marriage') came over to talk to me. Half an hour later, she was crying, and I was shushing her and stroking her hair. How have I ended up here? I eventually got rid of her and turned round to see Pete pulling Sarah, the class slut.

~~~

I hate this word. SaaaLUuuuT. There is no male equivalent, and it is invariably used to vilify and belittle strong women who are comfortable with their sexuality. It's a cheap and unimaginative word for a quick, nasty insult. I wish I hadn't been complicit in its use.

~~~

She pulls about a million people a night. Urgh. It's pretty insulting to think that Pete's bar is low enough for Sarah but not for me.

Barry then invited Mad Dog, Beth and I back to his for burgers. I was on the balcony when Pete and Kate arrived. Kate took me to one side and said that Pete's heard that I like him… ohh ohhhhhh. And he doesn't like me back. Wow. This feeling is starting to become pretty familiar. EVERYTHING IS RUINED… I can't stay with him anymore. I can't hug him without him misinterpreting it. I can't just hang out at theirs in a casual way anymore. Our friendship is kablamo.

I was a bit pissed, so I couldn't quite keep it together. I left and cried all the way home only to get back and realise I'd left my phone at Barry's. So I walked back to his and he told me that Mad Dog's got it and has taken it back to The Medic House. Merde - that's the last place I want to go. Barry walked with me to The Medic House, quick in and out (of the house… not with Barry), and I've just got home.

Pete didn't even look up when I arrived. This is exactly what I wanted to avoid! Him awkwardly ignoring me. I KNEW he didn't like me! I never wanted to actually hear it though. I didn't want it confirmed, and I never wanted him to know I liked him. Our friendship was far more valuable, and I knew I'd eventually move on to someone else. I liked Frank no time ago, and look what happened there… Frank who? If there's one thing I can confidently rely on, it's my endless ability to be fickle.

I can't stop crying. I've been plunged into such a deep melancholy.

MONDAY 13TH DECEMBER 2004 2.30AM
LISTENING TO DON'T MISS YOU AT ALL BY NORAH JONES

I met Mag Dog, Kate and Connie for brekkie in *Cuba* on Saturday morning but Pete arrived. I was civil and jokey, and no one could see my chagrin. I spent the rest of the day with the girls, and we went to *Union* in the evening, where Pete could (of course!) be found. He kicked my arse at pool and then enjoyed the rest of his evening with his arm around Mary. It was starting to upset me, so I left, only to realise I'd had my phone nicked. I lost one of my best friends, my pride, my heart and my phone in 24hrs. Fuck. I hung out with Mad Dog, Beth and Connie at theirs today. Pete was obviously lingering like a bad smell all day before cornering me in the kitchen.

'Is everything ok, Claire? I feel like you've been weird with me this weekend.'

'Everything's fine!'

I massively overdid how fine I was and must have looked completely manic.

'Cool. You're welcome to stay tonight, by the way.'

What the fuck? I don't understand. Yes, it's a bit of a trek back, and it's dark and freezing, but if he knows I like him, why would he send me mixed signals!? Does he want me to sleep in his bed? Surely this isn't simply an act of chivalry? I would love to sleep next to him, but… WHAT IS GOING ON?! Barry and Matt are convinced he likes me.

'Thanks, Pete, but I'll head home in a bit.'

How d'ya like them restraint-apples?

~~~

TUESDAY 14TH DECEMBER 2004 1AM
LISTENING TO SPITTING GAMES BY SNOW PATROL

I've blown it with Pete. I just HAD to be a massive twat! I couldn't help myself. Most people have gone home for xmas, and it's pretty much just Pete and I left to bumble around Plymmy. We hung out at his place and played poker, the two of us, for hours. We cooked dinner, had a bottle of wine and watched Spooks. We headed into town, played darts and had a few pints in a random pub, then went to *Bac Bar*. We were both pretty pissed when I unleashed the crazy on his ass.

'Look, Pete, I just want you to know that I know you know I like you and that the feeling isn't reciprocated. I never wanted you to know cos I value our friendship, and I didn't want to ruin what we had.'

'I don't disagree. I don't want this to become a thing. We're great friends. Please don't ruin that.'

'I'm trying not to! Don't worry, I'll meet someone else before you know it, and I'll wonder what on earth I saw in you.'

'Great. You're great, Claire, but I really like Mary and want to give it a go. You're making things weird now.'

I could feel my wheels falling off... I was losing control.

'Jeeeez. I know you like her! You talk about her a bajillion times a day...'

Just stop talking, Claire... but no. I can't. Fucking. Stop.

'It's sooooo boring! I hate hearing about her.'

And out came the drunken tears. I was a fucking disgrace, and he was maddeningly cool about it, which only served to fuel my emotions and stoke my psycho-fire. I started talking about short-term friends... in between my sobs. Fuck Gretchen! This is becoming a thing, and I'm developing quite the complex. Pete stayed pretty silent during this verbal onslaught... did he not care?!

'We should probably spend a little less time together, Claire. I don't want to upset you. We definitely need some space, and I'm not sure we should see each other again until after Christmas.'

'FINE!'

And once again, I stormed home, crying like a drunken twat. Why do I insist on behaving like this and annihilating all my friendships? What is wrong with me? I hate me. I don't deserve friends.

I've lost Miles and Pete this term, and IT'S 100% my fault!

TWENTY-FOUR
CHRISTMAS '04

THURSDAY 16TH DECEMBER 2004 10.55AM
LISTENING TO WHICH WAY IS OUT BY RAZORLIGHT

I'm trapped on the longest train ride in the world with only my dark and shitty thoughts as company.

I spent yesterday watching films with Ellie and Lou in our duvets and then found three texts from Pete basically saying he didn't want to leave things as we had and could we meet? So we went to the *Union* for a few games of pool, and we joked around, and everything was amazingly fine. It was a risky strategy (one that involved zero thought and planning), but it seems that I may, in fact, have cleared the air. Everything between us is going to be ok, I think.

~~~

FRIDAY 17TH DECEMBER 2004 1.40AM
LISTENING TO THE IMPRESSION THAT I GET BY THE MIGHTY MIGHTY BOSSTONES

And breathe. I'm home.

Had dinner with Chloe and the parentals before going out with the school lot (Maggie, Herbert, Al Winter, Douglas Macdonald, Hector McKellan and David Moore). I offered to drive, which was a welcome break from the total excess of the last few months. Maggie was shit-faced and soooo funny. I've missed everyone. I think of how I used to fancy Herbert and how similar it is to Pete Bond - and that turned out all right!

~~~

MONDAY 20TH DECEMBER 2004 4.10AM
LISTENING TO LONELINESS BY TOMCRAFT

Ouff WHAT A NIGHT! Had lunch in Helensburgh with all of Dad's family, then went straight to Next Door Andy's when we got back. His dad invited me to stay for dinner, and Big Sam arrived and joined us, too. Vino all round and the three of us then went to *Bannerman's* to watch *The Comrades* - Dan Jeffries' band! They were amazing - I was so impressed. Every inch of my being wanted to scream, 'THAT'S MY EX-BOYFRIEND! I KNOW THAT GUY' but just about managed to play it a little cooler and told Next Door Andy and Big Sam… and some random girl in the bogs.

We had a drink with them after their set. Dan Jeffries is SO COOL. Obviously I fancied him after he'd just played live, but I also wished I could have seen him then as I do now (with my marginally maturer eye). We were friendly, but he kept me at a safe (and understandable) distance! Apparently, him and Psycho Jane had only just broken up. Wow, that was a meaty relationship! What's that? Four or five years?

We then all headed to *Rush*. Sofia and all the St Catherine's girls were there. I feel so insecure the second I'm around them, even though the vats of fake tan and peroxide make them look like poo-coloured Barbie dolls. I hate them.

Next Door Andy, BS, and I then stumbled to *Cavendish*. Bloody William Macleod was there. How is Edinburgh so tiny!?! It's astonishing that I still get a visceral reaction when I see him.

A rush of shame, nostalgia, disgust and probably always a little bit of love. Next Door Andy stopped and said hi to him for a minute while I went to the bar with Big Sam. William and I have passed the point of civil liberties. Now that he's fucking dead inside.

The three of us went back to Next Door Andy's after closing. Big Sam was cooking some bacon, and Next Door Andy and I were dancing around in the kitchen when he suddenly burst out laughing.

'Wow. Claire! That's embarrassing. For a split second there, I wanted to kiss you!'

Big Sam and I stared at him. Big Sam looked even more horrified than me and dropped his spatula.

'What the fuck, dude?'

I had, almost instantaneous tears of laughter rolling down my cheeks. Oh, how the tables have turned. I scoffed at him.

'Ha ha! What? That IS embarrassing for you! You're drunk, but I hope I make a note of this so I can remind you of that time you wanted to kiss me!'

'Ha! I didn't want to kiss you. It was just a weird thought. Hence why I told you! You were just flirty dancing with me! You used to fancy me, remember!'

'Yeah, when we were five! We're pals now.'

'Yeah, I know. It's like we're your only friends in Edinburgh… and you've got off with most of MY friends anyway. You don't know how to be friends with anyone without flirting with them!'

The air turned to ice and I felt my entire body go rigid. That cut deep, and a silence descended upon us. We were all just staring at each other, and my heart was hammering in my chest. EXSCUUUUUUSE ME?! What the fuck has gotten into him!? He suddenly looked down a little sheepishly (very un-Next Door Andy).

'Sorry, Claire. I'm just drunk.'

CHRISTMAS 2004

I went home pretty sharpish after that. He can be such a dickhead sometimes.

~~~

HEY ANDY! REMEMBER THAT TIME YOU WANTED TO KISS ME?

~~~

SUNDAY 26TH DECEMBER 2004 3.15AM
LISTENING TO HOW TO BE DEAD BY SNOW PATROL

Been in Paris at Mamie and Papy's for the last few days. I miss hanging out with my friends. How awful is that?! I'm with my family, who I hardly get to see, in Paris, and I'm the grumpy teenager. I can't help it! I arrive, delighted to see everyone, and I want to tell everyone how happy I am to be spending time with them and how much I love them, but one wrong word or a slightly mistimed look and I am overcome with irritation. I then huff and puff, conceited and feeling desperately misunderstood. I want to leave and see my friends until it's time for me to leave, at which point I usually cry, never wanting to be parted from my Mamie and Papy. It's ridiculous. I miss them so much during the year, and then I'm being driven nuts within an hour of our reunion.

I got the ER box set for Christmas, and Chloe and I have been watching it. How on earth is knowing everything you need to know as a doctor even possible?! I'm so depressed by the enormity of it and how enormous I am. Pfff… big, hopeless, stupid, selfish, fatty. No wonder no one ever fancies me.

I'm going to spend the day at *Le Musée D'Orsay* tomorrow and just relax and do some sketches by myself. I want some space where I can smoke when I want and spend my time either overthinking or doing some art and thinking of nothing. My brain has felt fried since we arrived, unable to think through the clamour of family. I know I should make the most of them, but they're driving me MAD.

~~~

TUESDAY 28TH DECEMBER 2004 1.20AM
LISTENING TO NOT EVEN JAIL BY INTERPOL

I just found out that Pete Bond is in my PBL group until the end of the year! Gah! This is torture. I'll have to sit with and look at my rejection and humiliation dead in the eye for the rest of the year. I'll be followed by this nasty little cloud of embarrassment. How am I ever supposed to get over him if he's constantly by my side being a lovely friend? I don't understand why he doesn't like me - we get on so well, and I'm definitely better looking than he is.

~~~

Oh no, she didn't!

~~~

There's obviously something very wrong with me that I can't see! The unknown unknowns - the undoing of us all...

I punched Papy's old wooden, glass-topped bureau last night as I was dreaming that Robin had turned into a blue gremlin-esque monster and he was chasing me, trying to eat me cos I'd fed him some salt and vinegar squares (which was apparently a faux-pas). Hurts like a bitch.

WEDNESDAY 29TH DECEMBER 2004 4.30PM
LISTENING TO GLEAMING AUCTION BY SNOW PATROL

Ahhh... some peace. I'm sitting alone in a nice little Parisian bistro with a Diet Coke and as many fags as I can smoke. I went to 'the other Claire's' flat last night. Her brother, Fred and mother-blinking-Nico were there. Lovely, charming, fuzzy, sober-cheerleader Nico. I would have done anything to get with him. So rather than

CHRISTMAS 2004

prove him wrong and behave like a normal human being, Claire and I went fucking bananas. It was almost as if the thought of not drinking or smoking drove me the other way and allll the way off the ledge. I'm ready to go back to Plymouth now.

 Walking along with friends all around,
 In love with those on the rebound,
 Getting all I want without satisfaction.
 Getting who I want without the passion.
 Seeing but blind to everyone else's secret.

~~~

Jesus Christ, that's terrible.

~~~

MONDAY 3RD JANUARY 2005 3.30AM
LISTENING TO STUMBLE AND FALL BY RAZORLIGHT

I'm happy. I had an awesome New Year (Maggie and I ripping up the streets of Edinburgh) and everything feels calm and simple. I don't feel stressed, heartbroken or anything that I usually feel the need to vomit onto the page. I actually feel like everything is going to be ok. Actually, I don't even know what to write…

New Year's Resolutions

1. Drink less. Save money for music and presents. Stop making a dick of myself. This will lead to me slashing the hangovers, getting more work done and losing weight.
2. DO SOME GODDAMN WORK YOU LAYABOUT.
3. Read more.
4. Quit moping about like a sullen teenager and appreciate your family.

Finn just told me he slept with his house mate. Twat. Everyone knows the rules. Sucks to be him. I still get a little pang of jealousy when I hear he's with someone else. I have no right, of course. I wish he wasn't so much of a man whore. Fed up and ready to go back to Plymouth.

~~~

WEDNESDAY 5TH JANUARY 2005 4AM
LISTENING TO WHERE IS MY MIND BY THE PIXIES

I spent the afternoon drinking with Big Sam and Clyde then danced all night in Stereo with them. These guys, man... This is happiness.

~~~

SATURDAY 8TH JANUARY 2005 4.20AM
LISTENING TO GUNS DON'T KILL PEOPLE, RAPPERS DO BY GOLDIE LOOKIN' CHAIN

I will be a doctor. I WILL! I can't sleep cos I'm running through all the things I need to do and pack before heading back to Plym. I finally finished my portfolio analysis - oh shit just realised the floppy is still downstairs. Might go grab it now. I cannot forget it!

~~~

Were we really still using floppy discs in 2005? They were, without a doubt, the LEAST reliable saving medium. A hard disc - now that feels sturdy. Good old child-bearing-hipped hard discs. But pathetic, yellow-bellied, flimsy floppys - we should have expected nothing less.

'Hey, floppy, where's my work?'
'What work?'
'You know! The essay I've been writing and religiously asking you to look after in various different formats!? You had seven ver-

sions an hour ago. I didn't want a repeat of the French A Level saga!'

'No idea what you're talking about, love.'

I used to save each piece of work on three floppys, and carry my baby hand grenades in three separate, cushioned bags (there was an endless list of things that 'could interfere' with them). We lived in constant fear of losing all our work at the whim of a small plastic ARSEHOLE. No matter the precautions, it was the file-saving equivalent of playing Russian roulette with one empty chamber. You'd insert the disc, a deadline a mere hour away, only to discover that all three had inexplicably wiped themselves. Bang - you're dead.

TWENTY-FIVE
ED

FRIDAY 14TH JANUARY 2005 1AM
LISTENING TO CHOCOLATE BY SNOW PATROL

Amazingly: 2005 is not totally shit. Things with Pete are going really well - all friends and all forgotten. Phew. I feel like I just flicked a switch, and now I don't fancy him. It's weird. Taaa Daaah! And they said she never had a talent. Can you fall in and out of love as quickly as me? I didn't think so. The sonic of emotions, travelling at the speed of light and lust…

So, on that note, I was playing pool with Pete and Robin on Monday afternoon in between Jigsaw and Clinical Skills when I spotted this super fit guy that I really couldn't help but stare at.

Later that night, Mad Dog, Kate and I went to *Wonky Legs*, and he was there again, so I went over and spoke to him.

'Hey. Are you following me?'

What a line. It had the immediate effect of repelling him off me.

'What?! No! Why would you say that?'

A very good question. Why would I say that?

'Ah. Sorry. It was a stupid joke. I just saw you earlier in the *Union*.'

He laughed. If you can call it that. It was nervous and uncom-

ED

fortable. Wow. A-Z of seduction right there. Anyway, it got better after that, and he bought me a drink, and we exchanged numbers. He's called Ed, doing his third year in computing and blah blah blah… this guy is a massive hottie.

I saw him again in *C103* on Wednesday, and we had a bit of a dance before he came back here. We kissed and had a little fumble. Ah… ha ha … fumble… not called it that before. It feels like something Hugh Laurie would do. He is so beautiful, but in the words of the med school, his chat is 'borderline'. Not bad, I just wasn't sure yet, but if I'm perfectly honest, his looks could carry way worse chat, so who cares?

I saw him again tonight, and we kissed A LOT. I am seriously feeling this one! He's kind and bulky and strong, and ahhhhhh, just fuck me now Ed Louis Branagh.

~~~

Hopefully, my dad learnt his lesson reading my first book and is coming nowhere near this one.

~~~

Right. I need to go to bed and do loads of work on my SSU tomorrow. Fingers crossed for some awesome Ed-based sex dreams.

~~~

TUESDAY 18TH JANUARY 2005 1AM
LISTENING TO I PREDICT A RIOT BY KAISER CHIEFS

Went to the *Union* on Friday with Pete, Frank, Robin, Mad Dog and Kate. Ed was there lookin' fine… We had a really hot pull near the bar. I felt like I couldn't get enough of him as I let out a little moan and felt my knees buckle when he cupped the back of my head, his hands entangled in my hair and drew me in. Ouff, what a hot piece of ass. His smile curls up at the corners, and there's the sexiest divet in between his forearm… muscles… oh fuck you anatomy! Yes, I should know it. But I don't. FINE! I'll look it up. Ok. The bit in between the extensor carpi ulnaris and the extensor digitorum communis. Well, I do NOT feel that added to my story. Note to self: no more 'medical banter'.

~~~

TUESDAY 25TH JANUARY 2005 2AM
LISTENING TO BOULEVARD OF BROKEN DREAMS BY GREEN DAY

```
Text from Ed: Morning gorgeous. Just
to let you know that I cant stop think-
ing of you.

Text to Ed: Morning. The feeling is
very much mutual. xxx
```

Why won't I just go to sleep? I have to be up in seven hours and only slept three hours last night. Maybe I'll just die. That would save me some trouble. Argh! Not like that! I don't want to die.

Pete Bond, Robin, Kitty Harvey and I have decided to live together next year when we go to Exeter. Pete and I had a 'would it be weird?' chat and decided that no, it wouldn't. Robin suggested it (clueless to my previous infatuation), and nothing would have been weirder than saying no and Kitty... well, I'm not quite sure how that happened. I think we all thought it would be a good idea to have another girl, and 4-beds are easier. She's nice so it's fine.

~~~

There she goes again. Showing up all the other writers with an impressive display of adjectives.

~~~

She isn't the most fun person in the world; she's a bit earnest and body-obsessed. She goes to the gym every day BEFORE uni. Good for her. I guess I'm a bit jealous of that level of dedication. Getting to uni is my daily achievement.

~~~

FRIDAY 28TH JANUARY 2003 2.10AM
LISTENING TO TINY LITTLE FRACTURES BY SNOW PATROL

I've just been to see *Meet the Fockers* at the cinema with Ed. It's so easy and comfortable being with him. He smells so good: I love it. He smells like the glue they use in schools in France, sweet and almondy. I spent a good chunk of my childhood wanting to eat that glue, and Ed made me feel no differently. I have to stop myself from actively sniffing him like a psycho. He kept glancing over at me and giving me the kind of smile that made me feel like the only person in his world.

We were walking back to his when he took my hand. Wowa this feels like some girlfriend shit.

'I could get used to this. You're not who I thought you were.'

Talk of mixed signals…

'What does that mean?'

'You're more chill than you let on, Claire… I like it.'

I smiled and winked at him. Just wait until I start Hannibal-sniffing you, big guy…

~~~

SUNDAY 6TH FEBRUARY 2005 1.10AM
LISTENING TO EVERYDAY I LOVE YOU LESS AND LESS BY THE KAISER CHIEFS

Worked my bloomin' socks off this week then went to *Roundabout* last night with Pete and Frank, and bumped into Ed. Have his muscles got bigger? I felt myself blush when I saw him. He smiled his runaway smile and came right up against me, wrapping his arms around me and pressing his nose against mine.

'Hey, gorgeous. You bin ignorin' me or just playing hard to get?' He smiled with his mouth, but there was a smidge of cold in his eyes. 'I don't really like mind games.'

'What? Me neither!'

I have NOT been ignoring him. We'd text a few times last weekend, but I've genuinely been busy with work, and I was kinda waiting for him to message me.

'I went round to yours on Tuesday, but you were out. Your house mate said he'd let you know. I wrote you a note and everything.'

'What?! Which house mate?'

Not that I needed to ask! Bruce... you slimy beach bum.

'Err... the blonde surfy one.'

Fucking Bruce.

'Oh, Ed. I'm so sorry! He never told me.'

'Well, I guess, in a way, that's the best outcome for me. Can I get you a drink?'

And with that, he grabbed my arse.

~~~

Just when you thought chivalry was dead.

~~~

I spent the rest of the night chatting, drinking and kissing him. He came back to mine, and we stayed up until 5am messing about. No sex, though - I'm clearly getting more restrained as I get older!

ED

I went to the medics house tonight, and Beth and I cooked a roast for everyone. Pete was being very weird and looked so upset. He went to bed early, and I gave him a little knock before I left. He looked like he'd been crying.

'You ok, buddy?'

'No, not really, but I don't really want to talk about it, if that's ok. Thanks, though.'

'Course. Catch you tomorrow.'

Something bad has happened. Pete never looks like that - it broke my heart. Hope he's ok.

~~~

WEDNESDAY 10TH FEBRUARY 2005 8.30PM
LISTENING TO DON'T CHA BY THE PUSSYCAT DOLLS

It was the medic's pub golf last night. Fuck me, that was messy. Mad Dog and I managed seventeen holes, but we were an absolute disgrace. I could barely stand. Kate and Frank won again with a completed eighteen holes in one. It's impressive for sure, but this CANNOT be good for us. We all have massive blanks, and I spent most of today with everyone at the medic's house, trying to piece everything together.

I woke up this morning confused and disorientated. I was fully clothed, tartan golfing flat cap still firmly on my head. The pounding had gone past my head and taken over my whole body. My tongue was so dry it was numb and brittle, and my eyes scratched inside the sockets as I looked around the room. Where the fuck was I? Then I noticed the sleeping figure next to me and realised it was Robin Mills. I gave him a gentle nudge, and as I watched him wake up, I could almost hear the screaming start up in his head.

'Urrrghhhh. Claire! Ah! Why are you in my bed!?'

'No idea.'

'Did we…? I feel like I had sex last night.'

How very dare he.

'We most certainly did not. Jesus. I feel awful. Do you have any water?'

He ignored me and continued to stare into the distance, looking confused.

'I definitely had sex with someone. In the toilets.'

'Shut the fuck up. No, you didn't.'

There's no way. This is Robin. Lovely, sweet, Welsh farm boy Robin. Robin who hadn't even tasted curry until a month ago. Robin, who I'm fairly sure is (was?) a virgin. Kind, considerate, feminist Robin. Not 'fuck someone in the bogs' Robin.

'I did! I think I had sex with Lauren in the toilets in *Roundabout*.'

I was speechless and just stared at him as the memories just came in one by one to punch him in the face.

'Oh no! And then I was sick and got barred from the *Union*. Oh dear. And then I got lost in the park.'

'The tiny park round the cover from here?'

'I think so. I couldn't find the way out, and I was just crawling around, and I got chatting to the tramp… Neil, I think? He then gave me a leg up over the wall and… oh god…'

Just when you think you know someone. Then Mad Dog rushed in, covered in blood.

'WHAT THE HELL HAPPENED LAST NIGHT? I've just woken up to a blood bath, I can't find my phone, and I've shredded my plus-fours.'

Mad Dog had split her chin open, but we managed to steri-strip it back together. Pete was sick all over his room. Frank had smashed his full-length mirror and lamp. Kate lost her wallet and has a massive bruise the shape of a heart on her back. I lost my puffer jacket and my watch and broke my camera. HOW DO

ED

YOU LOSE A WATCH? I have a horrible feeling I may have also seen Ed at some point.

I'm never going to do pub golf again. I'm never drinking that much again. Soooo dangerous.

~~~

I'm a bit speechless and feel quite embarrassed by the booze culture and glamourising dangerous drinking habits. This was our currency and our language. Our world would have been so different if we'd fostered some hobbies rather than forever going down the pub and getting drunk. I don't like the slight hint of pride I can read between my lines.

~~~

SUNDAY 13TH FEBRUARY 2005 2.30AM
LISTENING TO OH MY GOD BY THE KAISER CHIEFS

I've just woken up having dreamt I was an artist, and I had a beautiful studio with floor-to-ceiling windows and shelves bursting with paints, brushes and art. I was so happy just painting all day. I WANT THAT!

~~~

24TH FEBRUARY 2025
LISTENING TO LAST NIGHT'S MASCARA BY GRIFF

Studio space confirmed. 20 years and ten days later.

~~~

MONDAY 21ST FEBRUARY 2005 1AM
LISTENING TO OVER AND OVER BY NELLY FT TIM MCGRAW

Ed came to mine last night, and we stayed up 'til about 5am sniggering and fooling about, which eventually led to us having sex. It was going GREAT when he suddenly stopped.

'Um, I'm really sorry, Claire. I've got a confession to make.'

Oh God. Married? Girlfriend? Hepatitis? Weird fetish? Good lord, don't say you want to suck my toes or something. WHAT-TTTT?!?!?!

'That sounds ominous… go on…'

'I've already cum. Sorry. That's so embarrassing. That was really short.'

PHEW!

He stayed the night, and we cuddled all night, and I was aware that he kept kissing the back of my neck throughout the night. He's so soft and yet strong… he smells sooooo good. I picked up new notes of clove cigarettes and Cerruti 1881 homme tonight, glued together with the scent of Parisian primary schools.

He woke me up this morning with a cup of tea and a kiss on the forehead.

'Morning, sexy. Just been chatting with Bruce…'

'Oh god. What did he have to say?'

'Said you were apparently a "fitty in the sack". Have you guys slept together?'

'Jesus. No. He's just messing. Ignore him.'

'Is he jealous?'

'No. You'd think. But no.'

We shared a sandwich at lunch, then spent the day walking about Plymouth, and I was rabbiting away. Must talk less.

We had sex again tonight, and it was wayyyyyyyyy better. Please don't let it blow up now.

ED

FRIDAY 25TH FEBRUARY 2005 2AM
LISTENING TO HOUNDS OF LOVE BY THE FUTUREHEADS

This week has been bliss. I wake up every morning feeling crap and exhausted, and then I remember that Ed is in my life, and I smile. Ahhhh, he makes me so happy. We've spent the week alternating between his and mine, and it feels very intense. I've not felt this way since Artie. EEEEEEEEEEEEE!!!!

~~~

SATURDAY 26TH FEBRUARY 2005 4AM
LISTENING TUMBLE AND FALL BY FEEDER

Fuuuuuuuuuck. (OBVIOUSLY) I spoke too soon, and it's all gone tits up. I'm so upset and angry with myself for falling for it all over again. OVER AND OVER AND OVER AGAIN.

I went to the *Union* tonight with Kate and Mad Dog. Ed was around, and he'd give me a quick kiss now and again in passing. It was caaaaaaaa-UTE! He rang me a few times at the end of the night as he wanted to catch me before I left. We walked back to his, all perfect and lovely, had very giggly drunken sex, and I was having a fag out his window afterwards.

'Look, Claire. I think we might need to have a bit of a chat. I don't want to ruin what we've got, but equally…'

'Right…?'

I felt my stomach drop. I knew instantly where this conversation was going. He's seen through to the real me. No good thing could ever have lasted…

'Yeah. So. I got messed around by my ex at Christmas, and I'm just not ready (or interested, to be honest) in any kind of relationship.'

I knew it. It's always too good to be true.

'And when did you have this epiphany? Have you been thinking this the whole time? You've not been acting like it… or have things changed?'

'Nothing's changed. It just feels like things are getting more serious, and I don't want a girlfriend. You're awesome company, and I have such a laugh with you…'

'So you thought you'd have one more shag tonight and then tell me?'

He looked a bit sheepish and then had the fucking AUDACITY to flash me his cheekiest of grins.

'I'm only human. I hope that's not the last time if I'm honest.'

'Fuck this.'

I threw my fag out the window and then got dressed in the least comfortable silence of my life before storming out.

Always the fuck buddy. Never the girlfriend. I feel so hurt. I'm home now and sat here like a loser, crying into my diary. You'd think he could have said something earlier.

~~~

SATURDAY 26TH FEBRUARY 2005 12.30PM
LISTENING TO LOCKED UP BY AKON

```
MSN Chat with Ed

Ed: you there?

Me: Yeah

Ed: Sorry bout last night, I was very
drunk. What time did you leave?
```

ED

Me: bout 330. I just wish ud sed smthg earlier.

Ed: It's not like I don't like you. I just don't want any commitment at the moment.

Me: I know. You said.

Ed: Im usually not much of a relationship person anyway, and my last screwed me over, so I think I'm cautious about relationships.

Me: That seems like a very stupid life philosophy. Look. I liked you and I don't think things were very clear from you. The amount of time we were spending together seemed like a commitment regardless of what you want to label it as - it's ridiculous. Look, never mind.

Ed: I like you too. I really enjoy your company, I think you're a wicked laugh, but it's just the wrong time.

Me: Like I said Ed. YOU SAID. I'm just pissed off as I feel like I've had this conversation a thousand times in my life and I'm only 19.

Ed: Bet you're even more pissed off about leaving your tobacco behind.

Me: yeah, I know. I was going to roll on the way back and could've licked myself when I realised.

Me: KICKED myself. Obviously wasn't in the right frame of mind to lick myself.

Ed: I've got your earrings too.

Me: FUCK

Ed: Don't worry I'm not going to do anything to them.

Me: Ha

Ed: Right I better go psyche myself up for rugby - so hungover. Sorry you hate me now. I just had to be honest with you. I hope we can still have a laugh together.

Me: You think you could drop my stuff back on the way to rugby?

Ed: Yeah. Sure.

Me: Ta

~~~

ED

TUESDAY 8TH MARCH 2005 3.10AM
LISTENING TO WIRES BY ATHLETE

Went out with Bruce, Mark, Rich, Trigger, & Tommo. Lou's away, so Rich is gracing us with his fucking presence again. We went to *Wonky Legs*, (there's something about *Wonky Legs*… legitimately not allowed to go without wonky legs). Anyway, Rich and I had a blazing row. We were all sat around the table with a fish bowl and I was just so happy to be out with them all again (even Rich!)

'Awwww, you guys… I've missed you all… We used to go out together all the time - this is so nice!'

Rich somehow decided to take offence to this. He's such an agro little bitch… He slammed his phone down on the table and stood up, wide-eyed and glaring down at me. I can't believe how intimidated he made me feel. Lovely Rich, who I used to stay up all night chatting with, who came to get me at the train station in the middle of the night… who shared a bed with me on countless occasions just for company, who I spent a week with in Coventry. There he was, looking like he'd love nothing better than to punch me.

'What the fuck is that supposed to mean, Claire?'

'Nothing! I'm just saying how nice it is!'

Fortunately I wasn't the only person to be shocked by his little outburst. Mark and Bruce weren't impressed, and Bruce (being a biggish guy) stood up and calmly put his hand on Rich's shoulder.

'Yeah. Chill out, mate. I think Claire was just enjoying the moment.'

'She meant something!'

And in the flicker of a second, it almost looked like he was going to go for me. Bruce clocked it and grabbed his arm. Rich was staring into my eyes with such a fury it flicked my own anger switch. Fuck him. How dare he make me feel threatened. I stood up to meet him and looked him right in the eye.

'Oh, you know what, Rich. Fuck you! Bit over-sensitive, aren't you? "She protesteth too much" and all that? I didn't actually mean anything, but now you mention it, none of us ever see you any more. You've been a shit friend since you and Lou first got together, and you've done nothing but get worse since. There. That hit a nerve enough for ya?'

I sat back down and started rolling a fag, feeling everyone's eyes on me. My heart was thundering around in my chest, and my face was on fire. Despite the deafening drum and bass, we could've heard a pin drop, and in that brief, delicious second before the storm, I felt great. Rich obviously went totally apeshit, and I genuinely think that if Mark and Bruce hadn't been there, he'd have hit me. Bruce was looking at me in an exasperated 'what did you think would happen?' way. Rich hurled every insult under the sun at me, but I didn't really care anymore. It felt good. We've not been friends for ages, and let's face facts - he got so bloody angry in the first place because it's true. SUCK ON THAT YOU WANKER!

~~~

SATURDAY 19TH MARCH 2005 12.30PM
LISTENING TO SOMEWHERE ELSE BY RAZORLIGHT

Haven't written in ages! I've actually been doing some work!
Well... Some.
Ok. Enough.
We went to Cardiff last Saturday for the rugby versus George's medics then back to *Roundabout* on our return. Ed Branagh was there - urgh. Why won't he love me? Ed's mates were so shit-faced and obnoxious.
'Hey, Claire! How big is Ed?!'
'Wouldn't you like to know...'

ED

Fuckers. I joked about with them a bit, but it descended very quickly into them being totally disgusting, saying things like 'I'd like to have a go' and 'Then you can compare us all', etc etc. Frank said nothing, but Pete told them all to fuck off. Ed sat there silently, not even acknowledging that I was there, and then, on the way out, whispered, 'Well, I hope you're proud of yourself. That was just... silliness.'

WHAT? I was speechless, and I watched him leave without a word. How dare he?

```
Text to Ed: What was that supposed to
mean? Your friends were being dicks.
Thanks for defending me btw. Oh and
don't you dare even think about mak-
ing me out to be some kind of slut.
I was the one that liked you and you
were the one with the one track mind.
Fuck you.
```

Also, Connie and Frank are a couple. I love her, and I don't fancy him anymore, but no matter what happens, there will always be a part of me that thinks, 'If I can't have him - no one can'. I mean, I don't resent her, but... ah, whatever. I'm a bit jealous.

AND Bruce's ex, G, is pregnant - WITH TOMMO'S BABY! TAAAAAAWIST! She was apparently not on the pill (and never told Bruce) because she wanted to see if she COULD get pregnant. I cannot understand this.

TWENTY-SIX
EASTER 2005

THURSDAY 24TH MARCH 2005 2AM
LISTENING TO YOU BETTER YOU BET BY THE WHO

Ahhhh, Edinburgh - how I've missed you.

I went out last night with Maggie, Herbert, Doug McDonald and Hector and FUCKING GRETCHEN CAME. Maggie and her are besties again. Streuth.

~~~

I like to refer to this as 'My Neighbours phase', and it lasted a bonza five seconds while I struggled to spell streuth, before vowing to never use it again.

~~~

I now have to make a choice. If I want to stay good friends with Maggie, I have to BOGOF Gretchen. I just can't bear to have her in my adult life infecting everything... but... it's Maggie... I love her! Surely I'm grown up enough to cope with the odd night of Gretchen in tow? But will she try to 'turn her' (bad not gay)?

We sat round the table all night and caught up and pretended we were all a lovely group of school friends catching up. Gretchen knew it was all a façade - we were just trying to outdo each other with our acting skills.

~~~

FRIDAY 25TH MARCH 2005 5.20AM
LISTENING TO ACROSS THE UNIVERSE BY THE BEATLES

Tonight was really surreal, and I can feel the anxiety crawling up my legs already. I picked Maggie up at hers, and we went back to mine for dinner, and Herbie joined. The three of us got through three bottles of wine. Then off to *Bannerman's* to see Thee Comrades (Dan Jeffries' band). They were fecking awesome, and I loved every delectable second of it. Why have I not married a musician yet? We had a few drinks afterwards, and Dan and I went to *Opium* and had a dance. This is when things got weird. I walked back to Dan's flat in the Grassmarket. He made us both a cup of tea and put on some Bach and the football on silent. I was sat there thinking: What is this? What am I doing here? Do I fancy him cos he's in a band now? I mean, yes, obviously a little bit. Fickle superficial Claire... He then monologued about Bach for hours, and it was weirdly the sexiest chat in the world! I then realised it was getting late and I was never going to try and kiss Dan... I can't believe it's been five years since I last kissed Dan! I really hope he gets to share his talent with the world. He is truly incredible. If he doesn't become world famous, I'll... ermmm... eat my pink tartan beret.

~~~

SATURDAY 26TH MARCH 2005 6PM
LISTENING TO FRIDAY NIGHT IN BY THEE COMRADES

I'd been listening to Dan Jeffries' band's EP that he gave me last night all day and it's insane. I messaged him, and we went for a coffee this afternoon, but the shine wasn't there in the cold light of day. His music, though...

> Text from Ed: I miss you baby. Miss
> your tits and your hot ass x

Good.

> Text to Ed: As you should but you can
> fuck off. Respectfully. X

~~~

MONDAY 28TH MARCH 2005 00.20AM
LISTENING TO SUNRISE BY ANGEL CITY

Last night was frantic. We all got whipped up into this overheated frenzy. I can't quite believe it happened. A bit like the (very) toned-down version of the Bacchanal in The Secret History: wine and madness…

Maggie hosted dinner at hers with me, Herbie, Al Winter, Hector McKellen, Doug Macdonald, Davie Moore… and fucking Gretchen, of course. We were all shit-faced. We played drinking games, and it turned into this vodka, stripping rampage till about 6am. It was awesome but definitely a bit weird. Hector jumped from a window on the first floor onto the flat roof on a bay window (legit could have died), then climbed down, came in through the front door and snogged me in a heroic, arm in the small of my back and sweeping me down, way. I do not fancy Hector but it was surprisingly hot and funny as hell. My god, the more I think about last night, the more I think we've lost the plot.

~~~

He did what? Ha. I don't think either of us remember this. Hector McKellen was like the others, brilliant but very silly. He was skinny but not unpretty and, like many of us, existed in an almost permanent state of hangover. When I last saw him, I said something totally forgettable (I have forgotten), and he looked me dead in the eye and said, 'Spoken like a true diarist.' It was everything I wanted to hear. I have struggled with the word 'writer' and I am paralysed with imposterism when I hear 'author' but diarist? It is perfect and makes me feel like I have found my little corner of society to nestle in.

~~~

THURSDAY 31ST MARCH 2005 4AM
LISTENING TO 14TH STREET BY RUFUS WAINWRIGHT

I went out with Next Door Andy, Clyde, Big Sam and their lot tonight. We went to *City*, and Maggie and Gretchen were there with Jamie, Grumpy 'Arseface' Toby, 'Lads' and the other St Felix's boys. At least Mish wasn't there - phew. I would almost definitely have made a tit of myself if he had been. I hate being around them all. I feel like I'm at school again and can't remember who I am now. I become small and embarrassed. Man, school was shit. They're all a mega bunch of twats. Apart from Mags... and Lads... and Jamie's all right... but they all come with Gretchen. GAH!

TWENTY - SEVEN
TOM 'THE TIPPLE' MORRIS

SATURDAY 9TH APRIL 2005 10.30PM
LISTENING TO POSES BY RUFUS WAINWRIGHT

I've been back in Plymouth for a week now, and it feels right. Pete Bond and I have been hanging out all week, and to think I ever wanted to ruin such a beautiful friendship!? I'm so glad he didn't let me.

As for Lou and Rich… pff I wouldn't want to ruin such a happy page, but they've been insufferable. It's been just the three of us in the house this week (Rich has basically moved in now), and their INCESSANT giggling and laughter have become part of the aggravating soundtrack to my life at Amity Place. Even the name of the road feels like it's mocking me. Friends?! Pah! Every time Lou laughs at something he says, I feel a pang. She has chosen him over me. No one ever told her about how Rich behaved in *Wonky Legs* before Easter. He has no doubt given her a warped 'Claire was drunk' version of events. I hope he's never like that with her, but closed doors and all that. I can't even see why I used to consider him my friend. Where is that guy?

BUT… (And I can't quite believe it wasn't the first thing I

mentioned)… I have met someone new. Tom Morris. I met him on the first night back in *Bac Bar* with Pete and Mad Dog. He is beautiful with bright green eyes and dark olive skin. He was quite drunk, though and ranting about the quality of their vodka shots (in a rather pompous way). He asked for my number, and to be honest, he could have said anything, and I would have given it to him.

~~~

Tom Tom Tom. A Mediterranean-looking Hugh Grant with a charm and assuredness in keeping with his elite Cheltenham upbringing. Tom had naturally well-defined muscles that screamed of good genetics and had nothing to do with the odd game of croquet and cricket that interspersed the perma-drinking culture of the super-rich. His (slightly too) unbuttoned white linen shirt exposed biscuity skin, and even his frontal bossing oozed success and power. But like a lot of posh boys, there was an inherent need to balance his privileged childhood and wealth with bad behaviour. It can't have been easy to blend in with the Janners* whilst continuing to appease his family's disappointment that he was studying at Plymouth University.

**Someone from Plymouth.*

Tom was unquestionably an alcoholic with an unpleasant disdain for anything middle class or below. Suede moccasins or boat shoes were the only acceptable day-to-day footwear, and the thread count on his student sheets was dizzyingly high. The look he gave Mark when he first met him in his orange Wolverhampton shirt was akin to if you saw a cat vomit and then start to eat it again. He genuinely asked me later if it was because he played for Wolverhampton (as this was the only reason that made sense to him).

'...Because someone is PAYING him to wear it?'

'Ha ha! Nope. And he has worn it exclusively aside from two balls since the first day I met him in September in 2003.'

'You're joking.'

'I am not. Although not EXACTLY the same. I believe he has three.'

'But… it's sooooo ugly and <shudder>…. chavvy.'

I've made him sound cold, liquored and aloof, which he was, but he was also affectionate and playful and the last man I loved before I met my husband.

~~~

He text me the next morning.

```
Text from Tom: Hey Ducky. What a pleas-
ure it was to meet you last night! Yep
yep yep… Would you like to meet later
today? Maybe for a drink or a game of
pool? I'm intrigued to see if you were
bullshitting me with your skills…

Text to Tom: Yep yep yep! (I'd love
to). 5pm at the union? Keen for vin-
dication. Brace yourself. x
```

And we played pool and had a few pints, and we kissed, and he came back to mine. We watched *The Manchurian Candidate*. Fuck me… NOT AN APHRODISIAC! It's horrible!

Tom is such a gentleman! And a romantic. We've spent every night together this week. That body, man! But managed to restrain myself thus far.

I'm getting so nervous about the ISCE (*Integrated Structured Clinical Examination*) now. Why haven't I worked harder? What did I think would happen? Drink through it, close my eyes and let the magic happen? Idiot. I almost considered sleeping with the Clinical Examination textbook under my pillow in the hope that some of the Calculator Annie* vibes would take effect and I would wake a medical genius. In your face, Doogie Howser**. Ahhhh, I'm so fucked.

~~~

*Calculator Annie by David A. Adler *was one of my favourite books as a child. It's about a girl who becomes a maths genius overnight after sleeping with a textbook under her pillow.*

**Another niche early 90s reference.* Doogie Howser, M.D. *starred Neil Patrick Harris as a teenage doctor balancing life-saving surgeries, homework and dating dramas. It was basically 'House' meets 'Clarissa Explains It All' with genius-level diagnoses and a lot of introspective, coming-of-age journaling.*

~~~

WEDNESDAY 13TH APRIL 2005 2.30AM
LISTENING TO IF THERE'S ANY JUSTICE IN THE WORLD BY LEMAR

I was staring at my life sciences anatomy tonight, wondering how important it really was? I mean REAAAAALLY? I spent an hour doing a detailed sketch of dermatomes (with a plan to label it at some point… maybe) when Ellie barged in.

'Come on, baby doll! We're going dancing! Colin's sent me two last-minute VIP passes for the Lemar gig tonight. You in? Lou can't make it.'

Ahhh, Ellie… she could have offered almost anything, and I'd have been game. Sure, Lemar isn't necessarily my musical Tetley, but no one can argue that he has the best set of eyes in the business… and dancing with Ellie… and probably some free drinks in the VIP section.

'HELLS YEAH! I. AM. IN. Take me to your leader.'

She grinned, shook her perfect, peachy bootie, dry-humped my door and told me I had twenty minutes.

We danced all night, then had drinks with Lemar and his crew afterwards. They were all swanning over Ellie as I drank the champagne. It was actually rather uneventful, and it all felt a little groupie-esque but not in the cool, Kate Hudson in Almost Famous way. I never did get round to labelling those dermatomes…

I've just got home and bootie-called Tom. He was soooo drunk but took the bait and told me he was on his way. I wish I hadn't now. I'm tired. Shit. Maybe I'll message him back.

~~~

THURSDAY 14TH APRIL 2005 3AM
LISTENING TO ALISON BY WHITMORE

Pete Bond turned twenty-one a few hours ago, and I couldn't love him more. I got him an engraved hip flask, and we all went to *Cuba* for midnight. He was hilarious. Silly Pete. I gave him his hipflask a bit later when we were sat out the back, and I was having a fag.

'Happy Birthday, buddy! I'm not sure what I'd do without you these days. You're without a doubt one of my best friends. I'm excited about us living together over the next few years.'

He leaned over to give me a hug and fell off his chair. We both giggled, and I tried to help him back up again. His eyes were all over the place.

'Ouff Pete. You are DAARRRRRUNK.'

He stroked my hair (in a very unromantic way) and smiled at me.

'At the end of the rainbow, Claire, is you.'

Haha. I love him to bits. I love my friends. So lucky. Shit, it's late, and I've got clinical skills in the morning.

```
Text from Tom: Hey Ducky. I just want
you to know that I'm thinking of you…
a lot x
```

TOM 'THE TIPPLE' MORRIS

SATURDAY 17TH APRIL 2005 11AM
LISTENING TO CAUGHT UP BY USHER

Tom Morris. You have been admitted to the inner circle.

<Retching noises>

I went to the *Union* last night with Pete, Kate, Mad Dog and Frank. Tom confidently came to join, and I could have cried with how happy I was not to see him intimidated by anyone. He just got on with everyone, played pool, bought some drinks and kissed me without any reservation. He came up behind me when I was about to pot the black, pressed himself against me and whispered in my ear.

'Ducky… I know it's not been long, and I'm not really a relationship kinda guy, but I would love to call you my girlfriend…'

Oh, the romance of it! Yep, yep, yep! I turned around and kissed him and told him that I'd like that too. The ducky thing is CAAAAA-UTE! Weird but cute. The night I met him in Bac Bar, he told me he thought I reminded him of the little dinosaur called Ducky in The Land Before Time who chirped a constant 'yep yep yep'.

Anyway, it's stuck and man, am I a sucker for a nickname!

SPOILER ALERT. I slept with him. A lot. He has not left my side since then. I'm excited. REALLY EXCITED.

Sex felt slow and soft and old fashioned.

~~~

SUNDAY 17TH APRIL 2005 3PM
LISTENING TO WHEN THE NIGHT FEELS MY SONG BY BEDOUIN SOUNDCLASH

Last night was completely ridiculous. Pete Bond had a party at The Medic House for his 21st. He'd bought 21 bottles of cheap cava and had 21 of his friends attempt to drink their bottle in 21 minutes. Needless to say, it was chaos. Kate, Frank and I managed to finish ours, but Kate and I were rocking together on the sofa whilst simultaneously burping encouragements to each other.

Pete vomited outside his front door with the final gulp. Robin (who normally can't drink for shit) suspiciously came back from the toilet with half left in his bottle... we knew, and he caught my eye immediately and knew we knew.

You'd think it'd be easy, but the bubbles...

Most people went to bed about 1sh, and that's when the fun REALLY started. I introduced everyone to Shagopoly. It wasn't long until Frank, Kate, Robin, Connie, and I were all sat in our pants. Beth came downstairs to get some water and found us all semi-naked, sat round the Monopoly board.

'What's going on here? Can I play? I'll catch up.' She proceeded to strip down to her pants, neck a glass of whisky and sit down with us. Brilliant.

~~~

19th April 2005 6pm

Tom just told me he doesn't want me playing Shagopoly again.

'I'm sorry, ducky, but no girlfriend of mine is going to be playing stripping games. It's uncouth.'*

'No boyfriend of mine will tell me what I can and can't do. Besides, I'm couth as fuck*. But I will take your suggestion on board. I kind of get it, but don't tell me what to do!'

~~~

*I'd waited my whole life to say that. Legend has it that my uncle (who had a slight tendency for the uncouth) once shouted someone down with that exact retort while drunk and (no doubt) behaving disgustingly. My aunts spoke of it often when I was growing up, and when I first heard the story, I longed for the chance to say it myself.

But it's not the kind of line you can force. You simply have to wait until someone calls you uncouth.

~~~

THURSDAY 21ST APRIL 2005 12PM
LISTENING TO APPLY SOME PRESSURE BY MAXIMO PARK

I'm falling for Tom. He drinks waaaaaaay too much. Sure. But the gentlemanly suaveness makes me weak at the knees. We've spent every night together, alternating his and mine, and yes, the sex is sometimes HOT, but I just LOVE sleeping with him... said no man ever. He strokes me and caresses me and kisses me in his sleep.

I'm going to the yacht club ball with him tomorrow, and I found a Karl Lagerfeld x H&M black sheer puff ball dress for £19.99. Boom. Basically Chanel. Ahh, I'm so excited about us. The only issue I'm slightly struggling with is his RaRa, posho, toffee-mouthed accent.

Right - must crack on with some work. ISCEs and SSU... fuuuuuck!

~~~

SATURDAY 30TH APRIL 2005 1.10AM
LISTENING NUMB / ENCORE BY JAY-Z AND LINKIN PARK

The last week has felt CRAZY. Tom and I are inseparable, but man, does he drink, and there's not an insignificant amount of coke. Coke is such a ballache. I am yet to meet someone on coke and think, 'Oh yeah, you're more fun now.' I usually stare at these verbal-diarrhoea-ed idiots, unable to get a word in. And that's me saying that!

I've spent most days and evenings working, and Tom then pitches up about 9ish every night, completely shit-faced. Being sober and (for once) working and conscientious has only made his drunkenness more obvious. But he's so hot, so funny, and so ridiculously romantic. He douses me with compliments.

How long can this last? Summer will be here before we know it, and next year, I'm off to Exeter. It feels like we're bound to end.

Anyway, he came round for dinner tonight. He, amazingly, wasn't drunk on arrival (but quickly smashed about two bottles of wine). He was swaying and staring at me, a little glassy-eyed.

'So, ducky. I don't want this to sound weird, but I'm falling for you. I was wondering if you'd like to come back to Cheltenham in a few weeks.'

I gave him my best faux shock.

'TO MEET YOUR FAMILY!?'

'Ermm... yeah?'

We smiled at each other and snuggled into bed as I told him I'd love to. Fun! His parents sound TERRIFYING, though, and there's another issue. Tom's been friends with this girl called Jules for years, and they apparently pulled over Easter, which then led to talk of them going out, but ta dahhhhh... I arrived and ruined everything! He had to break the news about me being his girlfriend last week, and she hung up on him. So Jules is going to be there and since 'the breaking of the bad news', she has apparently been really supportive and cool about it all and 'can't wait to meet Claire' as 'she sounds wonderful'. Tom is being a complete man about this and totally oblivious to the nightmarish undercurrent of this situation.

'Such a good idea! You two'll get on so well.'

Oh, Tom... it's a good thing you're good-looking cos this level of naivety is not sexy. Right, he's here now and pissing me off. Must stop writing.

Tom and Jules were together within the year and married within five.

~~~

SUNDAY 1ST MAY 2005 1.15AM
LISTENING TO YOU'RE BEAUTIFUL BY JAMES BLUNT

Tom has really got me into James Blunt (I'm terribly embarrassed to admit this… even to myself!). Of course, he has - big posh twat that he is. But I am loving it.

Tom read my diary after the last time I wrote. If you're reading this now, Tom - YOU'RE FUCKING DUMPED.

I am hating how much he drinks, though. And this is me talking! I know I can be a massive pisshead, but now I think about it, the last month or so with Tom… I've never drunk so little. It's totally put me off! Last night was one of the first times in ages we actually 'finished' having sex cos he wasn't too drunk to cum. Surely, that's a bad sign. Maybe it's me? No. It's him.

I can't make up my mind about him. He's so judgemental about everything. How people talk, how they dress, where they're from… it's such a turn-off, but then he's sooooooo adorable and chivalrous with me. I've never had real chivalry, and, well… feminism aside, I love it. He seems to be pretty future-orientated about us, too. He's keen to give it a go over the summer… I just don't know. I flit between 'I love him!' and 'what an alkie snob'.

We went out again tonight, and surprise surprise, he's wankered. Him and his house mates had had a bottle of vodka EACH before going out. WHAT? That's insane. He then kept doing coke, which was apparently 'only on special occasions'. Like this completely ordinary Saturday night out in Plymouth, you mean? I obviously can't say a word for fear of a repeat of Artie-drugs-over-me-gate.

Mad Dog, Kate and I have got a bit of a revision schedule going (thank god!). We're meeting in *Cuba* during the day… curly fries, diet coke and clinical skills. It's perfect, actually. It's empty, has plenty of room and there's no real expectation for us to spend much with just the right soundtrack to keep us from dying of boredom.

~~~

THURSDAY 5TH MAY 2005 1AM
LISTENING TO I DON'T KNOW WHAT IT IS BY RUFUS WAINWRIGHT

I'm falling for Tom more and more. He's still a full-blown alcoholic, sure, but I'm falling in love with him. I can't believe I'm actually saying this, but I'm dreading the summer. Is it going to end? I can't stand the thought of an enforced break-up. I've just asked him to leave cos I seriously need to get a good night's sleep and get some work done. I do not need drunk, snoring Tom in my single bed, pressing his useless, inebriated boner against me. We failed to have sex AGAIN tonight cos he was too drunk. I was then having a fag out the window with Rufus Wainwright soundtracking our failure to conjugate.

'Sorry, ducky. Just too much to drink, you know.'

I was singing along, and I turned to face him.

'I dunno where to goooooo, but you gotta be there… that's ok, Tom. Don't worry about it.'

'Christ, I hate your singing face. It's so weird.'

I felt so hurt. In a flash, I pictured the hundreds of people who had seen me sing in my life, and before I knew it, I saw their perspective through Tom's eyes.

'Charming. Fuck you.'

'Don't be so defensive, ducky! It's not stopping me falling in love with you. I just thought you'd like to know, your singing face is less than attractive.'

I have become THE most self-conscious singer since that moment. I used to sing without thinking. It was effortless. But now, I hesitate, wondering what everyone else thinks. He took that from me, in a single moment, and I have never managed to uproot his nasty little seed of doubt. No one should ever worry about how they look when they sing. Which is, of course, absurd.

~~~

MONDAY 9TH JUNE 2005 12.30PM
LISTENING TO GOODBYE MY LOVER BY JAMES BLUNT

I woke up to a little note on my pillow this morning from Tom. He'd taken it from a magazine and had written across the top.

```
'I can never find the words so I will
steal these instead.'

Love is all we need. We can conquer
the world, fly to the moon and fetch
the stars from the sky, and yet life
is nothing without love. And without
love, everything is really nothing.
```

It was the medic's summer ball on Saturday, and what a laugh. The ball was standard ball chat, and we left and went to *Cuba*, where I met Tom. On closing, Kate and I recruited a few people who were up for going to the Hoe for drinks and sunrise. Pete Bond, Kate, Mad Dog, Beth, Robin Mills, Frank, Tom, and I headed there with pit stops at people's houses to pick up supplies. Robin arrived with a camping stove and made hot toddies. It was a warm night but cool on the waterfront. We sat on the concrete steps, and I felt so content, nestled in between Tom's legs, listening to the sounds of the waves and my friend's laughter, friends I never thought I'd have. Tom and I swigged on a bottle of neat gin (which was foul and yet Tom managed to put a good chunk of it away). I BLOODY LOVE A SUNRISE! Is there anything more romantic? Clean slate? New day, new start… take a deep breath of sea air and start again.

We walked to McDonald's after sunrise and sat outside, drunk in our formal wear, waiting for it to open for breakfast. What a disgrace. Tom took the words right out of my mouth at one point.

'If my mother could see me now…'

I felt humiliated but also angry that he had sucked some joy out of what had, up until that point, been a perfect night.

~~~

I have one photo from this night, and it was taken at 8am of all of us walking barefoot down Plymouth High Street, heels in hand, happy, dishevelled and squinting in the early morning sunlight.

~~~

I went back to Tom's and slept for a few hours before heading to Kate's. Frank and I baked a cake for Mary's birthday, and oh god… we made such a mess, coating Kate's kitchen with flour and eggshells. Frank and I then slept for another hour on Kate's sofa before making our way back to the Hoe for Mary's birthday with a cake that looked like it had already been eaten. I tried to drink through the pain and enjoy another hilarious evening, but I just couldn't do it. The tiredness punched me in the face about 8ish, and I headed back to my house and messaged Tom.

> `'I am shagged. Heading home. Fancy coming round?'`

> `'Sorry ducky! Massive night out with the boys! It's going to be a late one. Sleep well my angel. X'`

It's probably the ticking time bomb of my imminent departure, but I want to be with him all the time. I want him to be holding me and kissing me ALL THE TIME. ARG! I'm falling for him way too quickly, and I can tell I'm going to get so hurt by this malarkey.

~~~

TUESDAY 17TH MAY 1.50AM
LISTENING TO ALL ABOUT YOU BY MCFLY

It's happened. I LOVE TOM MORRIS. Merde.

I survived my weekend in Cheltenham. Tom and I got the train on Friday and had a lovely dinner with his parents and his brothers in their MASSIVE manor house. We all got on so well, and his dad then gave us a lift to the pub where Tom's school friends were. Including Jules (or Jawls as Tom pronounces it). Obviously she was CHARMING and so pleased to meet me and see Tom so happy. And I was OBVIOUSLY charming back, and we were BFFs before the end of the night. God, I hate my woman-kindness.

Saturday: We went for a big walk and pub lunch with his parents.

Sunday: Tom and his parents had loads of friends and family for Pimms and croquet on the croquet lawn. They have a fucking croquet lawn! Nothing else happens on that particular patch of grass. Croquet is its sole and only purpose. OF COURSE THEY HAVE A CROQUET LAWN! Who wouldn't, right? I questioned what a lowlife like myself was even doing there, but the sun shone, the drinks flowed, and Tom looked dashing in a cream linen suit. He looked like Jude Law in *The Talented Mr Ripley*. He stayed close to me all day, holding my hand, kissing my cheek, hand in the small of the back, draping his jacket over my shoulder, pouring me a drink… I could get used to this way of life. God, I love him. I can't believe it. I love THE most English man I have ever met.

Monday: We had a leisurely brunch before getting the train back, and I realised I'd lost my train ticket home and had no money. It was mortifying, and his dad had to get me a new last-minute ticket at the price of £100! I felt awful.

~~~

This was on my 'sort out when I get a proper job' list, and after my third real payslip in 2008 (he was too far down the list to be done after the first two), I posted a cheque to Tom's dad.

~~~

We've decided to give it a go over the summer. I can't bear to let 'it' go. I want to spend every second with him, but I know it's only going to make things worse when we have to say our goodbyes on the 31st May. I really don't want to get heartbroken just cos of distance. It just hurts too much.

OH, and he's told me he's going to Cornwall with Cheltenham peeps, including Jules (Jawles!) (NIGHTMARE!!) and Ginevra (Ginny… or Ginné as Tom says it). Ginny is his first and only ex-girlfriend before me and best friends with Jules. DOUBLE NIGHTMARE. He ended it just before Christmas after a two-year relationship, and she still loves him and keeps sending him mixed CDs. I am not pumped about his little jolly away with these two hotties who want my man.

~~~

TOM 'THE TIPPLE' MORRIS

FRIDAY 20TH MAY 2005 2AM
LISTENING TO SOLDIER BY DESTINY'S CHILD (FT T.I. & LIL' WAYNE)

This Tom situation is out of control. It was the medic's 'S' party tonight, and I went as Spotty from SuperTed… full yellow spotted body paint and everything. Kate was a 'shadow' and completely black. We discussed whether or not it was appropriate but decided she was going as a shadow and not 'blacking up'.

~~~

Nothing says young and stupid like an inappropriate fancy dress outfit. Apologies for any offence caused. I can think back to a few low fancy dress points that I would rather not cement in writing. For perspective, this is only a few months after Prince Harry dressed as Hitler, which, we have now been told, was our future King's idea.

~~~

I walked back to Tom's at the end of the night… so drunk… barefoot in the rain with my face and body paint running. It was the first time that I was drunker than him. I actually don't think he was drunk at all, and he had to put up with me. I was soooo annoying.

I was lying in his bed spinning so asked him to tell me a story. I wish I could have recorded it as it was the sweetest, most sincere, loving story I have ever been told. My terrible drunk memory of it is as follows.

'There was once a very handsome duck called Dom. He was a bit of a slag and used to fuck all the other ducks until, one day, he met Cher, a beautiful duck from a northern pond. They fell madly in love and were the envy of all the other ducks in their pond. Dom wanted nothing more than to protect Cher and spend the rest of his little ducky life with her, but sadly, when summer came, Cher had to migrate back to her Scottish flock. Dom and Cher didn't see each other much for nearly three months, BUT they spoke every night, and like all absences, it made their hearts grow fonder. They were finally reunited after their summer apart and lived happily ever after.'

Oh, Tom. I hope that's true. We both said we loved each other tonight, and I think we're both REALLY determined to make it work.

~~~

SUNDAY 22ND MAY 2005 11PM
LISTENING TO NO BRAVERY BY JAMES BLUNT

Tom's a dick. He just came round totally shit-faced and really twitchy... clearly coked up again. On a Sunday. He went up to my room, staggering around and undressing on the way up the stairs. He got naked and then lay on my bed on his back with his flaccid penis, looking at me expectantly. He looked hilarious, and it made me laugh.

'Err... and what do you think you're doing?'

'Come on, ducky... a little lovin' for your boyfriend?'

'WRONG! Not tonight, I'm afraid. You can't just come here and expect sex! Jesus, Tom. You were all sweet and romantic and "I love you" last week and now look! Steep downward trajectory, aye?'

'Just to clarify, I didn't say "I love you" the other night. Just that I was "falling in love with you".'

I wanted to burst into tears. Taking back an "I love you" is the pits.

'You did say "I love you".'

'You were shit-faced. Do you really remember?!'

'Yes, I remember. But if you're actually about to take it back, go ahead.'

I stared at him with my most 'don't you fucking dare' look. He looked around shiftily and embarrassed, but he still had the nerve to power through.

'I just want you to know I'm falling in love with you, but I'm NOT IN LOVE with you.'

Naked. He had the fucking audacity to say that to me stark bollock naked.

'You've made your point. I think you should sleep in your own bed tonight. I'm tired and have a lot of work to do.'

I'm gutted.

~~~

WEDNESDAY 25TH MAY 2005 2.10AM
LISTENING TO BEVERLY HILLS BY WHEEZER

TOM IS SUCH A FUCKING ARSEHOLE! He came round last night, shit-faced (again) and kept saying weird stuff like 'I've heard some really interesting things about you… do you have anything to tell me?' He was really aggressive and kept looking annoyed and suspicious. It made me defensive, but I didn't even know what I was supposedly defending myself about. This went on for hours, and I didn't get anywhere. He eventually said, 'This is pointless if you can't even admit the truth,' and he left. I was left feeling weird and guilty EVEN THOUGH I HAVEN'T DONE ANYTHING WRONG! I was running through every conversation I'd ever had, everything I'd ever done. Had he read my diary again? I read through it again and checked, and there wasn't anything too bad. I tossed and turned all night, getting increasingly pissed off with him and his riddles. How dare he make me feel I've done something wrong without telling me what!

We didn't message all day and I went for a drink with Mad Dog and Kate at *Ride 2* tonight. Tom was there, completely ignoring me. FUCK HIM! So I smashed the 241 pitchers with Mad Dog and Kate. I was pretty drunk but not that drunk when I slipped coming back from the bar (pitcher in each hand), lurched forwards and whacked my head on one of the low metal coffee tables. I didn't knock myself out, but I was pretty stunned and bleeding fairly profusely from a rapidly developing egg in the middle of my forehead. I felt sick and awful, and there was a lot of fuss and hands and napkins being pressed into my face. And just when I thought I'd reached peak humiliation, Tom broke my heart. I saw him look over at me, sat on the floor, soaked in blood and Long Island Iced Teas, and we locked eyes for a split second. I registered what my paranoid android brain thought was disgust, saw him smirk and then turn his back on me. WHAT IS GOING ON? Every bit of me wanted to cry with the shame of it all. And just when I thought I couldn't feel more embarrassed, I looked up to see Artie and his beautiful blue eyes, helping me to my feet. I felt a bit dazed but ok and wanted nothing more than to get out of there and forget it had ever happened. Artie insisted on walking me home, and I assumed Tom just kept drinking.

'How's your head? It's looking errrr ... ok-ish. Should I let Bruce or Lou or Ellie know you're coming home? Or your boyfriend?'

'Thanks, Artie, but I'm ok. Tom was actually there and didn't seem too bothered.'

'You're kidding? Maybe he didn't see? You want me to stay with you?'

'Thank you, but I'll be fine... just a bruised ego.'

We then walked for about ten minutes before Artie broke the silence.

'I'm sorry how things ended with us, by the way. I know I hurt you, and I never wanted to. I wasn't in a great place last year. It's not an excuse, but I really did care for you and didn't mean for it to end the way it did.'

'That's sweet, but it feels like a lifetime ago now. No hard feelings.'

He gave me a one-armed hug, and it was as if Tom knew he had to break it up, for he rang mid-hug. He was drunk and slurring and aggressive.

'I just wanted to check you're not passed out in a gutter or something.'

'What has gotten into you? I'm fine, thanks. Artie of all people is walking me home!'

'That's just typical of you! Put him on!'

'Fine!'

I passed Artie the phone, who looked horrified and like he wanted to evaporate. I watched him listening for a while before he spoke. He was calm and… oh how I've missed him. Tom was blowing his top, and Artie… sweet, soothing and collected. Artie had no bravado to flaunt and didn't feel the need to wave his ball sack around (metaphorically).

'Look, Tom. I'm no threat, man. I'm just getting her home cos she's still bleeding, and her head doesn't look too good…'

I then heard Tom say, 'Well, I'm home, and she's not bleeding here, is she?!' before hanging up.

As soon as Artie dropped me home, I thanked him, waited five mins, then I turned around and marched to Tom's.

'What is going on?!'

'I heard you've been cheating on me!'

'WHAT?! I'M NOT CHEATING ON YOU. I HAVE NEVER EVEN A BIT CHEATED ON YOU!'

'Bruce told me that you were a liar and that you still love Artie and that you apparently love Pete AND Frank and you and Robin had sex recently, and you're shagging "other blokes"!'

I couldn't believe it. I had smoke billowing out of my nostrils. I wanted to kill him.

'We've all got a past, Tom, but the only person I have loved or been with since I've been with you, is you! Fuck this, Tom!

I'm not justifying myself. You're listening to Bruce over me! AND ROBIN! It would be like shagging my brother! Look at my head! Do you have any idea how it felt to be sat bleeding on the floor and have you look at me with such disdain before turning your back on me? What happened to 'protect you and live happily ever after?'. What happened to 'I'm falling in love with you?'.

I was furious. I was seeing red, but Bruce… wait until I get my hands on that fucking tubular mother fucker!

'I can't even look at you, Tom. Everything's ruined. I'm going to go now <deep breath> and we'll talk tomorrow.'

'Why? So we can break up? Let me save you the trouble…'

'Oh, it's no trouble. It's over. This is unfixable.'

'No shit. Cheating'll do that to a relationship.'

I stormed home, barged into Bruce's room and started to slap and hit his sleeping, lying cunt of a body! I hated him! How dare he ruin my relationship! I went full psycho. You think all women are mind-fuck-psychos? I'll show you psycho! I was shaking, I was so angry. Once fully awake, he was quickly able to restrain me and sat me in the kitchen for a chat. Apparently, he had genuinely believed all this. I've bullet-pointed below how Bruce 'THE FUCKING GENIUS' O'Neil came to these conclusions and, worse, took it upon himself to tell my boyfriend.

- 'I cheat on Tom': These very general, non-specific and bullshit claims had come from… drumroll… Detective Big Dick Dave. Sorry, what? I haven't seen BDD in over a year! As soon as Bruce said it out loud, he admitted that this was, on reflection, not a reliable source.

- 'I love Frank': Bruce and Frank had bumped into each other pissed in the *Union* a few weeks ago, and Frank then told Bruce about how I'd tried it on with him (twice). I reminded Bruce that he already knew this, and it was from ages ago and not recently. Ah yes…

- 'I love Pete': He had only said that Pete and I spent a lot of time together and that it was suspicious. Didn't I fancy him too? Well, yes, but… AGES AGO.
- 'I love Artie': I glossed over this one a little…
- 'Shagging Robin': Bruce stood there stroking his half-baked, baby face, looking puzzled, trying to remember about Robin. 'Didn't you tell me you'd shagged Robin?'

I was gobsmacked. WHAT. AN. IDIOT.

'NO BRUCE. I DIDN'T!'

He looked pretty sheepish.

'Ah. Sorry Claire. I'll call Tom. I'll sort this. I'm so so sorry! I'll sort it. I promise.'

~~~

WEDNESDAY 25TH MAY 2005 8PM
LISTENING GALVANIZE BY THE CHEMICAL BROTHERS

I woke up this morning with the mother of all headaches, and I looked HORRENDOUS! I had about a dozen messages from Tom apologising and the last one saying he was coming over.

Outside my door was a tray with orange juice, two paracetamols, a card from Bruce, an enormous bunch of peonies and a new dairy (with beautiful red and gold embroidery).

```
Card from Bruce: I just wanted to
say that I'm really sorry for being
a twat!! I never meant to say what I
said to Tom. It wasn't my place to
say anything and I should never have
thought that of you in the first place.
I was just being drunk and a dick
head! Don't expect you to forgive me,
```

```
but I needed to say sorry to you. Is
there anything I can do... just let me
know. I think I've sorted it with Tom.
```
Bruce xxx

Tom came round, and he was also very sheepish and apologetic. He told me he'd only believed Bruce cos he was falling in love with me and he used it as an excuse to get out of the relationship without being the dickhead. He realised he didn't want to lose me, and PLEASE, WILL I GO BACK OUT WITH HIM? How could I say no? I (of course) got back with him but couldn't shake the image of him looking down at me, bleeding, with a smirk on his face.

~~~

SUNDAY 29TH MAY 2005 8.30PM
LISTENING TO ORDINARY PEOPLE BY JOHN LEGEND

I finished my ISCE exam on Friday and phew - I think I didn't fluff it. It actually went quite well. Since Tom and I got back together, he's let me practise all my examinations on him. He thought it was 'sexy', which was weird. The egg on my head was flat-ish again, and I was able to cover up the bruising with some of Ellie's mega make-up. I am so relieved it went ok. Maybe. Just maybe, me being a medical student isn't a fluke. Maybe I could actually do this. MAYBE I could be a not totally shit doctor one day.

The medics and I then went to *Ride 2* for post-exams drinks. Boy, do I love post-exam euphoria. We sat, basking in the beer garden sunshine with enough cocktails to drown even Tom. It was BLISS. No more exams. Hello summer, give us a kiss. I danced all night, then went back to Tom's and had sex all night.

I spent all of yesterday in bed with him, and we even toyed with using Nutella, but my clean freak gene got the better of me… just think of the mess. So, normal sex instead. We had some strange conversations in our sleep deprived bedlam. We talked about what we'd change about each other.

'I wish you'd drink less.'

He looked at me, and for a split second, I thought he was going to get pissed off. But he just kissed me.

'I know… I wish your singing face looked different.'

I frowned.

'I find that weirdly upsetting. I can't change my singing face! The whole point is that I'm not thinking and just enjoying myself!'

'Haha, ducky! You're so sensitive! No, seriously, I would change where you're from so that you weren't going to Scotland for the summer.'

'And France…'

'Fuck. And France.'

'Well, you can't change that either. Just keep it together over the summer, and I'll be in Exeter in September.'

'It'll work, ducky. And actually, if I'm honest, I would never change you. I'd pay for you to be you, exactly the way you are.'

'Are you quoting films at me?'

'Nonsense.'

'Yes, you are!!!! That's what Mark Darcy said in Bridget Jones!'

'Never seen it.'

'Bollocks.'

We both spent the weekend ignoring the fact that the end was nigh.

I woke up this morning, and I felt ripped in half. How can this be the end? I helped him pack, and his dad arrived to finish up. Oh god. I had a huge lump in my throat, and we couldn't even look at each other when his dad fished the pot of Nutella out of the bed.

'You know they make chocolate for this purpose rather than wasting the good Nutella?'

Haha. Brilliant. We all laughed, and I kissed Tom goodbye.

I walked home listening to James Blunt and got myself into a complete state. Fucking Blunters…

I miss Tom so so much already. This is the first time where I feel like we like each other the same. With every single past relationship I can (without hesitating) say who liked the other person more. But with Tom, it's even. AH GAWD!!!!!! It hurts so much.

~~~

MONDAY 30TH MAY 2005 1.30AM
LISTENING TO NUMBER ONE BY JOHN LEGEND (FEAT. KANYE WEST)

This SUCKS! Tom just called, and we talked for nearly two hours. I miss him so much, and I'm terrified that it's not going to work. Absolutely petrified. Listening to John Legend and Blunters on loop isn't helping. Just to clarify for no one but possibly future me… I am saying 'Blunters' ironically. I'm not there yet. Let me be Mrs Morris for twenty years before poshisms like that pass my lips.

He's back in Plymouth on Friday for his disciplinary but I'll be in Exeter for my Induction to Clinical Care week. FUCK I'm going to miss him.

~~~

But of course! The disciplinary. I can't believe I didn't write about this. I only have the faintest memory of what actually happened, but it boiled down to arson. Tom and his flatmates set fire to something in their kitchen. They were drunk (of course), and I wasn't there, but I believe it had been started deliberately. I'm not sure I ever knew why, but it had got slightly out of control, they ran outside, and the relevant services were called. Terrifyingly, there was a sleeping house mate who no one had thought of and who was unaware of the fire. Fortunately, no one was hurt, but there was significant damage to the flat, and the potential repercussions were chilling.

The boys were threatened with expulsion and various serious criminal charges, but posh boys being posh boys never have quite the same consequences for their actions. They denied the hell out of it, the mummies and the daddies came to their rescue, and Teflon Tom The Tipple got away with arson.

~~~

I can't stop crying. This is awful. I LOVE HIM! Oh Tom, come back!

~~~

TUESDAY 7TH JUNE 2005 3.30AM
LISTENING TO MONEY DON'T MATTER BY THE MARTIN HARLEY BAND

I went to Charlestown in Cornwall for the weekend with Pete, Robin, Frank, Connie, Wej, Mad Dog and Kate. We went to see Red House play in a pub, having followed them from Plymouth… the most traject of groupies. We got a bonfire going on the beach and all slept cuddled up. We were lucky enough to sleep for about an hour before being awoken, covered in these hairy caterpillars that the fire seemed to be attracting and the start of an almighty downpour. WE DID NOT SLEEP. But what fun.

I'm losing Tom. Our chat on the phone last night was so weak and tonight was even worse.

'I really miss you, Tom.'

'Of course you do. Everyone does.'

Am I crazy to have hoped for an 'I miss you too, ducky'? I was not impressed. There was not one kind word from him. What's happened? Is it Jules or Ginny? He was so argumentative tonight, trying to pick a fight with me. The FUCKER. Is he trying to get me to break up with him? He's blatantly having doubts about me. I just need to see him and kiss him, and everything'll be fine.

~~~

FRIDAY 10TH JUNE 2005 3.30AM
LISTENING TO TEARS AND RAIN BY JAMES BLUNT

I just watched *Closer*. Is it the most depressing depiction of love and what it does to people? Yes. Yes, it is. It was all about unreciprocated love, jealousy and breakup. It was harrowing. It makes me never want to fall in love again. I don't think I could cope with an 'I don't love you anymore' or 'I love someone else now'.

I can feel my desperation rising with Tom. I'm going to blow it with my ugly insecurities.

~~~

SUNDAY 12TH JUNE 2005 11.20AM
LISTENING TO GHETTO GOSPEL BY 2PAC FT ELTON JOHN

Last night ESCALATED. It'll be a fucking miracle if I get my deposit back now. Everyone has pretty much left Plymouth, and it is bleak. Frank, Kate, Trigger and I are the only ones left, so I suggested we, once and for all, try to recreate the painting in Ride. It's basically the imprint of two naked bodies, and we've been talking about doing it all year. I have rolls of paper we could roll in the courtyard, and all my house mates have left… We also decided a little Dutch courage was in order before essentially getting naked and lathering ourselves up with paint. As it was our last night, we got all the leftover booze from our respective houses and got stuck in at mine. Urg… so many warm, half-open bottles of wine…

It got very silly very quickly. Frank had brought pink and

yellow poster paint, and by 4am, we were naked and squirting paint at each other in my shitty pebble-dashed courtyard. I'm not even sure what the painting looked like in the end, but I have never laughed so hard. I thought the 'damage' would be minimal given that we were outside, but I had underestimated the courtyard-to-shower transition with four drunk people covered top to toe in paint. The house looked like the scene of an Oompa Loompa massacre. I've just spent an hour trying to clean up and all I feel like I'm doing is smearing and spreading it around further. Goodbye, deposit.

Fucking hilarious, though.

TWENTY - EIGHT
EDINBURGH FRINGE

MONDAY 13TH JUNE 2005 00.15AM
LISTENING TO CARNIVAL GIRL BY THE MARTIN HARLEY BAND

I'm back in Edinburgh, and I feel bereft. I'll never live with Ellie, Bruce, Mark and Lou again, I might not ever see them at all! I'm not going to see Mad Dog, Kate, Robin and Pete until September! And Frank is going to Truro!

I'm missing Tom terribly, but that is such boring chat from me. Am I really going to write 'I miss Tom' every day this summer? Get a grip, Claire. Repeat after me: 'No, I won't'.

~~~

WEDNESDAY 15TH JUNE 2005
LISTENING TO DON'T PLAY NICE BY VERBALICIOUS

I've just realised that Tom is a disgusting cunt of a man. I am speechless by how opinionated, image-conscious and superficial he is. He told me that he would break up with me if I put on weight over the summer (even a little) or if I cut my hair short.

'The simple fact, ducky, is that all fat people are ugly. Looks ARE important, and anyone who says otherwise is lying. I wouldn't go near a girl if I didn't feel like she looked good on my arm.'

I'm horrified. He just wants a trophy girlfriend that other people would be jealous of. Admittedly, yes, it is a massive compliment to me (I've never considered myself like that!) but WHAT A DICKHEAD! Why am I still with him? He told me he thought 'our phone conversations are awful'. Why is he with me? My phone conversations ARE my personality! Does it really not matter?! The sheer shallowness is staggering. Guys like him used to ruin my life. How am I so easily letting my morals slide now? Stick some chocolatey abs and a cheeky grin on the devil, and I'm all his.

~~~

FRIDAY 17TH JUNE 2005 1AM
LISTENING TO HEY MAN (NOW YOU'RE REALLY LIVING) BY THE EELS

Oh, Tom is PISSING ME OFF! He's been a nightmare all week. Getting hold of him is bad enough, and then we have nothing to say to each other before invariably hanging up with a sour taste in our mouths.

```
Text from Tom 16/6/05 - Maybe we should
try having a chat rather than just
citing what we've done during the day!
```

Tom called tonight when Next Door Andy and I were on the way to the pub, and I said I'd call him back when we got there. Andy let me use his phone cos I'd blitzed my credit (again). I stood outside Scruffy's and called Tom back. I didn't mention anything about my day and told him I couldn't be long cos I hadn't been in and said hi to everyone yet, and I was on ND Andy's phone.

When I came out of Scruffy's a few hours later, I had two texts from Tom:

21.09 Fuck it. We'll speak Sunday. Not sure what u think a chat is but talking at me for 4 mins with the only question being what time can I call for a chat is hardly the foundation of a great relationship.

22.45 How can you tell your friends I'm fine if you have no idea what I do each day or how I feel? Been bothering me since we left Plymouth.

Text to Tom: How dare you? You're harder to contact than the bloody queen! I feel like I'm always making all the effort - I always ask how you are and what you've been doing. You're ALWAYS the one that doesn't answer / isn't in / has to go / can't talk / don't call back. You criticise everything and I don't know how to talk to you anymore! What do you expect?

From Tom: I expect a little give and take. Everything is always about you.

To Tom: That's not fair and that's not true. I feel like you're trying to pick a fight. You're making things so difficult with all this pressure to 'have a good chat'. It's not exactly relaxing.

He hasn't replied. I am DEFINITELY falling out of love with him.

~~~

SATURDAY 18TH JUNE 2005 2AM
LISTENING TO STAY WITH YOU BY JOHN LEGEND

So I'm the problem. Of course, I am. I have just spent the last few hours grovelling on my metaphorical hands and knees. Tom lectured me about how I talk too much and that he can't get a word in edgeways, and that even when I ask a question, I don't listen to the answer. Sounds like me. I know I do this. I'm such a dick. I get excited and chatty, and I know I get easily distracted in conversations, but it's not because I don't care. I'm going to make such an effort to talk less.

~~~

Although there is truth to my sometimes excitable distractibility (and this was not the last time I've been pulled up on it), Tom's intimidation here is disgusting. I am not blameless, but I don't want to hear nineteen-year-old me write, 'I'm going to talk less'. I don't want to use popularisms like 'gaslighting' or 'toxic masculinity'… they are overused and are losing their impact… however…

Maybe I could make up my own term? Poisoned manhood? Testo-warfare? Chauvinist dosing?

~~~

But despite it all, I miss him. Tom has weakened me. In fact, I think Edinburgh weakens me. I get home and remember how I was pre-uni, how I felt. Edinburgh is my kryptonite. Edinburgh makes me feel small.

~~~

SATURDAY 25TH JUNE 2005 1AM
LISTENING TO BEST OF YOU BY FOO FIGHTERS

Tom's pushing his luck. He's either breaking up with me, or he's lying, comatose, in a hospital bed following some freak accident.

'I'll call you tomorrow' was the last sign of life on Wednesday evening, and there has been NOTHING since then. He's told me he's writing me a letter too. Not a good sign, I don't think. I know he's a massive coward… surely he's not breaking up with me by letter?! If he does, I'll shred his fucking balls.

~~~

MONDAY 27TH JUNE 2005 2AM
LISTENING TO ALRIGHT BY JOHN LEGEND

Well, it happened. Tom and I aren't together anymore. My letter theory wasn't correct, but he FINALLY called today.

'I'm not sure this is going to work over the summer.'

'No, I'm not sure either. You're not coming to Edinburgh then? You said you'd booked a train?'

'I was going to*, I'm just not sure I can do this. I wonder if we should go on a break for the summer.'

*LYING PIECE OF SHIT

'If you can't 'do' the summer, it's over - we break up. I'm not pressing pause for the summer to allow you to have guilt-free fucks with Jules and Ginny before crawling back into my bed in September.'

'That is out of order! I don't want to break up.'

'Either we make an effort and stay together, or it's over.'

'I guess it's over then.'

'I guess it is.'

Did he just make me break up with him? I feel tricked. I can't believe it's over. Fuck. It's hit me.

```
Text from Tom: Listening to James and
thinking of you. Hope you're ok. I
don't think I am x
```

~~~

TUESDAY 28TH JUNE 2005 6PM
LISTENING TO PLEASE BY PETE MURRAY

Chloe and I walked into town together last night, and I was ranting and raving about Tom.

'...And he's probably going to start shagging *Ginerva* or *Jawles* again…'

'Hold on. Is "Ginny's" full name Ginerva? And she's from Cheltenham? And Tom is her ex? OH MY GOD, CLAIRE!!!! YOUR "GINNY" IS MY HOUSE MATE 'GINERVA' IN LEEDS! YOU'RE THE CLAIRE THAT STOLE HER BOYFRIEND?!'

Speechless didn't even come close. Neither of us had made the connection. I was not surprised to hear that the level of contact with Ginny has been much higher than I had been led to believe, and although I was the official girlfriend, the main fight was between Jules and Ginny. I was never a threat at all. A solid third place. Tom's a massive, MASSIVE fuck head.

~~~

WEDNESDAY 29TH JUNE 2005
LISTENING TO REFUGE (WHEN IT'S COLD OUTSIDE) BY JOHN LEGEND

```
Text from Tom: still constantly think-
ing of you. As far as I'm concerned
we're on a break. Not broken up xxx
```

How on earth are all these texts supposed to ease the transition? Man, I'd love some drugs right now. I wish they weren't bad for you. I have quite liked being off the weed this year, and I don't really want to, but I would love to just get off my face right now.

~~~

FRIDAY 1ST JULY 2005 3AM
LISTENING TO SUGAR, WE'RE GOING DOWN BY FALL OUT BOY

I am wrecked. Been drinking all day with Next Door Andy on his roof, then went to a comedy gig with Maggie, Herbert and Hector. I could barely see straight. I was so drunk I had to watch it all with one eye shut.

I'm annoyed with myself for texting Tom, too. Ahhh, I wish I could suck it back out of my phone.

```
Text to Tom: At a comedy gig and the
comedian is from Cheltenham. He is NOT
funny and keeps comparing Virgin Me-
gastore to Cheltenham Ladies College.
You'd probably guffaw. I miss you x
```

No text back. Fuck.

~~~

SATURDAY 2ND JULY 2005 2AM
LISTENING TO FEELING GOOD INC BY GORILLAZ

Chloe just told me that the fucking beautiful/model/billionaire Ginny got drunk, instructed Tom that they were 'almost definitely going to have sex tonight' and then confessed her undying love to him… one guess as to what happened there. It makes me sick thinking of him with someone else. They apparently used to spend

HOURS on the phone to each other every night when we were together. Time to move the fuck on, Claire. I think it's in part the rejection that's making me want him more. I'm such a 'want what you can't have' cliché!

Eep, I have to get up in three hours, Herbie and I are going to watch the Rugby early doors.

~~~

WEDNESDAY 6TH JULY 2005 5AM
LISTENING TO THIS MODERN LOVE BY BLOC PARTY

Maggie and I spent the day together and ended up in a lock-in at the *Bailey* with some hot guy called Grant, who got us free drinks all night. I had a cheeky snog with him before stumbling home with Maggie at 4am. She's snoring next to me now. I love her, and I want to keep her forever.

~~~

SATURDAY 9TH JULY 2005 2AM
LISTENING TO I FELL IN LOVE WITH A GIRL BY THE WHITE STRIPES

Hector Mckellen feels insulted… sorry… 'DISGUSTED', not to feature in my diary. He was so hungover at work in Millets today he vomited in a Wellington boot. Standard.

Hector and I went out with Herbert and Maggie tonight, danced all night and then came back and we're watching a film hoping to sober up pre-bed (the bed part shall not be together).

TWENTY - NINE
SEXY LAURENT

SUNDAY 10TH JULY 2005
LISTENING TO BAIL ME OUT BY PETE MURRAY

I'm in the south of France now, and I am going to do some work. There's nothing else to do, so I may as well knuckle down before going to Brittany, where there will be no knuckling down whatsoever. Knuckle up?

Just boshed through lung function tests and the aetiology of diabetes. Slap my thigh and call me doctor why don't ya.

```
Text from Tom: Hey. I hope you're ok.
I'm looking forward to seeing you when
you get back. Actually, I can't wait
to see you. I've written 5 letters to
you, all of which are in the bin. This
is bloody hard xxx
```

Good. I'm glad he's finding it 'bloody hard'.

~~~

WEDNESDAY 13TH JULY 2005 2AM
LISTENING TO SO BEAUTIFUL BY PETE MURRAY

I am soooo bored. Time is crawling along so slowly here.

Got a call from Sexy Laurent tonight. Him and Marie are 'on a break' (1998 called, and they want their Friends material back), so I, at least, won't have to deal with her this summer. We're going for a drink tomorrow. I bet he's got sexier.

~~~

The 'on a break' episode actually aired in February 1997. It doesn't matter of course, but for purist's sake...

~~~

THURSDAY 14TH JULY 2005 4.30AM
LISTENING TO I LIKE THE WAY BY BODYROCKERS

I've just had an amazing night with Sexy Laurent. Summer lovin' since 2001... He picked me up at 8pm, and it felt old school, and we slipped right back into it. He had a chilled bottle of wine and we went and sat on the beach in Nice and watched the fireworks. We chatted and it was so easy between us. Sounds like things are difficult with Marie. Then went to Villefranche, got a cocktail and stayed on the beach chatting until 3.30am. It was pretty wonderful. And, OF COURSE, he got sexier.

He's just dropped me off, and we kissed in the car... for the millionth time in our lives. Easy breezy. This is so exciting! Tom who?

~~~

FRIDAY 15TH JULY 2005 1AM
LISTENING TO ROAD TO NOWHERE BY TALKING HEADS

Just spent another night with Sexy Laurent. Went to his, watched a film, had a little cuddle and a kiss. Not a lot to report. Thinking back, I think we only ever had sex that one time... actually now I think about it, it was the 14th of July 2002? 2003? And my vague memory was that it was TERRIBLE. Something isn't quite right with him. He kisses weird for a start. But there are a lot of great things about him. But who cares? I'm not marrying him. Although I do kiss him a lot and this is the thing I don't love. Oh, for fuck's sake, Claire - stop over analysing.

```
Text from Sexy Laurent: Je passe vrai-
ment de bon moments avec toi. Je te
trouve vraiment super. Bonne Nuit.
```

~~~

SATURDAY 16TH JULY 2005 2.30AM
LISTENING TO LONELY BY AKON

Sexy Laurent and I had a scorching day at the beach in Monaco. We were having a drink this evening before heading back when out of the blue he gets a text from Marie saying she saw us out together and that she was going to take some pills cos there's no point being on this earth anymore. Not this again, surely? Does Sexy Laurent take the bait? Bien sur! He then spent the whole evening on the phone while I sat by myself and sipped at a single pastis for over 2 hours. I'd have gone home, but he kept throwing apologetic gestures my way... and I didn't have a car. So I waited. He then told me that I shouldn't leave the house by myself cos 'she'll get me'. My eyes hurt from rolling so hard. The tiny little French girl? She'd collapse if I exhaled at her. I'd like her to try 'and get me'... immature little bitch. I'd have her for my gouté.

~~~

Ohhhh, tough guy talk. Marie was tiny, but she was vicious, and if it had ever come down to it… who knows.

~~~

But I feel bad for Sexy Laurent. He's getting all this grief because of me, and I'm not worth it. I'll be gone again soon, and he'll be left with this natural disaster of a relationship to deal with. I told him as much tonight, and he kinda agreed.

~~~

MONDAY 18TH JULY 2005 00.10AM
LISTENING TO PUSHING THE SENSES BY FEEDER

Tom called this morning.

'Hey, ducky. How's France?'

Gulp. His voice… his voice that I used to hate so much, brings a lump in my throat.

'Hey, you. It's great, thanks. I reckon I've out-browned you…'

He laughed… beautiful little chuckle.

'C'est pas possible mon petit choufleur!'

'Oh ho! We're speaking French now, aye?'

'Indeed we are. We can't have French guys getting in my way…'

I didn't say anything, and the resulting silence went on for an eternity before he cleared his throat.

'I miss you. I'm still thinking of this as a break… It doesn't feel so long until we see each other again.'

'You know what I think about that.'

'I know. But I want you to know what I think. I haven't given up on us.'

And just like that, all the work I'd put into getting over Tom evaporated.

Sexy Laurent and I went to the beach today. I couldn't stop thinking about Tom, and he didn't stop talking about Marie. We didn't kiss or touch each other. We knew...

```
Text from Tom: Hey. No doubt you've
had another amazing, lazy day in the
French sun. Fantastic how midday
drinking ruins you (moi). P.s I can't
wait to win you back. Sleep well.
```

Goddamn him. As if he'll have kept his grubby little mits of Jules and Ginny. His little groupies worry me. They're all young, rich, stick thin and beautiful... and they all love Tom.

~~~

TUESDAY 19TH JULY 2005 00:00
LISTENING TO LOSE CONTROL BY MISSY ELLIOT (FT CIARA & FAT MAN SCOOP)

Well, slap my arse and call me Bob! Who passed year 2? This bitch baby! Oh Yeah! I am so relieved. Bring on third year - I NEVER thought I would get this far. I hope everyone else passed without any problems. Definitely going to do some work tomorrow.

```
Text to Tom: Greetings from the land
the Olympics forgot. Win me back aye?
A prize am I... careful now Tom... ps.
Had duck for dinner and felt terribly
guilty x

From Tom: Can't believe Ducky had Duck
for supper. No way I'm losing you.
Hence win you back. Would give one of
my arms to have you lying in the oth-
er. Sleep well Xx Xx
```

Surprisingly poetic. I'm like fucking putty in his hands. Right, I should probably head to Bedfordshire to have confused dreams about Tom, Sexy Laurent, and exams.

THIRTY
ST JACUT

FRIDAY 22ND JULY 2005 10PM
LISTENING TO IN THE MORNING BY THE CORAL

I'm on the train, and I'll be in St Jacut in just over an hour. I AM THE MOST EXCITED PERSON IN THE WHOLE WORLD. I MIGHT EXPLODE!

I had my last night with Sexy Laurent yesterday. We went to see Fantastic 4, then ended up in a grunge bar. Sexy Laurent is SUCH AN ANNOYING drunk. Then Marie called with her usual drama, and we headed home. We had a very brief kiss goodbye, but neither of us were bothered. See ya next year... unless I've met the love of my life.

~~~

Aw... which I had.

~~~

ST JACUT

THURSDAY 28TH JULY 2005 1AM
LISTENING TO MONKEY MAN BY TOOTS AND THE MAYTALS FEAT NO DOUBT

Early night tonight, so I'm going to take the opportunity to try and sum up the last few nights of drunken debauchery in St Jacut de la Mer. This place is my nemesis. Whatever Edinburgh does to me, St Jac does the opposite. It unleashes my angels… my demons… EVERYTHING. It turns me up, and I become an exaggerated (probably very annoying) version of myself.

Sat night: *St Awawa* bar with Marc and Les Marseillais (Seb and Ben). Ben, Marc and I got fucked, and poor Seb was left picking up our drunken pieces again, desperately trying to stop Marc and Ben from killing themselves. Yannick and Gael came and joined us later. Yannick is ageing well. He's one of those guys who'll always look good. Gael hasn't changed, and I'll always feel a little pang when I see him and remember how much I loved him and how terribly I treated him in Edinburgh… pauvre Gael.

My heart is twice as big when I'm with them all. The comfort, and love, and excitement I feel with Marc is unparalleled. I think he is my person. On *St Awawa* closing, we all went to a big house party at Charles' house. Nico was there looking hot and hairy and dishevelled… that 'I've just been windsurfing in a storm' look that I go gaga for. I had a catch-up with him, and although I felt myself drawn to him, I was conscious of my shit-faced level being high and how not up for that he was last year. Anyway, the night descended into pure chaos… messy messy. By 4am, I felt a bit overwhelmed, and Marc and I found a quiet room at the back of the house and spent the rest of the night drinking Ricard and playing caps. I think my heaven would be playing caps and drinking with Marc. It's astonishing that I don't fancy him really given that I love him so much. Would I kill for him? Given the right circumstances… I'm not ruling it out.

Sunday night: Got trashed again. Marc, Petit Flo, and I ended up stranded in this rural club cos everyone was too drunk to drive. Marc tried to convince me to drive us all home cos I was able to stand on one leg marginally longer than they could. I had enough sense, at least, to say no, what a terrible fucking idea. We slept in his car, the three of us giggling and smoking a massive spliff.

Monday night: Seb and I had a quiet night playing some pool at *Le Dauphin* with a pot of verveine menthe. Finally, some reprieve from the excess. I need Seb in my life.

Tuesday night: Marc and I teamed up for the pétanque tournament. We drank an absolute fuck tonne of Pastis in the sunshine and didn't do too badly at all. We had dinner at mine with the family, then back out to another drunken mess of a party at Charles'. Name it, we drank it. Aie! We stumbled to the end of the peninsula with Petit Flo and Ben for sunrise at 7am. It was perfect. It's the only time when my brain is quiet. The world feels still, the sun is peeking out over the horizon, and I am not thinking about anything outside that exact moment in time.

~~~

It's called mindfulness; give it ten years, and it's an inescapable concept.

~~~

Wednesday night: Went to St Briac for moules frites with Marc, Les Pernards, Les Marseillais, Petit Flo and Les Belges. I've just got home, and I'm so so tired... my bones throb from exhaustion. Not sure how much longer I can keep this up. And yet, I feel like we're only just getting started with François arriving tomorrow - YAY!

As for Tom, not a peep out of him in just over a week. Fuck him.

~~~

ST JACUT

SUNDAY 31ST JULY 2005 7PM
LISTENING TO PRESSURE DROP BY TOOTS AND THE MAYTALS FEAT ERIC CLAPTON

I'm dying... my liver, my head, my kidneys, my brain, my body... AHHHHH. Hosted my apero* on Thursday night, which was a big success. There were about thirty of us in the end, and I made a rum punch that was... punchy. There isn't actually much to say. Same same same. Drunk, stoned, bar, beach, bonfire, sunrise.

~~~

*An aperitif, bien sûr.

~~~

Friday night was chilled, and I spent the evening with Mamie, Papy, Mum, Chloe and the cousins - didn't even get pissed off with anyone.

Last night was carnage. Why do I keep doing this to myself? I'm unstoppable. I've got a bit of a crush on Clément. He's just so mature and charming, but the maturity probably comes with his age... is he nearly thirty?! I can't be arsed with any summer romance, though. Being single is so much simpler... you don't get hurt, and your heart doesn't weep.

François and I 'did' another bet, and we 'had' to pull. It was quite nice, actually. Dangerous territory, though. Then François and Ben both puked in the sea. What a disgrace.

~~~

MONDAY 1ST AUGUST 2005 1AM
LISTENING TO WISEMEN BY JAMES BLUNT

I miss my medic crew. I miss Pete and Robin and Mad Dog and Kate. It rained today, and with it, the joy in my life was washed away. It's like I'm solar-powered.

François, Marc and I chain-smoked through limitless espressos and games of pool at *Le Dauphin*. I think we were all a bit broken. I realised towards the end of the afternoon that we just continued on autopilot… smoking… another round of coffees… racking up another game… me to break… and repeat… without a word. It was easy, though, and so comfortable. I pulled them both in for a hug and nuzzled my face into their chests. Mes grands frères: I love them. They held me tight, and we all released and continued… another cigarette… Marc to break. We didn't need to say 'I love you'. It was obvious. I'll always love them.

Found out Clément fancies Chloe. This is new…

~~~

TUESDAY 2ND AUGUST 2005 4AM
LISTENING TO REDEMPTION SONG BY BOB MARLEY & THE WAILERS

Something's wrong. I'm feeling really off. It's probably cos I've drunk a year's worth of booze in ten days, but still… I feel so self-conscious about myself, and I don't feel like I've got the French to express myself properly. I'm only ever at 90%. It's making me calm (bad, boring, insecure, calm) and quiet, and I can feel myself not being fun, which I HATE. Spirit Claire is withering… as is this fucking pen… for fuck's sake. Pen two. Seb is leaving on Wednesday, and I should use him as an example of calm. I don't write entry after entry about him getting shit-faced and seeing yet another sunrise with me, but he is everything. I'm going to be miserable without him. OH MY GOD, NOW THIS PEN TOO. Marc and I feel more distant this year, although I'm fully aware that it's me who is distant. Don't die, Claire - get a fucking grip of yourself. Pen two is now allowed to die. It has served its purpose in allowing me to write FUCK ALL OF ANY CONSEQUENCE ONCE AGAIN.

~~~

WEDNESDAY 3RD AUGUST 2005 5AM
LISTENING TO SWEET AND DANDY BY TOOTS AND THE MAYTALS

I spent the day doing 18 holes of golf with Marc, Yannick, Ben, Seb, François and Nico. I was surrounded by the most perfect of friends, breathtaking scenery and a cloudless sky. We headed straight to the other Claire's for drinks, and I spent hours playing drunken badminton with some rusty rackets across a clothesline. Chloe and Clement pulled. She is LITERALLY half his age… ish… maybe. But she's beautiful, the sun shines out of her skin, and I love her… so fine!

THIRTY-ONE RIBS

FRIDAY 5TH AUGUST 2005 7PM
LISTENING TO BAM BAM BY TOOTS AND THE MAYTALS
FEAT SHAGGY, RAHZEL

I cannot even begin to describe the total carnage that was camping on the island last night. Just when I think I can't up the chaos, I up it… a lot. It started like all nights on L'ile D'Eshibiens. Bonfires, whisky, beer, pastis, rum, vodka, Red Bull and enough weed to kill Snoop Dogg. I'm not even sure how, but I think I've broken a couple of ribs… a stupid wrestle with François, Marc and Ben… I think…

I fell down to the sand and watched in slow-mo as Ben came falling back towards me, and all of his weight (which is a lot - maybe 100kg of pure muscle) landed through his elbow onto the front of my chest. I heard a loud crack. It was painful, but I was fairly well anaesthetised at the time that I gave it a little rub and went and sat back down by the fire.

My rib feels VERY FUCKING broken now. The pain just worsened exponentially this morning walking back from the island, but we were all probably still quite pissed. I eventually got into bed about midday today and I woke up a few hours ago. I got some food, and now I'm back in bed… the pain has gradually been building as everything else has been leaving my body. It's absolute agony, and I can actually see the break. There's some genuine chest deformity going on. When will I learn? Surely this is a sign, non? I'm lying in bed now, trying not to move… OWWWW! My mum is going to be super suss about me lying upstairs right now. Get up! Get up!

~~~

7.20pm

Nope. Got halfway down the stairs, and the pain was unbearable. I thought I was going to pass out. It was obvious for all to see. I've said that Ben landed on my chest when we were playing volleyball… not a total lie. Ahhhh… It's excruciating, and I'm tired, and the booze blues are creeping in. Why do I keep doing this to myself?

```
Text to Tom: Hey stranger. How's your
summer going? I'm feeling a little
sorry for myself. Overdoing it and I
think I've cracked a rib. I'm just go-
ing to say it… I miss you xxx

Text from Tom: I know. No matter where
I am or what I'm doing, I end up think-
ing of you. Take care Ducky and I'll
see you soon. xxx
```

~~~

Three separate people told me they went T-total after reading my first book. I'm starting to understand why. The incessant and over-the-top drinking culture of the early noughties is exhausting and humbling.

~~~

6TH AUGUST 2005 11.15PM
LISTENING TO SPEED OF SOUND BY COLDPLAY

Most depressing night ever. The pain in my chest has been ramping up since yesterday, but I decided that if I went out tonight, I could be distracted and drink through it (rather than focus on it at home like I did last night). Plus, I feel like I have to pretend I'm completely fine in front of Mum cos I don't want to hear about what an idiot I am (I already know that). It wasn't working, though, as I was clearly fighting back the tears all day. My mum insisted I went to see the local doctor today, who confirmed that I had 'une belle fracture' and gave me some codeine for the pain. He's also said I'll probably always have a visible bump there… right in the middle of my chest… a constant reminder of what a twat I was aged nineteen. Great.

We all had Festivalas tickets for tonight and I'd been invited for the apèro first at 'the other Claire' and her brother, Fred's house. I got there, and Ben, François and Nico were there too, but otherwise, I didn't know anyone. The other Claire suggested we share a spliff as that will definitely help my muscles relax and help with the pain. I had a small cough, and the sudden pain completely floored me. I felt like I'd been shot in the chest and couldn't take a breath in. I started to cry and panic, and I couldn't move. I was lying in the mud. I couldn't even sit up. Claire was just staring at me, and I heard Nico arrive.

'Bon, Claire. Ca suffit. Je te ramène chez toi.'

~~~

Right. Claire. That's enough. I'm taking you home.

~~~

He scooped me up in his warm bear arms and carried me to his car. I was still crying and said nothing. He plonked me in the passenger seat and got in silently.

'Have you seen what a state you're in? Why do you do this to yourself? It upsets me, you know. You're all the same. Do you really think you can carry on like this? Look at your ribs already. People like (the other) Claire will always be druggies, and she's going to waste her life, but you have prospects. You could be a doctor for fuck's sake!'

~~~

I had very pretentiously written this in French and had taken a great deal of time making sure my French grammar was on point. But it adds fuck all to this story.

~~~

Nico's right. He is so so right. I felt so embarrassed.
   'I know. You're right. Thanks for tonight.'
   'No worries.'
   He took me home and told me he'd sell my ticket for me. I took some codeine when I got home, and I feel so much better. I can hear the music pounding through my open window, and I am gutted. There is no way I can go because

   a. My mother has forbidden me from moving.

   b. I can't actually move without excruciating pain.

   c. I haven't got a ticket anymore anyway.

~~~

This was my last summer of total excess. I was pushing everything - limits, boundaries and my own body. It felt like I was always trying to make everything bigger, wilder and more intense. And for what? I don't even know anymore.

   The rib fracture was a wake-up call, though I probably wouldn't have admitted it at the time. Deep down, I knew Nico was right. He always saw it clearer than I did. He could see how dangerous it all was. I brushed it off then, but even now, I can almost hear his voice, that mix of frustration and concern.

It's strange to think about that version of me now. It almost doesn't feel real. How did I live like that? How did I not see where it was heading? It was always too much, but I just kept going and upping the ante. Maybe I thought I was invincible. Maybe I didn't care. Maybe I was just young.

But something shifted that summer and triggered the inevitable end of that phase of my life. Either way, I can't imagine being that person now. And honestly? I'm not sure if that's a relief or a loss.

~~~

SUNDAY 7TH AUGUST 2005 7PM
LISTENING TO RUN BY SNOW PATROL

I'm so annoyed about my rib. I can't do anything. It's so frustrating! I suggested going for some food tonight, but everyone is too knackered from Le Festivalas.

~~~

MONDAY 8TH AUGUST 2005 2AM
LISTENING TO HIGH BY JAMES BLUNT

Tom called tonight when I was a bajillion Pastis' deep with Marc and François at *Le St Awawa*. We chatted for a bit, and damn, it felt good to talk to him, but he sent a classic Tom text a little later.

```
Text from Tom: Wow. That conversation
didn't go as planned. Had a lot to
say and explain to you. Anyway, glad
to hear you're well. Speak soon. Take
care. Xx
```

Fuck off with your passive-aggressive little hissy fit. What am I supposed to think? He always does this! Sooo annoying. I know he's trying to get a reaction out of me, and he's succeeded. Fuck him and his games.

```
Text to Tom: Oh come on Tom. My life
does not revolve around you. If you
have something you want to say, fuck-
ing say it. I am not yours and there
to drop everything for you when you
deign me a phone call. You were the
one who decided you 'couldn't do' this
summer. We're not together remember -
cos that's what YOU wanted. Take care.
Xx
```

~~~

WEDNESDAY 12TH AUGUST 2005 5AM
LISTENING TO PON DE REPLAY BY RIHANNA

They must have put something in the water, for, all of a sudden, there appears to be a hell of a lot of attention being thrown my way. Last night at the fire, Gaspard, Nico, Romain and Jules were all over me. I stayed the night at Nico's - we just pulled, nothing major. I made a real effort not to drink much. There's something about his big bear-ness and the fact that he's 'told me off' that really humbles me and touches me. Someone like Nico would be good for me. He told me he wasn't interested in games, and I'm either in or not. In, I guess.

Then tonight, François of all people, seemed to be flirting more than normal. What's going on? I can't get Tom out of my head. Maybe I should just have sex with Nico... but he's got a tiny penis... François doesn't... oh my lord, I can't believe the thought just crossed my mind. I need some boundaries. DO NOT RUIN ANYTHING WITH François.

~~~

SUNDAY 14TH AUGUST 2005 11PM
LISTENING TO BILLY BY JAMES BLUNT

I'm off to Turkey with the fam for Mum's 50th in a few hours, and I can't wait! I've had the best last few days in St Jacut. I can't even begin to describe the joy. It flew by in a smoky haze of laughter, sun, sea and sand. François, Marc and I had the biggest three-way cuddle where we just spent an hour round the fire telling each other how much we love each other.

Tom just called, and we spoke for an hour, and it made me remember why I love (d?) him.

```
Text from Tom: It was really good to
talk to you. I might well like you
more than I thought. I hope our fire
hasn't died just yet.
```

~~~

SUNDAY 21ST AUGUST 2005 11.30AM
LISTENING TO EL CAPITAN BY IDLEWILD

Turkey has been epic. Sunning, eating, swimming and reading. Chloe and I have been out a few nights and met a lovely group of Frenchies. I feel relaxed, but I've got the worst cough. Probably a combination of the air conditioning and a hangover off the back of TOO MUCH in St Jac.

~~~

WEDNESDAY 24TH AUGUST 2005 1AM
LISTENING TO CRY BY JAMES BLUNT

I spoke to Tom last night, and I feel crestfallen. I have no right, of course, but… my heart. The conversation started in a very normal manner until he told me that Ginny wasn't speaking to him. I eventually convinced him to tell me why. Turns out they were both at a party and both very drunk (he could not stress this enough!). So anyway, she told her friends that she really wanted 'meaningless sex' and her little friends told Tom. He was 'so drunk' and 'not proud' of what he did, but to cut a long story short, he obliged, and they slept together… TWICE. My sympathetic nervous system went into overdrive. I FUCKING KNEW IT! The next morning she was apparently cuddly and saying things like, 'I'm glad we're together now'. Tom, obviously, being a massive cunt, didn't feel similarly and rather than kindly breaking the news to one of his best friends, he just disappeared. I don't want this coward in my life. Claire out.

```
Text from Tom: Hey. Just to say I
missed you so much this summer, I nev-
er stopped thinking about you. I've
actually been bloody well behaved this
summer, in the most part because of
you. I'm still wearing your bracelet.
Look forward to seeing you, hopefully
soon. Take care and sleep well Ducky
XxXx
```

Grrrr. I want to reply with something along the lines of, 'You want a fucking medal for shagging your best friend?!'

God I feel awful. Have I got this bloomin' bird flu?

~~~

SATURDAY 28TH AUGUST 2005 2AM
LISTENING TO GOLD DIGGER BY KANYE WEST

I did something very strange tonight. I've just been for a drink with Jules and Ginny. Yes, Ginny, the two-faced, snot-nosed cow that fucked Tom last week and Jules, his wannabe girlfriend. They're up in Edinburgh for the festival and messaged me to see if I wanted to go for a drink. I couldn't say no. I was so intrigued. Girls are weird. It was bizarre, but I felt in control. Jules said she was terrified of me. Considering they're best friends, they sure bitch a lot about each other... and they're both fighting for the same man. Jules told me that Tom is always talking about me... go on... and how it's obvious that he really likes me and that I have a fan club in Cheltenham and I'm too good for him.

~~~

Good enough for you to marry, though, Jules...

THIRTY-TWO
EXETER

MONDAY 30TH AUGUST 2005 1.20AM
LISTENING TO FIX YOU BY COLDPLAY

I arrived in Exeter, and I LOVE my house. I drew the big straw and have this enormous room. It is amazing to see Pete Bond and Robin. Kitty seems to live at the gym. Which is fine.

Mad Dog, Beth and Suzie are about twenty minutes down the road, and Kate is only about five minutes away. Perfecto.

Kate and I went out with Finn Ellwyn-Cox and his house mates tonight to *Arena*. We drank free cocktails all night, and Finn and I shared a little kiss. It's too easy with him… old habits die hard and all that.

Tom and I are fully over. He text tonight to say he wasn't going to come to Exeter until 'maybe October'. This isn't going to work. I properly ended it. We were over anyway, but I told him that it can definitely not be considered a break anymore. There is no way he's going to make the effort. He wasn't too happy, but it needed to be done. No more text, no nothing. Done.

~~~

THURSDAY 8TH SEPTEMBER 2005 11PM
LISTENING TO MY DOORBELL BY THE WHITE STRIPES

I have a new crush. A big one.

We were at the GP drinks the other night at the med school. It was a very weird 'opportunity' to meet the GPs we'll have our placements with. Crap red, warm white and an overlit foyer: romance 101.

Anyway, Pete was talking to some guy I didn't recognise so I went over.

'Oh, Claire. I was just talking about you. This is James. He's a third year, too, but was in Exeter the last two years. We've played football together. James, this is Claire, my house mate.'

He smiled at me and held out his hand.

'Hi.'

I couldn't help but grin back.

'Hi.'

Fin

SOUNDTRACK - FEAR & LOATHING IN PLYMOUTH

Pity Party by Ivory Layne

Where is The Love by Black Eyed Peas

Cry Me a River by Justin Timberlake

Rapper's Delight by The Sugarhill Gang

Inaudibles Melodies by Jack Jo

Just Like A Pill by P!nk

Beautiful by Snoop Dogg, Pharrell Williams, Uncle Charlie Wilson

When I'm Gone by 3 Doors Down

Crazy In Love by Beyoncé (ft Jay-Z)

Concrete Schoolyard by Jurassic 5

Glycerine by Bush

Seven Nation Army by The White Stripes

Mudfootball by Jack Johnson

Laid by James

Through The Wire by Kanye West

Bohemian Like you by Dandy Warhols

In Da Club by 50 Cent

Someday by Nickelback

Kingston Town UB40

FEAR AND LOATHING IN PLYMOUTH

You Can Call Me Al by Paul Simon

Family Portrait by P!nk

Let's Push Things Forward by The Streets

Graceland by Paul Simon

Flutter by Bonobo

All My Life by Foo Fighters

Gone by Jack Johnson

Pretty Green Eyes by Ultrabeat

Lonely as you by Foo Fighters

Smells Like Teen Spirit by Nirvana

Hard Candy by Counting Crows

Me and Julio Down by The Schoolyard by Paul Simon

Nervous In The Alley by Less Than Jake

Cocoon by Jack Johnson

Mr Brightside by The Killers

Black or White by Michael Jackson

Halo by Foo Fighters

Baby Boy by Beyoncé (feat. Sean Paul)

When Tomorrow Comes by The Eurythmics

Black and Blue by Counting Crows

This is a Call by Foo Fighters

Hey Ya! By Outkast

Tired of You by Foo Fighters

Taylor by Jack Johnson

Golden Slumbers by The Beatles

Back On The Chain Gang by The Pretenders

SOUNDTRACK - FEAR & LOATHING IN PLYMOUTH

Don't Worry Baby by The Beach Boys
Come As You Are by Nirvana
Automatic by Less Than Jake
Place Your Hands by Reef
You Make My Dreams by Hall & Oats
Hey Julie by Fountains of Wayne
Hurricane by Bob Dylan
This Love by Maroon 5
Are You Gonna Be My Girl by Jet
Somewhere Only We Know by Keane
Take Me Out Franz Ferdinand
My Sweet Prince by Placebo
The Reason by Hoobastank
Taste in Men by Placebo
American Idiot by Green Day
Comfortably Numb by The Scissor Sisters
Call On Me by Eric Prydz
Take Your Mama by Scissor Sisters
Piano Man by Billy Joel
Novacaine by Green Day
The Longest Time by Billy Joel
Laura by Scissor Sisters
Hammer to Fall by Queen
Pick Up by Bonobo
My Own Worst Enemy by Lit
Cryin' by Aerosmith
Sweet Child O' Mine by Guns N' Roses

I Miss You by Blink 182

We Didn't Start The Fire by Billy Joel

Aletheuo - Truthspeaking by DJ Krush, Angelina Esparza

I Want It All by Queen

Wake Me Up When September Ends by Green Day

I'm Lost Without You by Blink 182

Happy Alone by Kings of Leon

Take Me To The Clouds Above by LMC vs U2

Only The Good Die Young by Billy Joel

Swing Swing by All-American Rejects

Street Life by Randy Crawford

Too Much Love Will Kill You by Queen

Down by Blink 182

History of a Boring Town by Less Than Jake

Five Colours In Her Hair by McFly

Highway to Hell by AC/DC

Talihina Sky by Kings of Leon

Yeah! By Usher, Lil Jon, Ludacris

Sweetness by Jimmy Eat World

Inner City Life by Goldie

Tonight, Tonight by The Smashing Pumpkins

Noctuary by Bonobo

Fit But You Know It by The Streets

Come With Me by Special D

Look What Happened by Less Than Jake

SOUNDTRACK - FEAR & LOATHING IN PLYMOUTH

No One Knows by Queens of The Stone Age

Here Without You by 3 Doors Down

Easy Money by Billy Joel

Diamonds On The Soles Of Her Shoes by Paul Simon

Free by Donovan Frankenreiter

I'm Not Ok (I Promise) by My Chemical Romance

What'cha Know About by Donovan Frankenreiter

My My My by Armand Van Helden

1985 by Bowling For Soup

F.U.R.B. (FU Right Back) by Frankee

I Hear Talk by Bucks Fizz

Planet Telex by Radiohead

I Don't Wanna Know by Mario Winans ft. P.Diddy and Enya

Bend In The Road Donovan Frankenreiter

Sulk by Radiohead

It's The End Of The World As We Know It by R.E.M

2+2=5 by Radiohead

If You Could Read My Mind by Gordon Lightfoot

Every Little Thing She Does Is Magic by The Police

(Nice Dream) by Radiohead

We're Not Going to Take It by Twisted Sister

FEAR AND LOATHING IN PLYMOUTH

Paradise City by Guns N Roses
Times Like These by Jack Johnson
Bongo Bong by Manu Chao
Three Little Birds by Bob Marley &The Wailers
Je ne t'aime plus by Manu Chao
Amor pa'mi by Sergent Garcia
Tomorrow morning by Jack Johnson
Clandestino by Manu Chao
You Shook Me All Night Long by AC/DC
Easy Skanking by Bob Markey & The Wailers
Los desaparecidos by Sergent Garcia
Black Star by Radiohead
The Whole of the Moon by The Waterboys
Sunrise by Nora Jones
Jesus of Suburbia by Green Day
Playing with the Boys by Kenny Loggins
Mushaboom by Feist
Fall Line by Jack Johnson
Lithium by Nirvana
Breakthru by Queen
Slow Hands by Interpol
Turn The Page by The Streets
Stupidisco by Junior Jack
Move Your Feet by Junior Senior
Between Love & Hate by The Strokes
Too Much Brandy by The Streets
Date Rape by Sublime

SOUNDTRACK - FEAR & LOATHING IN PLYMOUTH

Creepin' In by Nora Jones and Dolly Parton

Last Night by The Strokes

Dreaming of You by The Coral

Love is only a Feeling by The Darkness

Club Foot by Kasabian

Next Exit by Interpol

Once in a Lifetime by Talking Heads

Pure by The Lightning Seeds

We Built This City by Starship

What Am I To You by Nora Jones

Molly's Chambers by Kings of Leon

Drop The Pressure by Mylo

L.S.F. by Kasabian

Humble Me by Norah Jones

One Love by Bob Marley & The Wailers

Swing Life Away by Rise Against

The Wine Song by The Cat Empire

Golden Touch by Razorlight

Evil by Interpol

Somebody Told Me by The Killers

The Long Way Home by Norah Jones

Brick by Ben Folds Five

Obviously by McFly

Leave Me Alone by Razorlight

Don't Mug Yourself by The Streets

Glamorous Indie Rock & Roll by The Killers

Those Sweet Words by Norah Jones

FEAR AND LOATHING IN PLYMOUTH

Vice by Razorlight

Don't Miss You At All by Norah Jones

Spitting Games by Snow Patrol

Which way is Out by Razorlight

The Impression That I Get by The Mighty Mighty Bosstones

Loneliness by Tomcraft

How to be dead by Snow Patrol

Not Even Jail by Interpol

Gleaming Auction by Snow Patrol

Stumble And Fall by Razorlight

Where is my mind by The Pixies

Guns Don't Kill People, Rappers Do by Goldie Lookin Chain

Chocolate by Snow Patrol

I Predict A Riot by Kaiser Chiefs

Boulevard of Broken Dreams by Green Day

Tiny Little Fractures by Snow Patrol

Everyday I Love You Less And Less by The Kaiser Chiefs

Don't Cha by The Pussycat Dolls

Oh My God by The Kaiser Chiefs

Over And Over by Nelly ft Tim McGraw

Hounds of Love by The Futureheads

Tumble and Fall by Feeder

Locked Up by Akon

Wires by Athlete

Somewhere Else by Razorlight

SOUNDTRACK - FEAR & LOATHING IN PLYMOUTH

- You Better you Bet by The Who
- Across The Universe by The Beatles
- Sunrise by Angel City
- 14th Street by Rufus Wainwright
- Poses by Rufus Wainwright
- If There's Any Justice in The World by Lemar
- Alison by Whitmore
- Caught Up by Usher
- When the Night Feels My Song by Bedouin Soundclash
- Apply Some Pressure by Maximo Park
- Numb / Encore by Jay-Z and Linkin Park
- You're Beautiful by James Blunt
- I Don't Know What It is by Rufus Wainwright
- Goodbye My Lover by James Blunt
- All About You by McFly
- Soldier by Destiny's Child (ft T.I. & Lil' Wayne)
- No Bravery by James Blunt
- Beverly Hills by Wheezer
- Galvanize by The Chemical Brothers
- Ordinary People by John Legend
- Number One by John Legend (feat. Kanye West)
- Money Don't Matter by The Martin Harley band
- Tears and Rain by James Blunt
- Ghetto Gospel by 2Pac ft Elton John
- Carnival Girl by The Martin Harley Band

FEAR AND LOATHING IN PLYMOUTH

Don't Play Nice by Verbalicious

Hey Man (Now You're Really Living) by The Eels

Stay With You by John Legend

Best of You by Foo Fighters

Alright by John Legend

Please by Pete Murray

Refuge (When It's Cold Outside) by John Legend

Sugar, We're Going Down by Fall Out Boy

Feeling Good Inc by Gorillaz

This Modern Love by Bloc Party

I Fell In Love With a Girl by The White Stripes

Bail Me Out by Pete Murray

I Like The Way by Bodyrockers

Road to Nowhere by Talking Heads

Lonely by Akon

Pushing The Senses by Feeder

Lose Control by Missy Elliot (ft Ciara & Fat Man Scoop)

In the Morning by The Coral

Monkey Man by Toots and The Maytals feat No Doubt

Pressure Drop by Toots and The Maytals feat Eric Clapton

Wisemen by James Blunt

Redemption Song by Bob Marley & The Wailers

Sweet And Dandy by Toots and The Maytals

SOUNDTRACK - FEAR & LOATHING IN PLYMOUTH

Bam Bam by Toots and The Maytals feat Shaggy, Rahzel

Speed of Sound by Coldplay

Run by Snow Patrol

High by James Blunt

Pon de Replay by Rihanna

Billy by James Blunt

El Capitan by Idlewild

Cry by James Blunt

Gold Digger by Kanye West

Fix You by Coldplay

My Doorbell by The White Stripes

ABOUT THE AUTHOR

Claire lives in Devon with her husband and two daughters. She works as a GP, lecturer and portrait artist. 'Fear and Loathing in Plymouth' is Claire's second self published book.

Printed in Dunstable, United Kingdom